Students and F.

The Abinger Edition
of E. M. Forster

Edited by

OLIVER STALLYBRASS

Volume 13

E. M. Forster dedicated
Goldsworthy Lowes Dickinson:

Fratrum Societati

G.L.D. *From the portrait by Roger Fry now in the Wine Room at King's College. Painted 1925*

Goldsworthy Lowes Dickinson

and related writings

E. M. Forster

Foreword by W. H. Auden

Edward Arnold

First published 1934
First published in the Abinger Edition 1973 by
Edward Arnold (Publishers) Ltd
25 Hill Street, London W1X 8LL

ISBN 0 7131 5692 9

Printed in Great Britain by
The Camelot Press Ltd
London and Southampton

Contents

Illustrations

(There is no satisfactory portrait of him in middle life.)

Foreword

I first read this book when it came out in 1934. Rereading it now, it seems to me even better than I remembered. I have only one criticism. If I had been Forster, I would not have quoted so extensively from Goldie's verses. In my opinion, poetry was an art for which he had little talent. This may, I realize, be a matter of personal taste rather than critical judgement. Goldie was devoted to the poetry of Shelley, which I have always found unreadable. On the other hand, he shared my admiration for Goethe, though, according to Forster, "he was soon confronted with the immense boringness of Goethe, and few Englishmen have faced it so frankly, and so successfully outstared it". I myself only find Goethe boring when, as in *Dichtung und Wahrheit*, he talks about his romantic attachments to a series of young ladies; on any other topic I find him endlessly fascinating.

That this biography should be the great book it is, seems to me a miracle. To begin with, it is not easy to write justly and objectively about a personal friend, a situation which, Goldie wrote, when asked to review a book by Forster, "leads us Cambridge people to under-estimate virtues and gifts for fear of being too partial". Then nothing is more difficult than writing an interesting book about a really nice person. The biographer of a monster, like Wagner, has a far easier task. Bad behaviour always has a dramatic appeal. Forster imagines Mephistopheles asking him why a memoir of Goldsworthy Lowes Dickinson needs to be written, and when he answers, "My friend was beloved, affectionate, unselfish, intelligent, witty, charming, inspiring," the devil says, "Yes, but that is neither here nor there, or rather it was there but it is no longer here." Forster can only reply:

> These qualities in Goldie were fused into such an unusual creature that no one whom one has met with in the flesh or in history the least resembles it, and no words exist in which to define it. He was an indescribably rare being, he was rare without being enigmatic, he was rare in the only direction which seems to be infinite: the direction

of the Chorus Mysticus. He did not merely increase our experience: he left us more alert for what has not yet been experienced and more hopeful about other men because he had lived. And a biography of him, if it succeeded, would resemble him; it would achieve the unattainable, express the inexpressible, turn the passing into the everlasting. Have I done that? *Das Unbeschreibliche hier ist's getan?* No. And perhaps it only could be done through music. But that is what has lured me on.

There were other difficulties too. Though Goldie travelled to America, India, China, a civilization with which he fell in love, he had no dramatic adventures there.

It is difficult to think of a life where so little happened outwardly. He was never shipwrecked or in peril, he was seldom in great bodily pain, never starved or penniless, he never confronted an angry mob nor went to prison for his opinions, nor sat on the bench as a magistrate, nor held any important administrative post, he was never married, never faced with the problems of parenthood, had no trouble with housekeeping or servants.

Normally, the chief source of material for a biographer is his subject's letters. Forster quotes from a number of Goldie's, and I find them most interesting, but he warns us that they are of small value compared with his conversation.

When he spoke to his friends or spoke of them . . . he vibrated to wave after wave, and as he turned his head from guest to guest at one of his lunch parties one felt that a new universe was seated on every chair. That was his strength, that was his glory, and if that could be communicated in a biography he would appear for what he was: one of the rarest creatures of our generation. His letters are a misleading substitute; they tend to exhibit him as merely sympathetic and kind.

In 1905, Forster tells us, Goldie's literary reputation was so high that it was believed that he "would easily beat Pater and Gobineau, and even creep up towards Voltaire and Mr Bernard Shaw". If he is little read today, this is not due simply to changes in fashion. He never claimed to be writing for posterity: nearly all of his books are concerned with the immediate issues of his time, political, religious, educational or what-have-you. Then his style when lecturing or talking to small groups seems to have been superior to his written prose. One of his younger friends wrote:

You know I always find a "but" about Goldie's writing. He would be so inclined to clarity in conversation (with me anyway) but so

beautifully unclear with his pen. I get mesmerized when I read anything he writes (except *John Chinaman*) and then have to read it all
over again.

On which Forster comments:

> There frequently is this hypnotic effect, although the argument is
> taut and the language apposite. Something is wrong—or perhaps
> too right—with the style.

It is only when he is describing Goldie's eccentricities that one
feels Forster has an easy job.

> He was not practical, and I can still hear him damning his sleeve-
> links in the morning because they wouldn't go in, or his hot-water
> bottle at night because it puffed in his face when he filled it. He
> swore constantly, and no wonder. For he was unhandy with "so
> called inanimate objects". They were always splashing or scalding
> him, or beating a merry retreat at the moment he needed them most,
> "Here you are, yes of course," he would say, lifting a sheet of paper,
> and there beneath it, after the locksmith had been sent for, would be
> the bunch of keys. . . .
> He is said to be the only man who could make a Corona type
> upside down. He struck the keys rapidly and violently, thinking of
> what he thought and not of what he did, with the result that he
> doubled lines, halved them, threw capitals in the air, buried numerals
> in the earth, broke out into orgies of ?????? or %%%%%%, and
> hammered his ribbon to shreds. George becomes "Geroge", Gerald
> "Gerlad", perhaps "perhpas", and there are even happier trans-
> formations such as husband into "humsband", and soul into "soup".
> A semicolon in the middle of a word means "1".

Forster first met Goldie at a lunch in 1898. Lunch was not a
success, and Forster left it "unprepossessing and unprepossessed".
A few weeks later, however, on Forster's returning a play he had
borrowed and confessing that he hadn't liked it, the smile on
Goldie's face came as a revelation of what charm could mean.

> Charm, in most men and nearly all women, is a decoration. It
> genuinely belongs to them, as a good complexion may, but it lies
> on the surface and can vanish. Charm in Dickinson was structural. It
> penetrated and upheld everything he did.

He seems, also, to have had the even rarer gift of creating charm
in others. In a letter he wrote "Lennie —— (?) gets nicer and
nicer", and Forster comments:

> Lennie's surname is indecipherable, but that he got nicer and nicer

there is little doubt: most of the people who constantly saw Goldie did that, though he did not realize why.

And I have never heard of a finer tribute to anyone than Forster's reaction when he learned of Goldie's death:

> He never staged himself as an invalid. He was chiefly occupied in saving us trouble and in sparing our feelings. Oddly enough he succeeded. A character of his strength manages to sustain those who cling to it, and I have "minded" more the deaths of people I have loved much less.

It must always be harder to draw a convincing portrait of a real person than of a fictional character, since, in the first case, the author is free to make the facts and situations what he pleases. I can only say that I find Forster's Goldie as living and convincing as any of the characters in his novels. Then, of course, one is frequently delighted by passages the authorship of which one would immediately guess, if one didn't know it already. For example, this passage about Goldie's unhappiness at his preparatory school:

> But these amenities lay at the edge of his life. Its centre was covered with rubbish and worry. And at its opposite edge lay an imbecile boy whom he sometimes kicked in order to ingratiate himself with his schoolfellows. He made no special confession to his parents about this; it was not a crime like the potatoes, nevertheless it haunted him.

One matter puzzles me a little. In view of Goldie's passionate interest in the League of Nations, I should have expected to find references to Count Kessler, the German who proposed that the League be made up, not of representatives of sovereign states, but of various interest groups, the professions, the churches, the trades unions, etc., on the ground that the League as constituted would be powerless to act in any case of serious conflict between the major powers. This idea, I should have thought, would have appealed to Goldie, but there is no mention of Kessler in Forster's book, nor of Goldie in Kessler's diaries, and it seems to be the case that they never met.

W. H. AUDEN

Editor's Introduction

E. M. Forster wrote two biographies: of his friend Goldsworthy Lowes Dickinson (1934) and his great-aunt Marianne Thornton (1956). About the writing of the earlier book more might have been known but for a rather curious reason. Shortly after 16 January 1931 Forster lost the key of his private diary. The keeping of the diary had always been spasmodic, and now for nearly four years it ceased entirely. Then the key turned up again, and on 7 October 1934 Forster summarized the intervening period, mentioning Dickinson's death and commenting:

> I am a worse speaker than I was and no creator. But a good journalist and my book on Goldie was good, always thought it would be. I will not do a book on Roger Fry.

The reference to Roger Fry is interesting. Fry had died on 9 September 1934, Forster had written an obituary note on him for the *London Mercury* (later reprinted in *Abinger Harvest*), and a full-scale biography had apparently been mooted by Fry's sisters; in the event it was written, not without fearful anguish, by Virginia Woolf. Two or three years later another biographical project of Forster's, this time for an edition of T. E. Lawrence's letters, made rather more progress but was also, eventually, abandoned. It would appear that, except for short biographical essays, biography was not a genre which came easily to Forster, that he was drawn to it only by motives of affection or gratitude, and that even these were not always sufficient to sustain him. This makes it notable that *Goldsworthy Lowes Dickinson* was completed with relative despatch—and that Forster "always thought it would be" good.

He had, of course, one considerable advantage. On his death on 3 August 1932 Dickinson had bequeathed to Forster what the latter describes in his Preface as "a quantity of autobiographical matter". This "was not to be published in its entirety, but might be used at my discretion"; and Forster "worked with the transcript of the *Recollections* at his elbow, following it closely in matter, in arrangement, and often in actual wording".[1] Although, as we shall see, the *Recollections* gave Forster some problems, they provided him with a framework, a large number of essential facts, and a source of copious—though always judicious—quotation.

Forster's statement that the "autobiographical matter . . . might be used at my discretion" suggests that he may have discussed with Dickinson the question of a biography; and this possibility appears at first sight to be strengthened by a letter to J. R. Ackerley of 12 January 1933:[2] "I continue . . . to hear him saying: 'Really my dear Morgan that you should have to do this.'" But, although one can easily imagine Dickinson making just such a deprecatory little joke, other evidence makes it much more likely that the imagination, and the joke, were Forster's, and that what had been in question between him and Dickinson was the publication of the *Recollections* rather than of a biography based on them. However this may be, Forster certainly discussed the project with Dickinson's two surviving sisters—"it would not have been begun without their approval" (page xxiii). Evidently this permission had been given by 10 November, when the *Times Literary Supplement* (followed two days later by the *New Statesman*) published a letter from Forster announcing his intention of writing Dickinson's biography, and asking for the loan of letters. The request met with a generous response.

Thus armed, Forster went briskly to work. He may already have been committed to the series of seven broadcast talks on books which he gave during the last quarter of 1932; but he took the opportunity of devoting the second entirely to Dickinson. For the next year he cut down severely on his occasional writing: in 1933 he published only three articles and two reviews (no broadcasts), as against twenty-four such items in 1932. As with almost every book he wrote, there were bad moments: "I have been feeling unusually restless and dissatisfied lately . . . I wish I could finish the Goldie Dickinson memoir. I have got so untidy and unconcentratish [*sic*]," he writes to William Plomer on 29 August 1933. But most of his references in extant letters are cheerful and positive in tone:

[1] Dennis Proctor, Introduction to *The Autobiography of Goldsworthy Lowes Dickinson, and Other Unpublished Writings* (London, Duckworth, 1973), p. vii. I am grateful to Sir Dennis, and to his publisher, Mr Colin Haycraft, for making available to me proofs of this volume (in which, despite its general title, the main item is captioned *Recollections*).

[2] Now, with other letters of Forster to Ackerley, in the Humanities Research Center, University of Texas.

I have an idea that I'm going to do the book rather gaily—anyhow I keep jotting down sentences that make me smile. (To J. R. Ackerley, 10 January 1933.)

But I must stop and get on with Goldie's book, which I find more interesting and occupying than I expected. (To Florence Barger, 9 February 1933.)

I must finish the Lowes Dickinson memoir. What its merit will be I don't know, I expect people will laugh at it for being sentimental academic stuff, and then ignore it. But I enjoy doing it and keep getting down things which seem to come from G. L. D. rather than myself, and please me. (To Forrest Reid, 4 July 1933.)

I am rather busy finishing the life of Goldie Dickinson. (To Siegfried Sassoon, 6 November 1933.)

There is also a letter to his publisher, Brian Fagan of Edward Arnold, dated as early as 11 December 1932—four days before the actual contract was signed:

I do want the book to be advertised and "pushed", in ways suitable to its character. I have got the idea that Dickinson, owing to his broadcasting, was on the edge of a much wider public, and I do want him to reach them.

In addition to enjoyment, affection, gratitude and a ready-made framework, Forster may have been speeded on his way by two further factors: an enthusiastic collaborator in the person of R. E. Balfour, who contributed the Bibliography, and—a spur to which as a novelist he would have been unaccustomed—a contractually agreed completion date. Originally 30 June 1933 (for autumn publication), this was modified at some stage to allow Forster a further six months. If the modification represented a reluctant concession on the publisher's part, it is not surprising that by 29 December he was, as Forster wrote to William Plomer, "taking up a strong line which I do not altogether resent". Less than four months later, on 19 April 1934, the book was published.

As I mentioned above, Dickinson's *Recollections*, while providing Forster with invaluable help, also posed him some problems. Their nature is explained in a letter to Forster which Dickinson wrote on 10 July 1932, less than a month before his death:

What I want to say to you is that I am sending the autobiography to Dennis Proctor, 5 Peel St, Church St, W.8. But I should like you, not him, to make any decision about it. My present feeling is that if anything were published (as to which I have no judgement) the sex part should be omitted. One can't trust people yet (nor perhaps ever) to be decent about those things, and anyhow my relations are still alive. Remember that my sisters have not seen this autobiography and I don't wish them to, except in a safely bowdlerized form. I must I am afraid leave all that to your judgement, but perhaps you would also consult with Dennis, though I want the final decision to be yours. There are other MSS which I have told May to send you but I doubt if there is anything that should be published and you have full leave to destroy or do what you like.

More than twenty years later Forster in turn gave Dickinson's unpublished writings to Dennis Proctor, with no restrictions over their ultimate publication; and today the *Recollections* in their entirety are available to all. In the less liberal climate of 1934 Forster decided to respect Dickinson's feeling and omit "the sex part" in toto. To quote Sir Dennis Proctor:

> One can well imagine how he must have chafed under the necessity of describing his friend's life without mentioning the rarest thing about it, the almost continuous experience over a lifetime of passionate love for another human being, merely because the other human being was always someone of the same sex.[3]

And indeed there is perhaps an element of casuistry in Forster's statement (page xxii) that "I have not tried to exclude facts about him with which I am not in sympathy or which might be held to decrease his reputation". If pressed, he might have claimed that at various points (pages 47, 56, 63, 64, 103, 151 in this edition) he *does* make it plain that Dickinson was homosexual. But at least one reader, in 1947, contrived not to realize this fact; and of Dickinson's shoe fetishism—to which both of Forster's relative clauses presumably apply—there is naturally not a word. To say this is not to dispute Forster's judgement; it is merely to point out "a serious omission in the portrait as well as a gaping hole in the narrative"[4]—an omission and a hole which may (such is human nature) partly explain the biography's comparative neglect. Certain passages—those where Forster voices his own feelings about Cambridge or public schools—are of course familiar and indeed famous; but largely through the frequency with which they have been quoted by commentators. But if *Goldsworthy Lowes Dickinson* is not one of Forster's best-

[3] Proctor, *loc. cit.*   [4] *Ibid.*

known works its admirers have been fervid as well as distinguished. W. H. Auden, for example, who reviewed it for *Scrutiny* and who has contributed a Foreword to this edition, has been quoted[5] as considering it Forster's best book. Christopher Isherwood was equally enthusiastic:

> I . . . am lost in admiration of your marksmanship in the G. L. D. book, which I have now read four or five times, and like better and better. (Letter to Forster, 26 August 1934.)

And Siegfried Sassoon has to pull himself up short:

> No one else could have done it, and the world will be a better place when, say, 5,000 thoughtful persons have read it. It just made me quietly grateful that "Goldie" existed and was "perpetuated" by E. M. F., whose existence also makes one gra . . . but I am waxing fulsome. (Letter to Forster, 17 July 1934.)

Reviewers, too, were almost unanimous in their praise; they included, apart from Auden, David Garnett in the *New Statesman*, J. A. Hobson in *Philosophy*, F. L. Lucas in the *Cambridge Review* and the *Observer* (identical reviews; such pluralism is, one hopes, a thing of the past), Desmond MacCarthy in the *Sunday Times*, Kingsley Martin in the *Political Quarterly*, Lord Ponsonby in the *Listener*, J. T. Sheppard in the *Spectator*, and H. M. Tomlinson (another who considered this Forster's best book) in the *News Chronicle*. Only three dissentient voices were raised: Montgomery Belgion, who made the book a peg for his famous onslaught in the *Criterion*, "The Diabolism of E. M. Forster";[6] Hugh Kingsmill in the *English Review* ("If Lowes Dickinson was indeed the best man who has ever lived, Mr Forster must be the worst of all biographers, for of the sublime qualities implied in Mrs Newman's praise Mr Forster has given us no hint at all"); and, in the *Vegetarian News*, Henry S. Salt, whose review hinges on a remark of Dickinson's (page 176) about abattoirs, and includes this acid footnote:

> Mr Forster devotes to me a dozen lines, which show with what amazing carelessness such memoirs may be compiled. I am described, quite untruly, as having been "a rebellious master at Eton";[7]

[5] By Paul Cadmus in a letter to Forster, 7 May 1944.

[6] Dickinson figures as "a man in some mental confusion . . . when he meant 'God' he had to say 'It'".

[7] Salt was a master at Eton from 1875 to 1884; and his own published accounts of those years lend some colour to Dickinson's adjective.

then, with Mr Cox (who was much my junior) as a magnet for "cranks"; and the general impression conveyed is that the Cox household, with its Kentish agricultural folk, was roughing it together with mine. This quite misleading story is taken, I understand, from Dickinson's "unpublished recollections", which, I venture to think, had better remain unpublished.

Broadly speaking, those (the great majority) who loved Dickinson have loved Forster's biography, while those who were irritated by him were irritated also by the book that portrayed him so sympathetically. The reader who never knew Dickinson, and has perhaps read few of his works, may be curious to see him—the man and the writer—through other eyes than Forster's. Forster himself (or possibly Balfour) catered for such curiosity by listing (pages 252–3) sixteen obituary notices; but the list is confined to notices written by "friends who knew Dickinson personally". The following paragraphs—which make no claim to comprehensiveness—mention both friendly and hostile witnesses.

As early as 1905 Dickinson had a chapter to himself in G. K. Chesterton's *Heretics*.[8] Triggered off by Dickinson's article "How Long Halt Ye?" in the *Independent Review* that February, the essay is far from being Chesterton at his most swashbuckling. A much more sustained attack on Dickinson's outlook (and style) is made by Wilfred Stone in *The Cave and the Mountain: A Study of E. M. Forster*.[9] These criticisms are based, of course, entirely on Dickinson's writings. Of the accounts based on personal knowledge the unkindest perhaps, for all its protestations of gratitude, is that given by Esmé Wingfield-Stratford in *Before the Lamps Went Out*,[10] where he sums Dickinson up as "the best type of old maid". Something of the same feeling is voiced by Virginia Woolf ("Always Shelley and Goethe, and then he loses his hot water bottle") and endorsed by Leonard, who refers to "a weakness, a looseness of fibre, in Goldie and in his thought and writing, which was subtly related to the gentleness and highmindedness". Among other remarks made or quoted in this passage from Leonard Woolf's *Beginning Again*[11] may be mentioned Virginia's "Always alone on a mountain top asking himself

8 London, John Lane, 1905.
9 Stanford and London, Stanford University Press and Oxford University Press, 1966.
10 London, Hodder & Stoughton, 1945. The author has some biting things to say about Forster's biography also.
11 London, Hogarth Press, 1964.

how to live, theorizing about life; never living." In the same vein are Michael Holroyd's view of Dickinson as an "almost perfect example of the academic millenarian"[12] and George Santayana's epigram: "He prayed, watched and laboured to redeem human life, and began by refusing to understand what human life is."[13] This, however, and the patronizing reference to "poor Dickinson" belong to Santayana's sophisticated old age; as an undergraduate he had described Dickinson as "the type of everything I like and respect in the way of intelligence and feeling".[14]

Much more sympathetic, again, are Bertrand Russell's comments in his *Autobiography*, the first volume of which[15] also includes six of his letters to Dickinson. Wholly sympathetic is the picture given in *The Life of John Maynard Keynes*[16] by Sir Roy Harrod, who twice mentions Dickinson's "absolute integrity". Christopher Hassall's *Rupert Brooke*[17] is notable for an amusing anecdote about a misfortune that befell Dickinson while bathing nude near Grantchester, and a charming one about the occasion when Rupert Brooke and Hugh Dalton disturbed Dickinson in the small hours by arguing loudly at the entrance to their staircase.

> "I wish you'd go to bed!" he called out, testily, "I can't sleep." Next morning the two . . . went up to apologize and were asked what they were talking about. "Immortality," one of them replied. "Oh," exclaimed Dickinson, seeing the incident in a new light, "now if only I'd known that, I would have come down and joined you." Dickinson was a being as rare for the breadth of his tolerance as for his learning, and when he was offered the Kahn Travelling Fellowship, the main purpose of which was to widen the Fellow's mind, Brooke exclaimed, "If they widen Goldie's mind any more, it'll break!"

Finally, an account of Dickinson that equals Forster's in affection may be found in Sir Dennis Proctor's long and moving Introduction to the *Autobiography*.

[12] *Lytton Strachey: A Critical Biography*, vol. 1 (London, Heinemann, 1967), p. 173.
[13] *My Host the World* (London, Cresset Press, 1953), p. 31.
[14] *Letters*, ed. Daniel Cory (London, Constable, 1956), p. 52; letter to Susana Sturgis de Sastre, 14 January 1897.
[15] London, Allen & Unwin, 1967.
[16] London, Macmillan, 1951.
[17] London, Faber, 1964. The bathing anecdote is told on p. 267; the passage quoted occurs on p. 170.

An explanation is perhaps needed for the appearance, in this volume, of seven appendices which formed no part of Forster's book as originally published. In a collected edition of his work, here surely is the place for anything else he wrote on Dickinson and his books; and Appendices A to F fall under this heading. Inevitably, Forster repeated himself; and I have excluded, as adding nothing of any significance, several pertinent items (C248, C255, C258, part of B21) from Miss Kirkpatrick's bibliography[18]—as well as, *a fortiori*, his contributions to a programme on Dickinson broadcast by the B.B.C. in 1960,[19] and an "Introduction" to a new edition[20] of *A Modern Symposium* which consists merely of linked extracts from *Goldsworthy Lowes Dickinson*. Appendix G is a letter from Beatrice Webb to Forster thanking him for a gift copy of his book. (It was doubtless to ask Sidney Webb about his visit to Cambridge—see page 80—that Forster paid the visit to Passfield Corner described in *Two Cheers for Democracy*.) The letter, besides offering yet another view of Dickinson, is amusing in a number of ways, and the Maharajah of Chhatarpur's request to Sidney Webb "to help him to save his soul" deserves to have been immortalized by a Max Beerbohm cartoon.

Notes on the text and on the Bibliography will be found on pages 225 and 230 respectively; and it only remains for me to express my thanks to those who in one way or another have given me generous and valuable help. First and foremost, on this occasion, comes Mr W. H. Auden, whose graceful Foreword will surely win new readers for this comparatively neglected book. To Sir Dennis Proctor I am deeply indebted, in ways which I have detailed above and on page 227. He is also one of three people who have made helpful suggestions concerning this Introduction, the others being Mr P. N. Furbank—whose knowledge and kindness I continue shamelessly to exploit—and Mr Roger Greaves. For help of various kinds at King's College, Cambridge, I am again grateful to the Vice-Provost, Dr Donald Parry; the

[18] B. J. Kirkpatrick, *A Bibliography of E. M. Forster* (London, Hart-Davis; 2nd, revised impression, 1968).

[19] Third Programme, 19 January. The narrator, Mr Frederick Laws, who kindly lent me a transcript, tells me that Forster "sulked when I left in the reference to homosexuality by Kingsley Martin, insisted on using his own ending piece and set me to read the Mephistopheles, saying it was type-casting".

[20] London, Allen & Unwin, and New York, Barnes & Noble, 1962.

Librarian, Dr A. N. L. Munby, and his staff; the Archivist, Mrs Penelope Bulloch; and Mr George Rylands. The British Library of Political and Economic Science has been generous in answering my inquiries, and more particularly in allowing me to quote in full the letter from Beatrice Webb to E. M. Forster which forms Appendix G; for permission to quote from other unpublished letters I would like to thank Mr Christopher Isherwood, Mr William Plomer and (in the case of Siegfried Sassoon's letters) Mr George Sassoon. Of previously published material, extracts from Dickinson's *Recollections* (including Sir Dennis Proctor's Introduction) are included by the courtesy of Gerald Duckworth & Co. Ltd; Appendices C and D by that of, respectively, Methuen & Co. Ltd and George Allen & Unwin Ltd. To Messrs Allen & Unwin, and more particularly Mr Rayner Unwin and Mr Ken Abbott, I owe additional thanks for giving me access to their archives in connection with the Bibliography. I am grateful like-wise, in this context, for information supplied by the National Libraries of China, India, Japan and the Netherlands. Their British equivalent—both the Bloomsbury and the Colindale sections of the British Museum—has also given me much help; so, once again, has the London Library. For assistance of various kinds, notably in the collating of editions and checking of proofs, I owe warm thanks to Mrs Sylvia McGeachie and to my wife, Gunnvor. Professor C. R. Sanders and Dr Martin Schor have generously placed at my disposal their great knowledge of, respectively, Carlyle and Goethe, while Mr Arthur Crook, editor of the *TLS*, has kindly verified Middleton Murry's authorship of an unsigned article in that journal. My final debt is to Mr T. S. Matthews, who has taken time off from more creative work in order to cast his sharp eye over a complete set of proofs. For any editorial faults that remain I alone am responsible.

OLIVER STALLYBRASS

Author's Preface

During the last twelve years of his life Dickinson wrote a quantity of autobiographical matter. He told me that it was not to be published in its entirety, but might be used at my discretion, so I have used it in writing this book. It will be referred to under the general title of *Recollections*; indeed all quotations may be assumed to come from this source, when they are not otherwise assigned. I have also worked part of the *Recollections* into the substance of the narrative; for instance, the details about his childhood and his various states of mind are not guesses of my own, but rest on his authority.

How good is that authority? To what extent can a man be trusted to review his own past? Something must always be discounted, and in Dickinson's case we must discount a thin veil of melancholy which interposed between him and the paper as soon as he sat down to type. He was aware of this and tried to neutralize it, and it is, I think, his only defect as an auto-biographer. For when he tried to look back at himself he was at the height of his power as a prose writer; his mind was active and clear, his outlook fearless and humane; intent on the truth, he never exalted himself, and even resisted the more congenial temptation of self-depreciation. Such a breadth of outlook would have been impossible for him in his pre-war days, such detachment would have been impossible during the war. It was only at the close of his life that he was fitted to record his life, and—except for the tendency to write it down as rather sadder than he felt it to have been—his record may be accepted.

After the *Recollections* my chief source has been his letters, a number of which I have read, thanks to the kindness of his family and friends. He was not, in my judgement, a great letter-writer, but he always provides interesting views, terse sentences, relevant information, and I have quoted frequently. His books have also helped, and though I have not attempted detailed criticism of them I have referred to them all in passing, and have also described the contents of his privately printed works and of some unpublished manuscripts. Most of his books are now published by Messrs Allen & Unwin. *The Greek View of Life* is to be had from Messrs Methuen, *Goethe and Faust* from Messrs Bell, the life of McTaggart from the Cambridge University Press. *From King to King* and *The Development of Parliament during the Nineteenth Century* are out of print.

I have not tried to exclude facts about him with which I am not in sympathy or which might be held to decrease his reputation. To do so would be to pay him a poor compliment, for neither did he care anything for his reputation, nor was he dazzled by the reputations of others. He admired a biography not when it treated its subject in a reverent spirit but when it made it come alive. I should like to adopt his own standard here. I should like to make him live for people who never met him in the flesh, and to whom his voice when he broadcast was sometimes the first indication of his existence. It is for the general public rather than for his friends (who need no words of mine) that I write this book, and for that reason he will be oftener referred to as "Dickinson" than as "Goldie". He was not merely intelligent, affectionate, charming, remarkable; he was unique. But how is this to be conveyed?

I knew him for thirty-five years, and knew him well for twenty, so feel qualified to write about him from the personal, and perhaps from the literary, point of view. But there my qualifications end. I can discuss him neither as a philosopher nor as a publicist, and these sections of the book are bound to be unsatisfactory. I thought indeed of asking others to undertake them, and to deal in particular with his League of Nations work. But it seemed better that one person should be in charge, however obvious his limitations. Collaboration leads to thoroughness but not to consistency, and it is only through unity of treatment that the underlying unity of Dickinson can be stressed.

The arrangement of the book has been rather a problem, for his life was not dramatic and does not divide into strongly marked periods. I have aimed at a narrative but a halting narrative, which is interrupted by chapter 11 (his extra-European interests) and to some extent by chapter 7. I have tried to write simply. Some of his friends, who do not know foreign languages, have suggested that quotations in them should be translated, but I was unwilling to interrupt the flow of his prose, and think that the few words of Greek, Latin, French and German which occur in it will be explained by their contexts.

My thanks are due in the first place to his sisters, Miss May Lowes Dickinson and Mrs Lowes. Although the responsibility for the book is mine, it would not have been begun without their approval, and it could not have been completed without their help. In the second place I desire to thank the Provost and Fellows of King's College, Cambridge. They have given me every possible facility, and I want, in this connection, particularly to thank Mr R. E. Balfour, Fellow of the College, for his Bibliography. Mr Balfour has done a lasting service to future students. In the third place special acknowledgement is due to Dickinson's main publishers, Messrs Allen & Unwin, for the assistance they have so willingly given. In the fourth place comes the list of those who have lent letters, supplied information, given photographs, and helped in other ways, a list which includes the names of:

Mr H. G. Alexander, Lord Allen of Hurtwood, Mr and Mrs C. R. Ashbee, Mr Julian Bell, Mr E. K. Bennett, Mr Bernhard Berenson, Mrs Bridges (for Robert Bridges), Mrs O. W. Campbell, Mr H. Corner, Mr J. J. Darling, Lord Dickinson, Mr Bonamy Dobrée, Mr O. P. Eckhard, Mr Leonard Elmhirst, Mr C. R. Fay, Mr Elliott Felkin, Professor Roger Fry, Professor A. J. Grant, Mr Gerald Heard, Mrs E. B. C. Lucas, Mr Edward Marsh (for Rupert Brooke), Mr Kingsley Martin, Mr J. H. Mason, Mr R. J. G. Mayor, Professor H. O. Meredith, The Misses Moor (for Mrs Moor), Lady Ottoline Morrell, Mr J. A. R. Munro, Mrs Newman, Mr Robert Nichols, Lord Passfield, Lord and Lady Ponsonby, Mr Dennis Proctor, Mr D. H. Robertson, Mr D. K. Roy, Mrs C. P. Sanger (and for C. P. Sanger), Mr Peter Savary, Mr F. N. Schiller, Professor G. C. Moore Smith, Mr Dominick Spring-Rice, Miss Melian Stawell, Mr Cecil Taylor, Mr N. Teulon-Porter, Miss Cecilia Townsend, Mr and Mrs R. C. Trevelyan, Mr Stanley Unwin, Miss Webb (for Mrs Webb), Mr N. Wedd, Mr H. G. Wells, Colonel E. J. Wighton, Mr and Mrs Leonard Woolf, Professor W. Perceval Yetts.

E.M.F.

chapter one
Family

Goldsworthy Lowes Dickinson (Goldie) was the son of Lowes
Cato Dickinson and Margaret Ellen Williams.

On the father's side the family was Northumbrian, and has
been traced back to the great-great-grandfather, Jacob Dickinson,
of Whitfield (*d.* 1773) and his wife Alice Alexander (*d.* 1800).
There is a story that this Jacob and his brother were foundlings,
who were dropped off a coach on the moors, nicely dressed, and
that a farmer of the name of Dickinson adopted them, but no one
can vouch for the truth of the story. The great-grandfather,
William Dickinson (1738–1819) had a farm near Bardon Mill;
he married Jane Lowes (1749–1811), and there are other instances
of marriage between these two families.

Goldie's grandfather, Joseph Dickinson (1782–1849), came to
London at the beginning of the nineteenth century, and set up
a print- and lithograph-shop and photographing business in
Bond Street. He was gentle, sensitive, artistic, considerate of
others, and what one may recognize as the family type emerges
with him. His wife, Ann Carter, was from Devonshire, and claimed
connection with Sir Humphrey Gilbert; Goldie always felt more
in sympathy with this Devonian strain in him than with the
Northumbrian. The children could just remember their grandmother and thought her formidable. She was certainly a woman
of character, if I may judge by her entries in the family bible:
"Hope this will be the last," she writes opposite the birth of one
of her babies, and opposite the next birth: "This must be the
last." As it was. Some of the babies were christened out of
Plutarch, for whom Joseph Dickinson had a great admiration,
Cicero and so on, and about halfway down the long list comes
Goldie's father, Lowes Cato Dickinson, born in 1819.

Lowes Dickinson (he dropped the Cato) grew up in the Bond
Street shop, and was earning his living by the age of sixteen.
He began as a lithographer. In 1850 he was sent by some friends
to Italy to study art, and the charming letters which he wrote

during his three years' tour have been printed for private circulation. In his day, to travel meant to live with the people of the country, and his delightful personality gained him a warm welcome from them. He made some attractive water-colour drawings of the scenery, which have been preferred by some critics to his more professional work as a portrait-painter. On his return from Italy he came into touch with F. D. Maurice and the Christian Socialist movement, and, together with Charles Kingsley and Tom Hughes and others of that group, he set himself to transform society in the intervals of his work, and if possible by means of his work. He helped to found the Working Men's College—which was then not the trim municipalized institution up in Crowndale Road but a lodge in the wilderness of Great Ormond Street. Here he taught drawing for many years, in the midst of discomfort and enthusiasm. Ruskin was a fellow teacher. Although never a fashionable painter, he was in steady demand among the intellectual middle classes, and many London clubs and Cambridge colleges possess examples of him. He specialized in posthumous portraits; the picture of one of his heroes, Gordon, now hangs at Khartoum, a replica of it being in the Gordon Boys' Home.

He married Miss Williams in 1857, and lived at first in a studio at Langham Chambers, where the four elder children were born. Then he moved out to Hanwell. His relations with them all, until school intervened, were perfect. He would go up to his work and return in the evening to play, or to read Scott, Shakespeare or Coleridge aloud, while Goldie and his sister May perched together on a stool by the wood fire. In 1877-9 he built a London house close to his old studio—1 All Souls Place, a tall, dark-red, wedge-shaped house all windows and hospitality, and it was there that I saw him once or twice towards the end of his life. He was then nearly ninety, and he walked round the rooms with a candle to show some pictures which he thought would give me pleasure. His courtesy and intelligence left a deep impression. Perhaps, like many happy natures, he was better suited for affection than for intimacy; Goldie, though he loved him, never felt that they knew each other well. Father and son were alike in one respect, they were both subject to fits of gloom. But, whereas the son could give reasons for his depression which are only too convincing, the father was vaguer about it; he would write a despairing letter, and be puzzled when a consolatory answer was returned. Despair in the nineteenth century was a male prerogative; there was held to be something noble and authoritative about it. The twentieth century has had to take a less romantic view.

When we turn from the father's side of the family to the mother's, we find much the same tradition of decency and sensitiveness. There seems to have been no notable clash of types in Dickinson's make-up, and he experienced none of the dangers or thrills which may be traced to war within the blood. His grandfather on his mother's side was William Smith Williams. Mr Williams was for many years literary adviser to the publishers Smith, Elder & Co.; he discovered Charlotte Brontë, and welcomed her when she made her famous first visit to London. His correspondence with Charlotte has been printed in Clement Shorter's Life. He was incapable of self-advertisement. After his retirement, he lived quietly at Twickenham, where he died in 1875. His wife, a Miss Hill, possibly had Jewish blood in her, and this would preserve Dickinson from the stigma of pure Aryan descent; otherwise the ancestry seems to have been English. The Williamses had several daughters, one of whom, Anna, became a famous singer. Another, Fanny, is said to have had an even finer voice.

The marriage of Ellen Williams to Mr Lowes Dickinson was supremely happy, and perhaps that is why their son came to regard marriage as the best attainable earthly state—a risky state, like any other, but promising a union of emotion and companionship which cannot be found outside. Mrs Lowes Dickinson was a woman of sweet but firm character, with strong opinions as to what is right and wrong, and with a narrow vein of piety running through the abundance of her natural goodness. She died when her son was only nineteen, so he never developed with her the close relationship which often exists, for good and evil, between a mother and a grown-up son. He looked back on her as he did on his father: with love and admiration, but with the feeling that there had never been any intimacy. There certainly was nothing which can be described as an exchange of ideas.

There were five children to the marriage: Arthur (now Sir Arthur Lowes Dickinson), May, G.L.D. himself, Hettie (now Mrs Lowes) and Janet. Arthur was three years older than his brother, and they were so different in outlook that they never became intimate, though there was friendliness and respect. On the other hand, Dickinson remained in close touch with his three sisters. His earliest companion and friend was his sister May. In their childhood May was "rather precocious. . . . She acted and sang and danced and certainly, to my remembrance, flirted." The "little ones", Hettie and Janet, seemed then to be separated by a great gulf of years, and he and May were anxious lest they should intrude. "However, we were all very friendly together, and, unless the sentiment of the past deceives me, the childhood of us all was on the whole very happy." He was in many ways well fitted for domestic life, and he never knew real misery until he was wrenched away from it.

He took his name Goldsworthy from Sir Goldsworthy Gurney, one of the Cornish Gurneys, who were related to the Carters. Sir Goldsworthy was an inventor, and considering how his namesake denounced motor cars it is ironical that he should have invented the first steam carriage and should have driven it to Bath and back at the rate of fifteen miles an hour. After his death, a stained-glass window was put up to him in St Margaret's, Westminster, which window is not as well known to visitors as it should be. Most of it is occupied by saints, but at the bottom of its central light two very graceful angels hold up a plaque on which is the little steam carriage itself, traversing an undulating landscape in grisaille. Sir Goldsworthy Gurney is aboard driving a party of passengers in top-hats, while some gentlemen admire him from an adjacent hill. In a separate compartment to the left of the angels he reappears on a large scale, thinking out something in his study, and to their right is a lighthouse amid a stormy sea. The inscription says: "He invented the steam jet and the oxyhydrogen blowpipe." Who could wish to trace the name of Goldsworthy back any further after this? Though a Miss Goldsworthy, ancestor to the Gurneys, is said to have been maid of honour to Queen Anne.

The origin of his second name, Lowes, has already been indicated; it came from his great-grandmother on the father's side, and it has been adopted by all his branch of the family.

chapter two

The Spring Cottage
1862-1872

Dickinson's *Recollections* begin as follows:

> The earliest thing I remember—or rather remember to have remem-
> bered, for that is how it now presents itself to me—is looking out of
> a pointed window, opening like a door and filled with small diamond
> panes of glass, at the people coming home from church through the
> little gate of our garden. I may have been two years old and my
> nurse was holding me. This was in our cottage at Hanwell, then a
> little country village, now part of the suburbs of London. One or two
> other memories seem to float vaguely at this threshold of conscious-
> ness. Once, for example, stars looked large, with points all round
> them, as they used to be painted on the roof of the old St James Hall
> in London. For I remember one night, later, looking up and feeling
> surprised and disappointed to see nothing but pale tiny points of light.
> That seems to be all I can recover of these earliest days. After that,
> memory proper begins, treacherous, complicated, stratum piled on
> stratum, reflection and comparison vitiating experience.

He had been born in London (6 August 1862), and his family
moved to The Spring Cottage soon afterwards. It was first thought
to be "Spring Cottage", and associated with the vernal season,
but this proved a mistake; it took its name from a neighbouring
residence, "The Spring", whose grounds contain a spring, and
its notepaper had to be altered. All his early memories centred
round it. It was—or rather is, for it still exists—the sort of house
which excites and charms a child, for it was small, and completely
surrounded by a garden. When the family arrived there were
only two sitting-rooms, two bedrooms, a kitchen, and a veranda
covered with white roses, but they added a dining-room on the
ground floor and nurseries above it, and since the new dining-
room was connected with the old drawing-room by a greenhouse,
no conceivable delight was lacking, not even panes of coloured
glass. Then there was the furniture: the library table and the
Hepplewhite chairs which followed him finally to Cambridge;
the black clock; the Collard piano in a boxwood case, "sweeter,

5

I think, in tone than pianos have since become"; the Sheraton sideboard; the green velvet chairs; a vase supported by two little cherubs; the books, dark in colour, and including *Curiosities of London* where a boy was blinded by tying across his eyes two shells in each of which was a live beetle. . . . The children dashed quickly up to bed past the books. And above the white roses on the veranda grew a wistaria, which his mother, leaning out of her window, plucked to put in her hair. The whole picture, as he recalled it, has the graciousness and the solidity of a woodcut belonging to the period. It is a childhood of the 'sixties.

> The garden hangs in my past like a vision of light. Flower-beds are brighter than they have ever been since; shrubberies more mysterious; spaces larger, storms and rain more exciting. How I recall at this moment the oncoming of a storm, the black sky, the still air, and us in the twilight garden running and screaming with delight. And then the lightning, hour after hour, the sky opening and closing like an amazing flower, as I lay and watched it from my bed, till at last some elder pulled down the green venetian blinds, and there was nothing to be seen but the flicker of light at their edges.

The various trees in the garden had their characters. The fir tree was smothered in ivy, the chestnut commanded a view of the road, the sycamore dropped seeds onto the fernery, the cherry was covered with double white blossom, and under it his mother sat and sewed while they read aloud to her; to the end of his life this particular image recurred whenever he saw the double cherry in the Fellows' Garden at King's. There was also a kitchen garden, a shed, and a swing in which he and his brother and his sisters would impersonate the broad-gauge engines of the Great Western Railway. And outside the garden began in easy processes the world, reached by the trains, or by the new village cab upholstered in purple velvet, or on foot, or in a perambulator.

When Emma their nurse took them into the world, the expedition usually ended at a cemetery. Hanwell was happily placed for cemeteries: there were two large ones, besides the churchyard, and Emma liked to see the hearses come slowly down from London. Under her supervision, the children watched the interments from a distance, and spelled out the inscriptions on the tombs, and observed that the hearses called at a public-house on the return journey, and then proceeded less sadly. A young grocer who was courting her sometimes took them for rides in his cart. This was a great delight, and they gained lessons in deport-

6

ment too, and learned to refer to people mysteriously and by initials only: Mr A., Mrs C.—a method to be extended later to royalty. They learned too that tea should be drunk with a loud smacking sound. Emma married her grocer, and Dickinson kept in touch with her until her death, which occurred a year before his own. She was a most warm-hearted and affectionate woman.

The children were by no means left to run about with servants. They moved in the first circles of Hanwell society as soon as they could move at all, for although their father was not rich he was an artist of repute and position. "There were the people you knew and the people you only knew about, and the tradespeople, who were outside the pale, and the poor who sat in what were called free seats in church, and were visited and helped if they were good." Their chief friends were at The Spring—Sir Alexander Spearman and his family—but they were constantly at the rectory too, and this is important in view of later developments. The rector of Hanwell, Derwent Coleridge, was a son of the poet. He was a learned old gentleman, with a shaven chin and white side-whiskers, who knew several languages, and preached an annual sermon beginning "Reading Plato the other night . . .". He had a son Ernest, a daughter Christabel, and a niece Edith, who knew Greek, and taught the children's mother, who, in her turn, taught them. The most interesting feature of the rectory was not the Coleridges but the long succession of young Americans who came to be initiated by them into English niceties; seated upon the knees of one of these kind young men, Dickinson asked him why his face was so spotty—a piece of innocence which it horrified him to recall, yet it was not uncharacteristic. There was also an ecclesiastical crisis. Mr Coleridge took to turning east during the creed, and this involved him in a dispute with the squire, who turned west as a counterweight. The Dickinsons took the rector's side, and their father, who was fond of writing letters, sent one in which he rebuked the squire for straining at the gnat of turning to the east while swallowing the camel of unchristian feelings at the communion table. But the children visited at the squire's house too—if indeed he was the squire: there was a little doubt, he was melancholy and had an organ. And there were other figures who seemed, in retrospect, almost too fantastic to have lived: the lady who sang but could not shake until she heard Grisi sing "The Nightingale", and then "I shook and shook and have shaken ever since"; the lady who was shocked because work was done on the new railway station on Sunday, and cried:

7

"Believe me, Mr Dickinson, God's blessing will never rest upon it"; and the rector calling to his wife in the middle of a party: "Mary, my dear, we must keep a small Poe in the drawing-room." The chief drawback to all these kind people was that they were elderly and had no little children. For purposes of play, less eminent families had to be commandeered.

"In this place and society I passed my earliest years," and then follows a long list of little memories. Among them are "Lying in bed in the dusk, listening to the Moonlight Sonata played below; lying in bed in the morning . . . ; playing at Fairies with my father, which meant stealing up and tickling his bald head, while he pretended to be asleep; . . . singing, in a little piping voice, a song about a little fish . . . ; singing hymns on Sunday evening"; composing a hymn of his own—

> Woe unto ye pharisees,
> Woe unto ye scribes,
> Walking in the darkness
> Of your darkened eyes.

—and reciting it to his mother; "being sent to bed, and crying for hours; being spanked (once only)". And then lessons, based on *Little Arthur's History* and other textbooks of the period, and not at all interesting, though not repellent.

My mother, with infinite patience, conducted us through this routine, as well as running the house, providing her little dinner parties, learning her Greek, and adoring my father who also loved her, yet, as I think, not as she loved him.

Then, every year, a month or so by the sea, sands and donkey rides, sea-anemones, bathing, blackberries and cream. . . . A happy life, as I look back on it, and the happier because it was followed by such misery. For the time came when I was sent to school.

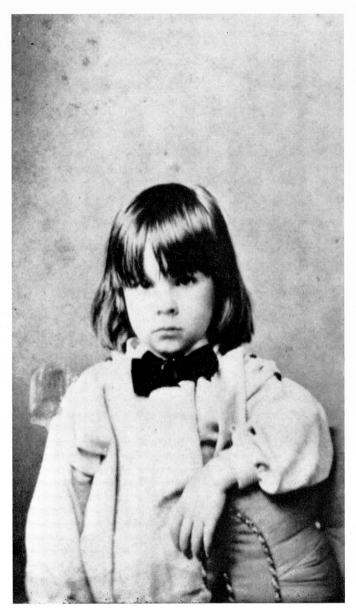

Age 6. *Photo by Dickinson Bros, his grandfather's firm*

Age 14. *Photo by Thorpe, Hastings*

chapter three

The Misses Woodman's Morning Class
1872-1874

The first school was not alarming, indeed it was only an extension of his home life. It was a day-school kept by two sisters called Woodman at 13 Somerset Street, Portman Square. He never forgot the address, because he got a prize every term, and on its cover was stamped the Misses Woodman's monogram surrounded by their address and by the words "morning class for the sons of gentlemen". Tom Hughes's sons, Pip and Plump, went to the same school, and it was evidently the best that Christian Socialists could provide for their young. Tradesmen were excluded, except when they were definitely rich, like Tab, afterwards Lord Brassey, and vice should have been excluded too, but it crept in and there was an appalling scene one morning during geography when a red-headed boy was detected telling a lie. "William Watson!" said Miss Woodman in terrible tones, "You have told a lie!" "I thought," said the assistant mistress afterwards, "Miss Woodman would have fainted."

To this snobby, conscientious and harmless establishment the child went up daily, taking the early train from Hanwell to Paddington, and returning in the afternoon, to be welcomed at the garden gate by his nurse. He had a pleasant time, and was "well grounded". Education, as we understand it today, was scarcely attempted. Everything was learned by heart. His mother had taught him Greek and Euclid by heart, and the Misses Woodman continued on her lines. Before long he could repeat a number of sentences like "Common are to either sex Artifex and opifex", and "Syllaba longa brevi subjecta vocatur iambus"—sentences to which neither he nor the Misses Woodman attached any meaning. In geography, when a country was outlined on the blackboard and round blobs were put for its towns, he could name the blobs as long as he looked at the board. No one suggested to him that "iambus" had to do with poetry, Greek with literature, and geography with Hanwell or Paddington. They were incantations which his preceptors desired him to memorize.

There were two Miss Woodmans, Miss Woodman proper, who was stern and ironical, and Miss Maria, with a cast in her eye, who was violent and ugly. When we said our irregular verbs to Miss Woodman, she would repeat: "Yes! Fatiscor. Fatiscor, I am weary. I am weary of you boys." Meantime, from the room above, out of the floor of which a circular hole opened into the room below, would come the smack smack of Miss Maria boxing someone's ears. Miss Woodman would pause with a sigh and then resume operations. "Fatiscor, I am weary." About these two great goddesses the lesser mistresses revolved deferentially. . . .

Only later on was a man introduced, as an experiment. He was called "the graduate", but he wasn't a success, I don't remember why. At any rate, one term saw the end of him; and at the prize-giving Miss Woodman remarked, with caustic wit, that should he turn up again it would be as an "uninvited guest".

Miss Woodman was a remarkable character. His sister Hettie taught in her school some years later and got the same impression of her love of the dramatic and her disciplinary power; "Lay not this flattering unction to your soul" was a favourite and a mysterious exclamation.

Once his parents went to America, the Hanwell cottage was shut up for a term and he was sent to board at the school. He became a favourite, and the mistresses cosseted him. He enjoyed scripture and breakfast in the morning, for he was a pious and hungry little boy. In the afternoon there were walks in Hyde Park, where a steam engine was seen, not Sir Goldsworthy's but an object in a vermilion box. Midday dinner was served in the gas-lit basement:

We were expected to provide the Miss Woodmans with what they wanted without their having to ask for it, and terrible it was when we heard a voice "I have to *ask* for the salt". I learned to say "thank you" instead of "please", and became conscious of a much improved style. A curious thing is memory. For now there comes back to me a picture of Miss Maria, in the water closet, trying in vain to flush it, and screaming "Someone has been using much too much paper". Many years later Miss Woodman married and Miss Maria separated from her.

The term passed rather slowly and he was glad to be back at The Spring Cottage again. He found that his sisters had grown out of all recognition, and he felt much more important himself. His childish outlook continued. He still loved playing at engines, he still thought education meant learning by heart, and, instigated by his mother, he was still very "religious". Every night he read a chapter of the Bible, sitting in his nightgown out on the landing under the gas jet and wishing someone would come and see how good he was. He must have been at the same time a charming and a morbid child. The charm was immense. All the visitors loved him and tried to spoil him. The morbidity may have been fostered by misguided training. The piety of his parents was, in his later judgement, unhelpful. It checked his instincts for enjoyment and gave him nothing with which to take their place. Yet how delightful life was—until the age of twelve. Then came the last childish holiday, at Croyde in Devonshire, and the news that he was going to a "real" school. His heart sank, but there was nothing to be done. The Misses Woodman and The Spring Cottage itself faded away, and he was carried off by his mother and left by her in a large, newly scrubbed room, there to await the arrival of real boys.

chapter four
Beomonds
1874-1876

Dickinson once took me to see his old preparatory school. It is at Chertsey, not far from the poet Cowley's house, and stands with its flank to the road. It is still a school, but for girls. We rang the bell on the chance, and were let in. He told the young mistresses how unhappy he had been there once, and how cold, and how he had scrambled in the morning for hot rolls, and they patronized him, but they were impressed when he told them that Charles Kingsley had once attended a prize distribution in the room where we were all standing. It was the room on the right of the entrance, and perhaps it was here that his mother left him to face the world. Frail, distinguished, and in the eyes of the mistresses doubtless somewhat absurd, he looked sadly round his former prison, which had become romantic because it was so far away. Then he thanked them with his usual gentleness, and returned to the world—a place which, for all its horrors, had never quite fulfilled the preliminary threat. "One suffers more later, but one has at least experience to correct it and character to fight it. At school a timid boy like me has no aid and no hope."

When he went to the school it had just been started by Ernest Coleridge, the son of the rector of Hanwell. He was a pompous fattish man, who "later found his proper work as an editor of Byron", and his letters to Mr Lowes Dickinson about his pupil make ironic reading, when one thinks of the black pools of misery beneath—decent prim letters, such as schoolmasters always will be content to write and parents to receive. He likes Goldie and reports that he can be taught anything, "and has more or less mastered the style of Horace", but is inaccurate, and "not an ascetic in regard to his dinner". The housekeeping was first done by Mr Coleridge's sister, Christabel. Then he took to himself a wife, whom he was said to have courted for years. There was rather an awkward silence when he brought her into the school-room to be introduced. None of the boys could think what to say. At last Charles Kingsley's son, who had a certain amount of savoir-faire and had previously been at Harrow, said, "I am sure sir we all congratulate you very much," and the situation was saved.

The wretchedness began at once. When it is recorded it looks like nothing at all, and seems to constitute no real indictment of the boarding-school system. There was no physical bullying to speak of, and no revolting orgy; indeed to the normal boy and the complacent grown-up Beomonds must have seemed quite a sound place. But, like most boys who have any imaginative contribution to make, Goldie was not normal. He suffered from torments which assail the spirit, from moral bullying, of which there was a great deal, and from his own timidity. Sometimes he gave in to schoolboy ethics as in the crisis of the potatoes, which shall be recorded presently, and then he was tortured by remorse. Sometimes he held out, but at great nervous expenditure and with none of the glow of martyrdom as a reward. He managed to get the worst of both worlds, to appease neither his darker angel nor his brighter, and for the reason that the third world—the world of Ariel—was excluded. Instead of the Moonlight Sonata, floating up through the floor of The Spring Cottage, sounds like these assailed his ears:

> Sitting round the table in the evening, supposed to be preparing unintelligible "work", I was disturbed and perplexed by the talk of older boys. "Bitches." What was a bitch? Did I know? "It's a female dog, isn't it?" said Kingsley, and I said yes, and thought perhaps it was. But then, why talk about it? Then someone put something cold down my back. Then prayers in the hall, all the servants trooping in, and Mr Coleridge in great form. Prayers, I think, always ended with "For so he giveth his beloved sleep". That sounded soothing. But then one went up to a bedroom with three other boys, one older, and inclined to bully, and there were many pains before sleep was given to one who I fear was not "his beloved".

What with the sinister hints, what with his top-hat, which had belonged to his brother and turned Sunday into a catastrophe, and what with his habit of washing thoroughly at night and only a little in the morning, whereas the other boys washed only in the morning and not at all at night, he was instantly reduced to despair, and before a week had elapsed he wrote home and asked to be taken away. Very characteristically he wrote on a post-card. It was intercepted, much to his surprise, and he was summoned by Miss Coleridge to the drawing-room. Buxom and effusive Christabel took him on her knee, cosseted him, talked to him like a mother, and ended with: "And now we will destroy this unlucky postcard." It went into the fire, and with it his last hope of escape. His letters home were henceforward read by the masters, indeed he no longer thought of escape: after the unlucky postcard had been burnt, there was nothing to be done, and time stretched forward endlessly, without a gleam to vary its monotony.

The gloom was increased by Mr Coleridge's attempts to deal with what was still termed "the mystery of sex". Serious and incompetent, he had summoned Goldie to the rectory at Hanwell before school opened, and had made some vague remarks that had no meaning whatever. Later on, hearing that he had had a bath with another boy, he called him to his study and cross-questioned him. The child was absolutely bewildered, he had no idea what the conversation was about, and Mr Coleridge soon became scared at the absence of response, and then dismissed him with the words "I don't know whether you are more fool than knave". He never heard one sensible word from any grown-up person on the subject. Once at home he had noticed that the cat looked larger than usual, and hazarded the guess that she had kittens inside her—not that he really believed anything so preposterous. His grandmother, who heard him, became humorous and sly, and changes in sleeping arrangements were the only answer.

His parents loved him and they had good instincts. But it was an age in which principles, not instincts, were valued, and they harnessed their love to the chariot of a narrow morality. The boys at Beomonds, for instance, were forbidden to buy sweets from the tuck-shop in term time; they all did it, so did he, and he referred to it in the holidays. His mother was deeply distressed, she spoke to his father, there was a painful lecture, and he returned to school with the feeling that it was definitely "wrong" to buy sweets or break any rule whatever. "Wrong", and at the same time "right"; he felt for the first time the fascination of disobedience for its own sake.

> The effect was far greater than might seem probable. It formed a kind of complex which haunted me all through my school life. Perhaps it is at the root of my impatience now of most current rules of conduct. But now I have reason and character to justify myself to myself. Then it was a mere fetish, which had got hold of me to my undoing. *Why*, though, did it get hold of me, when most boys would have let it pass indifferently? That, I suppose, goes deep into my character. At any rate, a confusion of conscientiousness, timidity,

hypocrisy seized upon and held me for many years. I emerged from it ultimately a rebel, and at bottom have been so all my life. But by what strange and devious routes the approach was made!

We can see from the above passage (if indeed its evidence were necessary) that he was not the ordinary sensitive boy. He was sensitive, but he was not ordinary, for he had the power of turning his unhappiness to account. There was something pretty tough in him—something which he consciously developed in later life. He could draw strength from the most unpromising objects. And though he regrets the "strange and devious route", and the apparent waste of energy and time which the fuss about the tuck-shop caused him, we may surmise that he could not have reached his final position by any other route, so that his parents were guiding him better than he knew.

The immediate consequences were, no doubt, most enervating. Here is a letter which reveals them in all their force. Note that he is writing not from Beomonds but from Charterhouse, some months later.

Charterhouse, Godalming
22 October 1876

My dearest Mother,

I want to tell you of something wrong that I did at Mr Coleridge's. I only remembered it the other day and thought that I should like to tell you. We used to cook things in the school room on Saturday evening and once or twice they sent me to get potatoes out of the stables and I did not like to refuse and so I went and I suppose it was as bad as stealing as they were Mr Coleridge's and I took little things like slate pencils too but I suppose that didn't matter. Please write to me soon.

Ever your affec^{ate} son
Goldie.

His mother evidently dealt with this letter as a parent in the 'seventies would, and she seems to have declined to distinguish between potatoes and pencils. Anyhow she elicits a second agonized confession in which the boy assures her that he is suffering over his wickedness quite as much as she can suffer and prays God to pardon him. A parent of today would have been bright and brief and, without condoning theft, would have managed to censure self-consciousness. Though even today has the recipe for handling sensitive children been formulated?

Beomonds had its pleasanter moments. He spouted Tennyson's "Dora", and Miss Coleridge said: "Well done, little Goldie." He acted Mrs Bouncer in *Box and Cox* amid great applause, though when he cleaned himself up one of the guests remarked: "What! Was it that little whippersnapper!" There was skating and walking, and bathing in the Thames without costumes— the middle classes had not yet adopted this fetish. And, occasionally, though more rarely than before, he caught sight of the glory of literature. "I have seen the sea," said Mr Boyd, a much admired master, meaning by those words that he had seen Salvini in *Othello*, and the words thrilled Dickinson, and in after years he echoed them. And when he had to translate Horace into verse —even if it was not the Horatian style it was not so bad for a boy of thirteen:

> Why love the pine and poplar white
> With mingling boughs sweet shade to spread?
> Why does the murmuring brook delight
> To hurry down its zigzag bed?

But these amenities lay at the edge of his life. Its centre was covered with rubbish and worry. And at its opposite edge lay an imbecile boy whom he sometimes kicked in order to ingratiate himself with his schoolfellows. He made no special confession to his parents about this; it was not a crime like the potatoes, nevertheless it haunted him.

chapter five

Charterhouse
1876-1881

Of Charterhouse he writes:

> I was there the other day, an elderly stranger, and had still the
> remembrance of prison and the joy of one released. Charterhouse
> was the same thing as Chertsey, only longer and worse. . . . The
> house was left to the monitors, who had powers to punish by boxing
> the ears (called "swingeing") and beating with sticks (called "cocking
> up", from the attitude assumed by the victim).
> The house in my time was what would be called a "hothouse of
> vice". The odd thing is that, though in a sort of way I knew this,
> I wasn't interested in it and didn't attend to it.

There follow some mournful and bitter reminiscences. He was
worried by sex and by the evasions of his elders on the subject,
and he was still more worried by the fetish of rules. One Sunday,
Dr Haig Brown preached a sermon about the importance of
keeping rules, and revived the tuck-shop trouble in Dickinson's
anxious mind. What rule had he broken last? He had been
guilty of talking in the dormitory after dark. The dormitory
was divided into cubicles, and the boys used to chat over the
partitions although they were told not to. That night, half dead
with terror, he announced that he would talk no more, then he
put his head under the clothes expecting martyrdom. Nothing
happened. When he listened again, the dormitory chattered as
usual, on other topics, though later on one boy did remark
"Funny thing him saying that", and another replied "Yes".
Nor was he persecuted next day. He felt both relieved and disappointed, and before long he resumed talking himself. All that
emerged from his effort was the feeling that he was alien, and that
whether he talked or was silent the rest of the dormitory belonged
to another world. "I have never lost it [this feeling]. Indeed, in
my old age I feel it as I never felt it before. Men become to me
simply unintelligible."

Then there was another address from Dr Haig Brown on the
mysterious subject of Collecting. "I pity that boy," boomed the

authoritative voice, "who has never been a Collector," and Dickinson, who was that boy, felt ashamed. "But I pity still more that boy who has remained a Mere Collector," and he felt he must be that boy too.

Then there was Confirmation, for which he was prepared on a manual drawn up for domestic servants. Another vague and alarming sex-talk accompanied it. He became more devout and attended Holy Communion with unreal but conscientious religiosity, liking to feel good, and sometimes longing to be bad. He was in a complete muddle, without any standards except what were imposed from outside, and even his rebellions were conventional. Left to himself he would have escaped into the lost world of Ariel, where neither obedience nor disobedience existed, and the only sacrament was beauty. And on one occasion that world was rediscovered. He was doing a dead language, Greek. Suddenly the smut, the moral tension, the meaningless lesson vanished and

> At length, in the dreary chaotical closet
> Of Erebus old, was a privy deposit,
> By Night the primeval in secrecy laid;
> A Mystical Egg, that in silence and shade
> Was brooded and hatched; till time came about,
> And Love, the delightful, in glory flew out,
> In rapture and light, exulting and bright,
> Sparkling and florid, with stars in his forehead,
> His forehead and hair, and a flutter and flare
> As he rose in the air, triumphantly furnished
> To range his dominions, on glittering pinions,
> All golden and azure, and blooming and burnished.

What had happened? Why, Mr T. E. Page, the Sixth Form master, was reading out to his class a passage from Frere's translation of the *Birds* of Aristophanes. Yes, but what had happened? What was this new existence? These words which came in the middle of Greek and had nothing to do with it, this magic which had nothing to do with chapel, this music which kept its measure apart from rules or the breaking of rules? Mr Page stopped reading, Greek was resumed, the door shut. But Dickinson had had a glimpse of the land which was his home.

One wonders, sharing his exultation, and knowing that in later life he could enter that land at will: one wonders why he did not stay there constantly, always with Ariel and Love the delightful, and rapture and sunlight and the Moonlight Sonata, where

sorrow is transformed into grace. Here was his home, and he
admitted as much. Yet he entered only to withdraw, and to return
to the anarchy whose dark premonition had been shown to him
at school. Was it that school, acting on his raw character, had
warped him? Or was it, as he came to maintain, that the world
of Ariel will not satisfy us until Caliban is tamed, Antonio
reformed, and Prospero restored to his kingdom? Perhaps the
difference between his boyhood and manhood was that as a boy
he could not escape from the horrors of existence, and that as a
man he would not escape from them. To a man of his character
this constituted a profound difference, and he was never again
to be as unhappy as at Beomonds and Charterhouse.

His social career was obscure. He made only two friends—
J. A. R. Munro and H. T. Bowlby. Munro was moved by the
great protest in the dormitory, came up next day, congratulated
the hero on his courage. "The reward of virtue, I suppose."
Later on Bowlby joined them. They formed one of those alliances
which are not uncommon between unpopular boys, and which
spring largely from circumstances. In any community it is necessary to have someone with whom you can consort and who will
not turn against you when you are attacked, and it is most
necessary in the community of school, where attacks are so
capricious, and so relentless when they start. Dickinson, Munro
and Bowlby clung to each other through the perils of Charterhouse, played fives together, looked on at games, which were not
at that date compulsory, and shared a study where they sat up
with cold feet till past midnight, doing work which they did not
understand. They were all highly good boys, they worked hard
and rose from form to form till they were made monitors, and the
school showed them what it thought of them by calling them
"The Three Graces". Munro is now Rector of Lincoln College,
Oxford, Bowlby became headmaster of Lancing and is now a
canon at Chichester. Dickinson kept in friendship with Munro,
who has preserved several sympathetic memories of him, and
thinks that his own memories are somewhat too pessimistic.
He lost sight of Bowlby.

Another slight alleviation was acting. His sister May acted
well, and he himself had performed with applause, at Hanwell
and Chertsey. At Charterhouse the visit of a Miss Volkes developed
in him a passion for the stage which, subsiding into an interest,
was maintained all his life. Miss Volkes was a professional actress,
who had come down with a company of Old Carthusians, and

her rendering of "My Johnny was a shoemaker" threw the lad into unusual agitations. He mooned about the court in the hope of seeing her again, and even wrote out by heart the play which she had given, with a view to performing it during the holidays. She echoed as it were the chord struck by the Aristophanes passage, "sparkling and florid, with stars in his forehead". She had "a wonderful laugh, a kind of ripple", and the boys declared she got a little tight while stopping with the Haig Browns. She went, and her gaiety with her, but she had shown him the way to the footlights, and a tendency in that direction which never proved fatal gathered strength after her visit. His music developed also: a more permanent possession. Munro still remembers his Mozart and Beethoven on the piano. He took up the violin for a time and performed in the school orchestra. And there were anemones and bluebells on the hill in spring, but he couldn't feel they belonged to him, for he did not yet belong to himself.

In this dim and unsatisfactory fashion the years wore away. Of course there were the holidays, but they were overshadowed by the masses of the departing and of the approaching terms, they were like a valley between high cliffs, into which the sun has no time to penetrate. No sooner had he got rid of Charterhouse than he had to get ready for it. Some pleasant things happened: one year his father took him and Arthur and May to Switzerland. It was the first time he had been abroad. He enjoyed himself, but he could not remember much afterwards except that they had argued about the names of mountains, and that his father, when trying to pinch his ear in the hotel, had pinched a young lady's by mistake. Other holidays were spent in London; when he was sixteen they left The Spring Cottage and moved into the house in All Souls Place. Memories of the *Messiah* and better still the *Elijah* . . . excerpts from a queer new thing, *The Ring*, and the composer embracing the conductor afterwards. . . . May liked *The Ring*, he could make nothing of it . . . the Bancrofts in *Caste* . . . Irving in *The Lyons Mail*, and, most moving of all, a play (name forgotten) in which a steamer ran down a row-boat on the stage. But each day nearer came the fortress on the hill above Godalming, ready to imprison him, and that was really happiness, people told him, he could never hope to be as happy as at school.

I curse the time as I look back upon it. It seems to me all evil and no good. Cut off from home life, unknown to them and they to me, without a root to hold me that really sprang from myself, yet tormented

by external ties of mere superstition, with not one of those passionate
friendships or loves which redeem school for many boys, despised,
and, as I think, rightly, yet by people who themselves were despicable,
with no intellectual interest and no moral conviction, alone as I have
never been alone since, physically unfit, mentally undeveloped—
was ever a sadder, drearier, more hopeless entry upon life? And no
one knew. And so, of course, no one cared.

It is interesting to compare this indictment with that of Robert
Graves, who was at Charterhouse thirty years later, and has said
what he thought about it in *Good-Bye to All That*. There is no
reason to suppose that Charterhouse either was or is worse than
our other leading educational hotels, but as generation after
generation of sensitive boys record their experiences in them
one marvels why the boarding-house system continues at all,
and why the middle classes still insist on so much discomfort
for their children at such expense to themselves.

chapter six

Cambridge
1881-1884

O Cambridge! Cambridge! small the need
Of plighted faith to honour thee;
Thine is the hand that sowed the seed,
The gathered fruit thy guerdon be;
'Twere wasted breath to bid thee take
The creature thou thyself didst make.
              G. L. D. (written in 1887)

Dickinson went up from Charterhouse to Cambridge in the autumn of 1881. Since he was in the popular estimation a typical don, it is curious to reflect that only by chance did he go to the university at all. His father could not afford to send him up unaided, and he was only "proxime accessit" on the list for entrance scholarships at King's. But one of the successful candidates went elsewhere, and he was given an exhibition of £40 a year. Unobtrusively and indifferently he began a connection which lasted over fifty years. He had no idea what Cambridge meant—and I remember having the same lack of comprehension about the place myself, when my own turn came to go up there. It seems too good to be real. That the public school is not infinite and eternal, that there is something more compelling in life than teamwork and more vital than cricket, that firmness, self-complacency and fatuity do not between them compose the whole armour of man, that lessons may have to do with leisure, and grammar with literature—it is difficult for an inexperienced boy to grasp truths so revolutionary, or to realize that freedom can sometimes be gained by walking out through an open door. The door had been opened before, to be closed. People, music, books and scenery—the four gifts he loved most—had been shown to him tantalizingly in childhood, and then withdrawn. Now he saw them again, all filled with a new vigour, they beckoned to him, they were all four alive, and their recapture fills the next years of his life. He was often to be exquisitely happy. He was always to have a choice before him which alleviated his miseries. To be a man was, in itself, a satisfaction to him, and he set himself to occupy, so far as he could, our heritage.

When he went up to King's there were only sixty under-graduates and a few resident dons. The Eton connection was still very strong; indeed it was not many years since the college had been open only to Etonians or since its members had had the right to claim a degree without sitting for an examination. King's was, and one hopes still is, a peculiar place. Eton, its twin foundation, gave it a tradition for which all non-Etonians must be grateful: a genuine instead of a faked tradition. And mingling with this were the oddities and the crudities—people who had not enjoyed their public schools or had been to the wrong school or even to none. They too contributed, and though the college tended at times to divide into what has been called the smart and the smarting set no fatal split occurred. Brains are not everything, as we all keep telling one another, still they do counteract social silliness, and the fact that all undergraduates at King's have to read for Honours has ensured a certain level of intelligence, upon which mutual comprehension can seize its chance to build.

His brother Arthur had preceded him to King's, was kind, and launched and lunched him at once, but "some of his friends were with him, and everything still breathed the wearisome air of the public school. I wasn't at home with that kind of man and I hardly knew there were other kinds." Healthy, practical, and destined for worldly distinction, his brother's friends could only intimidate him, and he was slow to find friends of his own. For a year or more he didn't really know what he wanted, and was dazed "like a boy recovering from a long illness". One of his friends, Graham, afterwards told him that he had been a very insignificant freshman, "and I am sure he was right". He worked ahead in the torpid, pseudo-industrious way he had acquired at school, taking classics because he was advised to, making notes, keeping lectures, counting hours. He went down to the river to be tubbed because it was the proper thing, and writes to his mother (22 October 1881): "I am getting on pretty well with my rowing but it is much more difficult than I thought, the coaches are very nice and don't blow one up nearly as much as I expected." The letter continues on a more genuine note: "I am getting on beautifully with my bicycle." He loved the bicycle even in its penny-farthing edition, and when the wheels became equal in size he was constantly astride. On this occasion he got no further than Newmarket, where he arrived "after several falls just too late for the train", and bathed in mud.

By the age of nineteen his desire to serve humanity was already strong, but it took inappropriate forms, like his work and his exercise. We find him, for instance (13 February 1882), joining the Cambridge University volunteers. "What, would you shoot your superior officer, sir?" is the legendary exclamation of the sergeant at whom he had pointed his rifle; and anyhow he was struck off the strength on 8 June 1884. Then he practised bell-ringing; he took a class of poor boys at Barnwell; he decided to reform prostitutes and asked freshmen for subscriptions for that purpose; he tried to reform his equals, and invited an atheist who had been drunk to join the Church of England Temperance Society. The atheist was headachy and polite, "but he declined the siren's voice". In all this activity we can trace the tradition of the Christian Socialism in which he was brought up, and he was in his own way to continue that tradition, though Frederick Denison Maurice would disown him, and Charles Kingsley turn in the grave. After several failures he realized that he could not serve humanity by the old methods, so he turned to new methods, and sometimes they were revolutionary, but he never abandoned the notion of service.

His rooms as a freshman were in Benet Street. Here he was able to escape and be alone, and the experience was so delightful that he began to wish for company. Undergraduates interested him very little during his first year, but he was impressed by two of the dons. One of them was his tutor, J. E. C. Welldon, who exercised on him an influence which he could not define. "I was at once shy and hero-worshipping." Welldon performed his duties conscientiously, but made no attempt to draw his admirer out. "I doubt whether he deserved the hero-worship. At any rate he and I have moved too far apart since then for any mutual comprehension." He remained a burly and enigmatical figure, uneasily balancing on a bicycle along the Ely road, and his subsequent career, as Headmaster of Harrow, Bishop of Calcutta, Dean of Durham and critic of the working classes, provoked little enthusiasm.

The other don was a very different story and a longer one. In the letter to his mother quoted above, he goes on to say that he is hearing and playing music at O.B.'s. This is the famous Oscar Browning, friend and enemy to so many generations of Kingsmen. Some people loved him—and Dickinson was to join their number. Others have disliked him so much that they have denied his greatness, and indeed the adjectives describing him do produce a confused effect in their totality. "Falstaffian, shameless, affectionate, egoistic, generous, snobbish, democratic, witty, lazy, dull, worldly, academic" is Dickinson's list, and he might have added that his hero could be a bully and a liar. He does add that he had "the Socratic gift of maieusis"—the gift which he himself was to combine with selflessness. O.B. was never bothered with that, still, whatever his make-up, he did manage to educate young men. His information might be erroneous, his method of conveying it intolerable, but he did lead them to discover themselves, and to bring to birth what would have lain in embryo. It was he who brought Dickinson out of the seven years' darkness, and set him upon his proper road. The *Recollections* have much to say about this, and I quote from them with the more pleasure because I agree with what is said. I came towards the end of O.B.'s glory, nor was I ever part of its train. But he shines out with a magnificence which has been withheld from his admirable detractors, he remains as something unique in the history of the university, a deposit of radium, a mass of equivocal fire.

I will set down some things I remember of him. He came down to my brother's room, which was on the same staircase as his, when I was a freshman of only a few days. He came rollicking in, already stout, already middle-aged, but with an air of equality with youth which I could not then comprehend. . . . Then I spoke at a debate when he was present. It was about ghosts. He was interested in my speech, came up to me afterwards and said: "I didn't know you were such a clever fellow." This was characteristic, for his principal gift was the power of making men believe in themselves. . . . After that, I remember playing duets with him, on his grand piano, how his bulky form crushed me into a small corner of the seat and the tempo was judiciously manipulated to suit his not too agile fingers. We played, I remember, the slow movement of Beethoven's 7th sonata [symphony?], and it became very slow indeed when we reached the demi-semi-quavers. . . .

He always had some boy or young man as a secretary, and for many boys and youths he did much to start them in life. His interest was in the young aristocrat, on the one hand, and the obscure struggler on the other. His rooms at that time, and for many years, were the centre of all that was most sociable, genial and stimulating in Cambridge. Every Sunday evening he was "at home"; and I heard at that time really good music there. . . . Later, he got together some curious kind of harmoniums supposed to represent the different instruments of an orchestra. Undergraduates called them O-Beophones, and I cannot pretend that I ever heard anything from them except cacophony.

He (O.B.) was secretary of innumerable clubs, including the swimming club, where his corpulent person was constantly to be found in the state of primitive nudity which, in those early and happy days, was characteristic of Cambridge bathing. For even in the meadows open to view, where the members of the town bathed, they ran in crowds quite naked, over the green grass. O.B. conducted at that time the Political Society, which he had founded and of which I, though then studying classics, not history, became a member. A paper was read, during which the President reclined in his armchair, a red pocket-handkerchief of enormous size covering his face. Then we all spoke in turn according to an order dictated by lots drawn out of a bag. I have passed many dull evenings there, but some that were interesting. And interesting or dull, O.B. produced his usual effect. We felt that we were men, and history a serious subject. Mr Browning's ambition was to produce statesmen. The only one I remember as emerging from his hearth-rug is Mr Austen Chamberlain, perhaps not the most intelligent of men, but always, so far as I know, kind, friendly and honourable.

Later, when I became a teacher at King's, Mr Browning was my senior colleague. I cannot honestly say that I found it easy to work with him, for I often disagreed with him, and never was there a man more incapable of seeing another man's point of view.

And then comes a picture more appropriate to the Italian Renaissance than the age of Victoria.

I found him once in his inner room, where he slept behind a screen, in the act of getting up. On one side of him was a secretary writing letters to dictation, on the other another secretary playing the violin. O.B. was seated in dishabille, between the two, and he began to speak on a subject always congenial to him, himself. Once, he said, he had his horoscope taken. He was born in the ascendancy of two planets, Capricorn and Saturn, the one elating, the other depressing. But, however much crushed by Saturn, he always knew that Capricorn would toss him up again to the sky.

One speculates, in passing, whether it was Oscar Browning or Dickinson who termed Capricorn a planet; either was capable of it. Their friendship is pleasant to remember. O.B. always liked "Gouldie" as he insisted on calling him, and regretted that he had not become more influential. And Goldie, as a rule so fastidious, could thank, with more than usual gratitude, the Silenus who had awakened him from nightmare.

How many young men did he stir to life who afterwards turned against him! They were wrong, though not without excuse. The man was more than his foibles; and I greet him here as many others might greet him, as one of those who discovered me to myself.

Since he wrote the above there has been a biography of O.B., by his nephew H. E. Wortham. He admired it greatly, and indeed it is one of the best biographies of the last few years—quite unsparing and completely sympathetic.

At the end of his first year at Cambridge (May 1882) a tragic event occurred which moved him deeply and finally marked his transition from the alien life to the real one. It shall be told in his own words.

One day, returning from a bicycle ride, I found a telegram telling me my mother was dead. . . . She had long been ill, but I was expecting no change. The effect of this telegram, perhaps, I do not justly recall. But, as it seems to me now, it was a curious blend of conventional and real feeling. The incredible had happened—for is not death always incredible?—and I had not come across it before. There was something about that that stunned. Then there was the effort, as it were, to feel more than one did or could; a curious sense of the melodrama of the position. And grief? Yes, I think so; and yet that not prominent and exclusive, as I supposed it would be. I rushed across to my tutor, showed him the telegram, and burst into tears. He was very kind, came back with me to my rooms, and helped to send me off to town.

I see myself now ringing the bell, the door opening, my sister coming downstairs in tears, my own tears, the whole distressing scene. I remember mother, lying on the bed, looking calm and beautiful. I remember my father's grief. Yet, after the funeral, I remember also sitting at one of our drawing-room windows with my sisters in a state of almost hysterical laughter, and one of my aunts remarking coldly that we had better not laugh so much as people might think it heartless. Then I remember lying on the sofa, trying desperately to realize the "never again", the indubitable and yet inconceivable fact. I returned to Cambridge to finish my term, oscillated between the grave demeanour I felt to be appropriate and the natural forgetfulness and cheerfulness produced by the company of my friends. I had to stay up late to keep my term, and there comes back to me a long solitary expedition to the fens. With this event, the death of my mother, I connect my definite passage into a new phase of my life.

It is difficult to analyse more fully than he does himself this very intricate experience. Love, rather than knowledge, had bound the boy to his mother, he had never desired to be frank with her, and perhaps that is why the emotions of the man were so conflicting. His laughter is easily explained—it is a common safety-valve. But why the enhanced feeling for Cambridge? From that time he tended to inhabit the university spiritually. The interests and emotions acquired there began to fill the vacations, although the house at All Souls Place remained his headquarters for many years.

> From now on my mind was in a ferment, a kind of ferment, however, which would hardly, I think, be intelligible to a contemporary under-graduate. It was as though, at last, the door that had once or twice swung ajar now opened and let me out. What I saw was a dim and moonlit scene, infinite, exciting, perilous, full of adventure. It presented itself to me as the problem of existence, at once felt and thought about —if indeed what one did then can be called thinking. It was exciting, to a degree that no modern young man of intelligence could com-prehend, to discover that Christianity was not, as it were, an inexten-sible box, very small, in which the whole world was packed, but that an immense world extended quite outside of it. That world I began to try to grasp in ways that seem now ridiculous but that had nevertheless an intensity, a passion and a romance that it is only given to youth to experience. It was exciting, then, to conceive that perhaps Jesus was not God but only an exceptional Being. It still seemed shocking at first that anyone should conceive him as only man. Then interest in him (such poor ignorant interest as it had ever been!) began to fade.
>
> Shelley suddenly gripped me. . . .

With the arrival of Shelley the door swung wide and never closed again. Shelley's influence was so important, it so dominated Dickinson till the day of his death, that it will have to be described in a separate chapter, and the same applies to two other arrivals from the world of books, Plato and Goethe. "Books" is an in-adequate word to use in so personal a connection. It was rather that three people who knew his language proved willing to speak to him in it and to say sentences which he could not have framed for himself. He entered a world which was an extension of his own heart. The habit of awe and reverence was always suspect to him, and he did not humble himself before his great writers, or exclaim (except in the first excitement of his youth) that he was not worthy to unlace their shoes. The world into which they called him was the world of freemen, where there is no bowing down before thrones or chanting outside shrines. What joys did he find in it? He communicated them as well as he could. But we can best share them if we have known his identical longings and pains. The *Prometheus Unbound*, the close of the *Phaedo*, Galatea and the Homunculus—they are only sounds in the air and marks on a page unless we have learned their language and been preparing to speak with them from childhood. And one of my limitations in discussing Dickinson is that the three writers who meant most to him have never particularly appealed to me, so that I can only divine by analogy what he found in them. One fact at all events emerges: he discovered these writers and human beings at the same time.

> While the mists were thus drawing up before religion, poetry, politics, like curtains of gauze on the stage, I was gradually finding, for the first time, real friends. . . . We feasted on ideas, on speculations, on poetry, music, or what not? The best of our life was long talks in our own rooms, or, in summer, pacing the grounds of King's, still, as I think, one of the loveliest spots in the world, and open still all night to talk, as well as to more noisy enterprises. The dedication to my unpublished volume of poems recaptures the feeling of those hours better than anything I can say now, when I pace the same ground half a ghost and more haunted by memories than realities. But always the same beauty, as perhaps may be the case even centuries from now.

Then he recalls the friends of this early period: A. J. Grant (afterwards professor of history at Leeds), "with whom I associate . . . a moonlit evening spent in the grounds of Trinity, after we had climbed a locked gate to get in"; J. W. Graham (afterwards principal of Dalton Hall), "older than the rest of us, . . . believing so ardently in progress that he would not have it doubted that art too must have steadily progressed"; A. P. Laurie (now principal of the Heriot-Watt College), "then the most speculative and bold of that little sect, a chemist, a Henry Georgite, a perpetual talker"; and C. R. Ashbee, afterwards an architect and designer. Ashbee is recalled as "a long youth, enthusiastic, opinionated, *schwärmerisch*", who jumped into a college eight and made a hole, and started a "Speculative Society", which was to spread through the world but collapsed after its first term. Ashbee had a gift for practical organization and for sympathetic contact with the working class which Dickinson admired but could not emulate. With him, as with Grant and Graham, he kept in touch all his life. The greatest of his Cambridge friends, Roger Fry and Ferdinand Schiller, become important at a later date, and mention of them must be postponed.

As Cambridge filled up with friends it acquired a magic quality. Body and spirit, reason and emotion, work and play, architecture and scenery, laughter and seriousness, life and art— these pairs which are elsewhere contrasted were there fused into

29

one. People and books reinforced one another, intelligence joined hands with affection, speculation became a passion, and discussion was made profound by love. When Goldie speaks of this magic fusion, he illumines more careers than his own, and he seems not only to epitomize Cambridge but to amplify it, and to make it the heritage of many who will never go there in the flesh.

> Others of that set have gone almost out of my mind, and some of them out of the world. But still their forms appear in the golden mist of dawn and almost I catch their voices through the talk of younger generations, heard under the same chapel walls, under the same chestnut grove, over the same great lawns, under the same stars reflected in the same sluggish yet lovely stream, that will hear perhaps for centuries yet the same voices at the same budding time of youth; unless perhaps—who knows?—they fall silent even before the eternal silence closes upon me.

In a meditation such as this the old dry little upper-class notion of an Alma Mater vanishes, and the university becomes for a moment universal.

chapter seven

Shelley, Plato, Goethe

I

In an early sonnet to Shelley, Dickinson compares him to a song, floating out of an attic at dusk over a sultry city, and transporting the listener into a land of streams. The sonnet exemplifies what he required from poetry. He did not care for pure poetry; that is to say, perfection of expression brought him only a passing pleasure. Nor did he care for poetry which conveyed a view of life hostile to his own. What he wanted was a song which would transport him out of the world in the right direction, wings that would carry him out of the body into a region where good and evil are more clearly opposed than on earth, and where good triumphs everlastingly. Sincere, enthusiastic, and fired with the same social hopes, Shelley provided him with exactly the right pair of wings. It was possible, in that enchanting company, to shake off the flesh. It was possible to shake it off in the company of many other poets, but Shelley remained unique because, however high he soared, he never rejected humanity.

Dickinson loved humanity—so far as the phrase has any meaning; and it still has some meaning, though not as much as it promised in the nineteenth century. He believed, furthermore, in something more definite: in love between two individuals. And it is because Shelley welcomed both sorts of love into the white radiance of eternity that he desired to follow him there. Beyond, or beneath, the human he was reluctant to travel; and it is significant that, while adoring Shelley, he should on occasions have maintained a stiff upper lip towards Walt Whitman. Whitman's mysticism sometimes repelled him, like D. H. Lawrence's later on. It tended to obliterate boundaries which he felt should be preserved. To "let oneself go" under the stress of emotion is all very well, but, O my brethren, in which direction? Towards "Kingless continents sinless as Eden"? or down into a uniform orgy where anything is everything, and blackberries and pismires indistinguishable from Socrates? Escape is only the first step towards salvation. It is useless, unless we take the right turning after opening the door. Now Shelley knows the way. Shelley is sustained in his airy quest by human love. Hence his supremacy.

> Shelley suddenly gripped me; I don't think as a poet, but as a visionary about life. His landscapes, always shimmering with moonlit streams, his loneliness, his passionate and ideal love were what seized me— "Alastor" and "Adonais" and the more ethereal and musical lyrics of *Prometheus*. I read Hogg's life of him (still in my deliberate judgement one of the most fascinating biographies in existence) as though it were a new gospel. Shelley at Oxford especially appealed to me. And then his political ideas! I thought with rapture and reverence of the youth of 19 dropping his leaflets among the crowd from a balcony in Dublin. I leapt with indignation and contempt at Godwin's solemn cry "Shelley, you are preparing a scene of blood". No one who has not felt Shelley once like that can know, I think, what Shelley is. I still recover those first feelings when I turn to him. And I still resent (rightly, as I believe) the elderly view of him as a man of genius gone astray, ignorant of life, wild and utopian. He had, in fact, a clear logical mind, a courage of conviction almost unique, and a burning passion for truth which is only not appreciated because it is of all passions the rarest. If there were indeed that world beyond, of which the Platonic Socrates used to dream, there is no one I would sooner meet; of all men of letters he is, I think, the most lovable, humane and genuine.

Shelley's immediate influence was enormous. It operated in two ways. In the first place it turned Dickinson to politics and schemes of social reform. Turning from his crude missionary attempts, he began to study conditions, particularly the problem of the land, as set forth in the work of Henry George. Henry George—a freelance economist who is almost forgotten today— was then a living force among the young men, and the transition to his *Progress and Poverty* from *Prometheus Unbound* was not as abrupt as it may appear. George was a sincere man, with a simple view of social disorders and their remedies. He came and lectured at Cambridge with success, and though Dickinson was never a fanatic follower he hoped for a little that the World's Great Age might begin anew through the taxation of land values. He never reread *Progress and Poverty* in later years, but he remembered it as a genuine piece of work, and it led him to make the agricultural experiment which will be described in the next chapter.

Shelley also influenced him in a more obvious way. He began to write poems himself. "Certainly they had no value, but nothing

I have written since has filled me with such excitement, such a sense of being inspired." The first of these poems, "Doubt", was sent to the *Carthusian*, of which his friend Bowlby was editor. Many others followed, he improved in technique, and in 1884 he won the Chancellor's Medal for a poem "supposed to be about Savonarola". The necessary facts about Savonarola were supplied by Mrs Oliphant, but all else by "Adonais", and the monk's fate is celebrated with a pagan melancholy which would not have consoled him and would have been more intelligible to his persecutors:

> But all too brief thy triumph, all too soon
> Thy heavenly kingdom perished, all in vain
> Thou climbedst to the splendour of thy noon
> To sink in night eternal. . . .

Dickinson rightly remarks that the poem "was hardly about the subject; a way prize poems have, and no doubt a good way". It is really a tribute to Shelley, at whose photograph he gazed while composing it. In accordance with the university regulations he was obliged to read it aloud in the Senate House, wearing his dress clothes for the occasion and addressing an audience largely composed of his own relatives. With this bizarre scene his public career as a bard came to an end. He wrote poetry subsequently, but as a vehicle for his private emotions, and, severely self-critical, he has not chosen to give much of it to the world.

> Though these [early verses] have, I think, no merit as poetry, they are of interest in my biography, as most young men's verses are. The other day I looked through a collection of mine with very curious feelings. Some I had quite forgotten and could not recall having written them, even when I read them. Some brought back an immediate vision of the place and circumstances where they were written.

Few of us have felt Shelley's fascination as he did, or else we have outgrown it and taken to "business or Keats". But, granted that that strange poetry and even stranger prose keep in touch with human beings, the fascination is easy to understand. Even when he was afraid of human beings, as at school, or bewildered by them, as in the War, he refused to escape from them, and it was only by a poet who maintained an earthly connection that he could be lifted into the empyrean. All through his life the devotion continued. Here is a typical extract from a letter to May (August 1893):

Deep down under the beefiest and brutallest disguise there lies the same tragedy which was the essence, unveiled and undisguised, of Shelley. "I think one is always in love with something or other; the error consists in seeking in a mortal image the likeness of something which is perhaps eternal." *Hinc illae lacrimae*—divorces and all the rest of it. "The desire of the moth for the star, Of the night for the morrow" is the epitome not only of Shelley but of all mankind."

And there are many other references, all grouping round the idea that though Shelley was exceptional he was not uncanny, and interprets the average man, if only the average man had eyes to see.

In some correspondence exchanged in 1906 with his friend Mrs C. R. Ashbee he goes further than this, and emphasizes the bodiless quality of his god:

Shelley never got *incarnate*. That's what gives him his unique quality, which people either love or hate, according as they are more or less incarnate themselves.

Mrs Ashbee replies with vigour that she must certainly be incarnate herself, for she cannot stand Shelley at all:

I am *poles* from Shelley, and that is probably why the elusive . . . soap-bubble quality—spirit—does not find any ring of answer in me. He was supernatural I think. It is very astonishing that women were so fond of him; it must have been I think the physical fascination and charm; for though women are attracted by intellectual power, I don't think that they can *ever get into line* with the "Children of the Soul" idea. I believe it is outside their range of consciousness; they can only look on in silent wonder.

Somewhat concerned, he replies:

About being "incarnate"—what I had in my mind was that spirit has to enter matter, to create; and in so doing loses its own purity and essence. And Shelley, as I feel him, never *did* enter matter— which is . . . what fascinates, and what, in your case, repels. All women, I think, have more need of, and love of matter than men. Men are the idealists. That's why they so often make a mess of things. Women would run the world more sensibly. But then—so *deadly* sensibly! A woman's first cry is "How will it affect the children?" A man says "How will it affect the soul, or the race, or God?"—What rot! Pray forgive me.

She forgives him.

He edited the *Prometheus*, but Shelley's real apotheosis is postponed until *The Magic Flute* (1920), where he appears as a morning star in the Castle of Sarastro—the castle from which Dante had been excluded, because he preferred authority to truth. Shelley is the poet of freemen. He helped to free Dickinson at Cambridge and he gives one more denial to the accusation so foolishly brought against poets, that they are not practical. If they are not practical, how is it that they have accomplished so much? And why have legislators and officials from Plato onwards kept such a watchful eye on them?

2

If Shelley rose like the morning star, Plato was heralded by the dubious twilight of Esoteric Buddhism. Like many young men who are discovering themselves and the world, Dickinson wondered whether there may not be a supernormal path to knowledge. He was by no means credulous or unable to sift evidence, and he had taste and humour, so that Esoteric Buddhism could not detain him long, but for about a year he was intrigued with it. "My idea, I believe, was that one must first discover absolute standards of Good and Evil, and then descend . . . to govern mankind." So he attended the meeting of the Society for Psychical Research to hear Colonel Olcott describe how he had once been visited by a Mahatma who had dematerialized through a closed door, but had left his turban behind him as a proof. "And here," said the Colonel passing it round, "is the turban." This sort of thing does not go down at Cambridge. More impressive than the Colonel and the turban was an Indian called Mohini. For a short time his letters are full of Mohini; "if he were proved a humbug, I would hide my face and believe in nothing no more," he writes to Grant. He was diffident of approaching, but finally begged for an audience, which was majestically accorded. Mohini refused to shake hands with a creature so gross, but was understood to approve the study of Plato and to recommend meditation upon the One. "I retired feeling really that I had got at nothing, but refusing to admit as much to myself." Ashbee wearied of Mohini and suggested that a little work for other people might be a good thing. "To which I find myself replying that living for others is a means to mysticism, not vice versa, and continuing to speak of Esoteric Buddhism and Mahatmas."

This being his state of mind, he approached Plato not as a writer of dialogues, or as a depictor of Athenian society, or a logician, or politician, or a publicist, but as an adept who was in the possession of absolute truth, which he had concealed in his writings, probably in his myths. At any moment the universe might open. And, though he modified this view, it tinged his future studies with poetry. Here is a letter to Grant describing his original attitude—though "attitude" is too cool a word to use for the fervour and the ecstasy which filled him. He had just taken his degree at Cambridge, and gone to Germany with Ashbee; at the time he writes to Grant, he was alone at Heidelberg, radiantly happy, and living upon vegetables. The date of the letter is August 1884—that is to say, he was just twenty-two. After some preliminary gaiety he says:

I've just descended from a seventh heaven, so to speak, i.e. from something considerably above my ordinary grovelling existence. That is to say, for the last two hours I've been sitting on the slope of a hill, looking out over the town and the Schloss and the mountains and the river, with a "whispering wood" all about me, reading and meditating on Plato's *Symposium*. Never again will I regret that I've spent years over Greek. I'm "sitting at Plato's feet" at present, and have really never experienced such "ecstasy" in the literal sense: why I can't tell you, but so it is. I seem to have got a new light for reading him, and it seems all clear and quite necessarily and incontrovertibly true. And moreover in the *Phaedrus* is much palpable "Esoteric Buddhism": do read it again, if you haven't lately, and there you will find the indestructibility of life, and the successive incarnations, and the one great consciousness, or ψυχή: and the joys of the adepts, and many such like. I'm getting desperate; I must discover somehow how to keep up to the highest point in the midst of all these necessities of eating and drinking and sleeping and conversing, and I must discover what is αὐτὸ τὸ καλὸν, and οἷα ἐστὶν ἡ ψυχή: else how can I ever deliver a respectable set of lectures? How can I explain, for instance, why Shakespeare's characters are natural and marvellous, and Jonson's aren't, unless I know what character is, and all about it. Now, being much at peace and in perfect surroundings, I can see clearly that until one has learned perfectly to control oneself, and to understand these mysterious laws that give rise to different opinions and passions, one has no right to expect to do any work that shall be necessarily wise and good: therefore if indeed an "Adept" would speak with me and give me hope, I would vanish to India, at least I hope so. I suppose, otherwise, all this will pass and I shall come down and muddle along, doing a little accidental good among much accidental harm, and cursing as fools all who don't agree with me. This isn't mere talk: I can't tell why, but parts of the *Phaedrus* and *Symposium* have come to me in this week like Revelation, and just for an hour or so a day everything has seemed "stale and unprofitable" except somehow or other to follow out Plato in the paths he hints at as leading to "the life of the gods". It's worth having felt, if it all subsides to nothing.

Forty years later, his memory of the Heidelberg experience was still vivid, and he describes it in the *Recollections* in much the same words as he uses to Grant at the time. It was not the only experience of the sort, for we shall find that he was visited several times by similar intimations of reality. Except perhaps once, at the very end of his life, he never had the mystic vision claimed by his friend McTaggart and by some of the saints. But he often went beyond those vague feelings of awe which represent the furthest most men go from the track of common sense.

Such being his approach to Plato, it is natural that he should be involved in Plotinus. There he found mysticism slab upon slab, without any alloy of Athenian dinner parties. He began to read Plotinus that same summer, and the first work of learning composed by him is a dissertation in which the doctrines of Plato and Plotinus are compared and harmonized. On the strength of the second version of this dissertation he was given a fellowship at King's in 1887. He never published it, and it remains in manuscript in the college library. In later years he regarded it as of little critical value, because it made no attempt to discuss the mystic experience upon which the assertions of Plotinus rested. "Plotinus does claim to have had this experience, and I daresay he did. The question would be, what value has it as truth."

Since, however, Plotinus is a thinker as well as a mystic, and reasons from his assumptions, there was plenty to say about him, "and granting my standpoint, the dissertation is, I expect, pretty good"; Dean Inge asked for the loan of it when he was preparing his Gifford Lectures on the same subject.

What I recall now is the curious state of mind in which I was when I wrote it. It was written mainly in the reading-room of the British Museum; in one sense not a bad environment for this Oriental-Italo-Egypto-Greco writer! But I really think that, for the time being, I was almost abstracted from the actual; and I mooned about the wintry and foggy London with a feeling that it was all an illusion and that some day, any day, I should awake into the real world. From the moment I finished the dissertation to the present time I have hardly looked into Plotinus. I wonder whether I ever shall again, and if so what I should make of it.

He lost interest in Plotinus, but not in Plato, to whose non-mystical side he then turned. From about 1890 on, he began to care about education, politics and conduct. The Greeks had also been interested in these subjects, and Plato was the most intelligent of the Greeks, and, at all events in his earlier dialogues, the most human. If Shelley dashed and splashed through the country of Dickinson's mind like a mountain stream, Plato was, so to speak, responsible for the irrigation system. He saw to it that the study of modern institutions and conduct should be fertilized by knowledge of the past. He provided breadth of treatment and aptness of comparison, and that subtlest help which comes from affinity of style. Two of the latest books are about him and he also dominates *The Greek View of Life*. He was also responsible for the dialogues, and the "dialogue" with Dickinson does not merely mean *A Modern Symposium* and *Justice and Liberty*, but all the unprinted and sometimes unprintable occasions on which he talked. In his talk, as in writing, he had the evenness of temper, and the power to state the other side fairly, which are supposed to characterize Socrates. Indeed, to a Goth like myself he seems much more Socratic than Socrates. Socrates—as Plato presents him—would have emptied any modern room at once. Dickinson kept every room full, never nagging, never setting traps, never reducing the company to silence while he demonstrated the supremacy of his intellect, the justness of his opinions, the aptness of his wit, the profundity of his vision. Even without Plato, he would have known how to converse, and how to handle life, but he was strengthened and confirmed by the presence of his companion—less beloved than Shelley, but more serviceable, for in this world there are many mansions, and a guide through them is needful. The Greeks—and Plato particularly—understand our political and social confusion, but they are not part of it, and so they can help us.

3

His love for Goethe dates from the same fruitful summer of 1884 when he read Greek in the pine woods above Heidelberg.

Oh Grant [he writes at the time], I've begun *Faust*, of which indeed I will not speak, for is it not as yet unspeakable? Such a rush of music and passion and thought as I have not known for long takes me out of this miserable self into heaven. Just suits me now; Faust with his weariness of books and all things does appeal so *strongly* to a bit of me; he's studied everything "und leider auch Theologie" *frustra*; and then the earth spirit who "sits at the roaring loom of time" (you'll remember in Carlyle). But have you not read *Faust*? Yea, I remember thou hast.

The "rush of music and passion and thought" was, he discovered before long, not continuous. He was soon confronted with the immense boringness of Goethe, and few Englishmen have faced it so frankly, and so successfully outstared it. After a forty years' interval he writes to Grant again:

I continue to be intrigued by Goethe and to think him a man of vision in spite of the disquieting fact that there is very little of him I can read. Only a German, perhaps, could manage to be at once a pedant and a genius, an official and a poet, a novelist and a preacher, etc. etc. He achieved anyhow the greatest of all triumphs, which is continuing to live to the last moment instead of dying prematurely at forty and then lingering on as a rather malicious and obstructive ghost, as most of us do.

At the very end of his life he paid homage in *Goethe and Faust* and in an unpublished *Faust* translation, and all his last utterances and letters are full of allusions. These will appear in their course. Here I would indicate three reasons for the attraction. In the first place there was Goethe's acceptance of science—acceptance in the sense of willingness to approach the riddle of the universe by any path which is available, scientific or otherwise. Goethe belonged to the tradition of the early Greek philosophers and of the Renaissance humanists, and was closely akin here to Leonardo da Vinci. His own scientific work, his theory of colour, for instance, might be as absurd as the attempts of Voltaire to weigh heat, for it was not to be supposed that he, or any other untrained worker, could perform laboratory experiments of value. But he could direct the spirit in which science could be used; he had not only curiosity but imagination and the capacity for wonder. Dickinson thought that this was an attitude which the modern man should try to share. He himself, though superficial observers dismissed him as dreamy and wistful, was constantly striving to decrease the dark. He hoped for a small circle of light which science would gradually enlarge; beyond this circle stretches a region which, so long as it is unconquered, belongs to imagination and poetry.

In the second place, he admired Goethe's many-sidedness. He was aware of his own limitations, and here was a man of congenial character, who had been not only a poet and scientist, but art critic, theatrical director, courtier, administrator, financier, soldier, philosopher, etc. He never wasted time in regretting that he was not equally various, for he knew that to measure oneself in this way against one's hero is futile, and is indeed a form of conceit. But Goethe was certainly his ideal as far as worldly conduct and scope of practical activities were concerned. Had he been permitted to take a leading part in European affairs, he would have worked in his spirit.

In the third place, Goethe had managed to grow old properly, and the older he grew himself the more he valued this. Most men —though not most women—become intolerable in old age, but here was a sage whom experience never ceased to make wiser, and whose very love-making remained free from senility. It is heartening to remember such a man; he has escaped the shadow of death—and it is the advancing shadow of death, not the actual blackness, which is such a disgrace and terror. Dickinson himself escaped it. Though the fates were to be unkind to him in many ways, they allowed him to keep his strength and sanity to the end.

This admiration for Goethe was connected with a general tolerance for the Teutonic. He liked in the Germans the qualities which endear them to the average Englishman, their good temper, their frankness and their romanticism; and he pardoned, as the average Englishman cannot, their heaviness, pedantry and docility. If his instincts yearned for the Mediterranean, his sentiments still clung to the forests and streams of the North, and in this dual allegiance he recalls that child of Helen and Faust, Euphorion, who symbolized the modern world.

Age 23. *At Cambridge.*
Photo by F. Hollyer

Manuscript of "Dedication" for a sonnet-sequence. Written about 1893, privately printed in *Poems*, 1896

Here, where the dews of sorrow
  Drop from a sky of lead,
I set myself to fashion
  A garland for thy head.

Perhaps on that tomorrow
  When we are counted dead
By some diviner passion
  It will be perfected.

chapter eight
The World of Matter
1884-1887

Between 1884, when he took his degree, and 1887, when he was
elected to a fellowship, Dickinson was in an uneasy state. A first
in classics, following on the Chancellor's Medal and other distinctions, gave him an excellent academic record, but what should
be the next step? He wanted to support himself, since his father
was not well off, and he wanted to help the human race and to
impart to it the truth and the beauty which he had discovered.
How should he begin? How, and also when? He writes to May
that it is a shocking thing to have reached the age of twenty-one
without knowing what to do, and to Ashbee at a later date that
"we're all too anxious . . . to begin 'doing something' before we've
learned even to shape our own characters". If his education was
finished, how should he utilize it, and if it was incomplete what
should he learn next?

Connected with this problem was a second one, which arose
out of his desire to help humanity. If he held aloof from ordinary
people, how could he help them, and, if he threw himself into
their lives, should he not become like them? He did not want to
become like ordinary people. Here he was definite, and he
remained, in this sense, an aristocrat to the end. To abandon
culture and blunt sensitiveness in the hope of breaking down
barriers always seemed to him a desperate expedient. He solved
this particular problem in later life by developing the power of
entering into other people's positions while he retained his own,
but it is impossible for a young man to have this power: he must
either abandon himself or hold aloof, and consequently there is a
slight touch of arrogance in his dealings with average humanity
which does not wear off until he has visited and endured America.

He spent the three years of uncertainty partly in Cambridge,
and partly at home or in the provinces, and there were visits
abroad. It was a period of experiment, and his general state of

mind at the beginning of it can be seen in the following letter to Grant (10 January 1885).

> At Cambridge it was as if we stood all in the light and shook hands bravely and cheerfully and then went out into the night, each in our different paths. And the old myth of meeting again in the light expresses a real need, whatever its underlying truth may be. You see I find it rather necessary to cultivate a hard outside in order to keep alive my fire within; men are so sceptical, so essentially "faithless"; and one has such tendencies that way oneself. For the sad thing to discover is that there is so little *conscious* vice; that the evil is done (or at least the good undone) by men whose position is absolutely logical and righteous in their own eyes; there is a gradual dropping away of the Truth . . . until it becomes impossible to conceive even of a higher Right. And keen [?] argument loses force and sympathy becomes impossible; one falls back on dogged and apparently unconvincing assertion. All this is very vague, but expresses somehow what I feel about "people in general", and the danger of assimilating their ideas.

He needed above all things to defend his newly won individuality, and although he desired to help and understand "people in general" his sympathy with them was still in abeyance. This comes out clearly in the three experiments now to be recorded.

The first experiment is a most fantastic one, and takes him quite outside his usual beat. Full of Henry George, of the social question, of the general ferment of things, he determined to go and work on a cooperative farm.

The farm had recently been started by Harold Cox, afterwards an uncompromising champion of individualism, but at that time a socialist. He had acquired some acres of barren heath in Surrey, which were to be reclaimed, and he had imported from Kent a family of farm-labourers by name of Gibbs with whom he lived in a newly built cottage. It was a strange establishment, which the arrival of the B.A. from Cambridge did not make less strange, for Goldie had no turn for manual labour, and only a theoretical affection for the working classes. However, he did not arrive with great expectations; there were some lectures which he hoped to prepare between the plough and the cow; also he was studying Plotinus. The economic position of Cox's enterprise was already desperate, but he was not interested in economics; he came because he had half a hope that he would now begin to lead the right life— physical work on the one hand, and intellectual creation on the other. The walk up from Farnham station to the farm, the scents of the country—how vividly he remembered them! "The great commons with the fern-owls sounding upon them in the dusk, the Frensham ponds, the bracken and the heather were silent witnesses of much passionate brooding in those short weeks." It was on the human side that he failed to get into touch, because he was choosing an inappropriate method.

He wrote long letters about Craig Farm to his sisters and to Ashbee. The following is to Ashbee, who was then in Germany:

Craig Farm, Farnham
2 May 1885

Dear Ashbee,

I've been waiting to write till I was a bit settled, otherwise I should have sent some scathing reply to your last, and now alas! it's too late. Things are good here, especially for working purposes (8 hours pretty easy to get in) but with a distinct tendency to dullness. Cambridge talk etc. was very distracting, but stimulating too, and the conversations and ways of the rustic are a poor substitute. You would laugh to see me seated solemnly at meals in the kitchen talking ineffectually to "George" and "Will" and "Tom" about them there peas and how the dung rotted them, but 'Arold would have his way; and how there ought to be hops here, and beans there, etc. etc.; with occasional jests about Annie's suitors and Paget's debts. (Paget! Call 'isself a gen'leman! I dun call him no gen'leman! What does 'e go for to ... etc. etc.)

A slight interval in which I've been fetching beer from the pub in an enormous brown jar; the men all sowing soot (for manure), and no one to get them beer, so I had to go. It's really very funny; if there were someone to laugh with I could laugh all day.

The family is George Gibbs, silent and humorous (at times), fond of grumbling and hard work: details to me Harold's little mistakes, and has a habit of making the same conversation do several times over, in which case of course I make the same remarks, with as much interest as possible: Mrs Gibbs, deaf as a post, with whom I communicate mainly by signs: she, however, converses much, being answered in dumb show. . . .

Then there's Will, fat and stupid, and Alick, silently devoted to Annie, who pities him; and Tommy cute and self-assertive, with dormant propensity to lying and juvenile fondness for a gun: and then there's *Annie*! . . . Suffice it to say she's superior in culture to the rest, and is considered by some very pretty. Harold I like much at present and admire. We get some decent talk over our hoeing and digging, but don't agree much, I think, at bottom. He is a socialist (Dem. Fed.), but not violent or unreasonable, seems to think in fact they won't do much; but "anything better than this". Says it was a great drawback to Mazzini that he believed in a God, which again will show you how we differ. Rather tired of the farm, I think, that is to say has learned from it all he will do: very doubtful if it will pay; all new ground and bad ground, which he has first brought to cultivation. Says it isn't possible to combine agricultural and student life, unless you take your agriculture as you do your exercise, for an hour or two a day (as I'm trying to do now). . . .

[12 May] . . . I've just had the sweetest good-night chat with Annie; but then she is so catholic; for instance a minute ago I saw her reclining in Alick's arms. . . . Good God! Ashbee, as Stone would say, there came here the other day one Dr Elizabeth B[lackwell]! All my ideas of higher education and the like for women are pushed back at least a century by the event! How that woman talked; flowing periods, elaborate parentheses, scarcely a pause for breath, words articulated like the snap of a pistol, gratified smack of the lips at each semi-colon! Unfortunate female companion reduced to positive deafness and imbecility by constant association: I should think she was paid listener-in-chief! "Come here, my dear, and sit by me! . . . Can you give her a low chair?" And we did, and there she sat, poor wretch, at the feet of the monster! Miserablest of females! "It is my profound conviction—though, mark you, I profess myself . . . a land nationalist —that it is idle, nay injurious, to advocate extreme reform before public opinion has duly matured . . ." etc. etc. etc. Ach Gott! Talk of mental diarrhoea. . . . As to Annie's opinion of her, that you may imagine. "These people evidently have not in any degree developed their intellect," quoth the learned Dr. "Thank heaven, no!" one felt inclined to say.

Mrs Gibbs is becoming painfully friendly: she bursts at all hours into my studious retirement, crying: "Oh Mr Dickinson, I've cut open that chicken and its liver is all diseased—come and look. . . . Now what would *you* do with it?" I, good heavens! And the woman is *deaf*, no getting at her! There's no denying that the family quarrels a good deal; Tom for instance "is such a little beast! I do 'ate 'im!" This alas! from a sister. And then Will! He will talk so freely at the dinner-table about "kicking your ass"! But these drawbacks will occur. I've tried my hand at ploughing with signal success: what a hardy son of the soil I should have been, if I'd been born to it! As I wasn't I remain a puny son of the pen, much in need of a sleeping-draught.

But I couldn't milk the cow. No, it may look simple, but I assure you there is an art in manipulating the teat of a domestic cow not easily fathomable! It will ever be a sorrow to me, but the fact remains: I can not milk a cow! . . .

Oh, mein lieber, how I would like to hear that nightingale! But I know 'em of old, and how the chapel sleeps in the moonlit water, and the limes are steeped in fragrance, and all the world asleep. . . .

He stopped at Craig Farm for a couple of months. Endowed

with a sense of humour rather than a zest for comedy, he did not abandon himself fully to its absurdities. Plotinus claimed him. In a cottage hard by vegetated the Salts—Henry Salt had been a rebellious master at Eton, and was to write a book called *Seventy Years among Savages*. Salt and Cox were both magnets for cranks, and queer people would call on a Sunday, amongst them young Bernard Shaw. The Gibbses mingled freely in this company, but without pleasure, and became obstreperous and critical. There were musical parties at the Salts, where culture demanded one sort of song, and agriculture another. There was a homeric meal at the farm where Will Gibbs routed Dr Elizabeth B. by chanting that there were worms in the soup. Dickinson's own table manners were called in question. Then he left, the experiment collapsed, the Gibbses were re-imported into Kent, the desert resumed its own, and Harold Cox went to teach mathematics in India. "I have met him since and found he still retains the personal charm he always had. But over the farm experiment a great ox sat upon our tongues."

About a year later, he wrote a story about this little experience, which still exists in manuscript form. It is a naïve transcript of events, where Gibbs becomes Biggs, and it is not surprising that Kegan Paul, to whom it was submitted, should have declined publication. But in the last few pages it sails into twilight and poetry. "Crankie Farm" has been a failure, and the two young men who have been muddling there sit by the edge of the great Frensham pond and watch the moon passing slowly down through heavy clouds and out again into clear sky. Their talk drifts towards immortality, and they agree that it exists here and now, and the trouble of an hour ago becomes nothing; "we knew it had been, and it was not: while we stood there complete without it." The night is filled with little sounds, not only the birds but the trees and the water seem to speak, the moon sets behind the trees opposite, and the Surrey landscape, without losing its own beloved and homely character, is absorbed into the cosmogony of Plotinus. All through his life Dickinson had this hope that, at a touch, the world of matter would be—not annihilated but transformed.

> No, not the hand of death! some other power
> Summon to aid thee in the day of doom;
> Earth shall reveal in one immortal hour
> More than was ever garnered in the tomb.

The hope was both a support and a distraction to him during the period of his immaturity.

2

The lectures on which he had been working during his stay at the farm were delivered during the winter of 1885–6 at various provincial centres under the auspices of the University Extension scheme. They were on Carlyle, Emerson, Browning and Tennyson. For all these writers, except Tennyson, he had unbounded admiration. His idea was that he should reveal their beauties to enthusiastic working men, who would be grateful for any crumbs from the academic banquet. It is an idea which other Extension lecturers have shared, and it seems even to have flitted through the minds of the originators of the scheme. His audiences were actually composed of women of the middle classes, women who had read their Tennysons and compared them with their Brownings for years, and who pointed out his shortcomings with provincial mercilessness.

> I had no notion how to speak, and no idea at all how ordinary people felt and thought. . . . I had my lectures written out in full and learned them by heart. They naturally fell very flat, and I still remember the cheerful schoolmaster who was my chairman at my first remarking at the end that we ought to be very grateful to Mr Dickinson for "even trying" to communicate his ideas on these great authors. Worse however than the manner of my lectures was the matter, for I did not conceal the unorthodox nature of my opinions. I also dressed very badly, fed very badly, and was still involved, whenever I had a chance, in my philosophic and mystical studies. . . . The travelling from place to place was fatiguing, and altogether, looking back on myself, I seem a sad, outlandish, stranded and alien figure. I had no notion how to get into touch with ordinary people, and no desire to do so, for I thought I was the bearer of a message which condemned all actual life.

The message was sometimes inaudible, and according to one of his friends he would turn his back on the audience when he became interested and toddle away over the platform on his heels, patting himself meanwhile with both his hands behind. *Si ce n'est pas vrai c'est bien vu*; one endorses the gesture. Nor was he more successful with the weekly classes, the question-papers and the personal contacts which are an important part of University Extension. "My sister has a bone to pick with you, Mr Dickinson: you wrote *Fool* on her paper!" Perhaps he had written "Good", but it was too late; his handwriting was already getting him into trouble. For the first term, his lecturing centres were Mansfield, Chesterfield and Stamford; for the second term Chester and Southport. He writes to May: "It is all very disgusting, and I'll never talk about poetry again. It's difficult to say which annoys me most, the people who don't like it or the people who do." And to Ashbee: "Going to lecture now, to which I am gradually becoming calm and indifferent. Life is so *much* bigger than anything one does in it." Such language suggests that a crisis is approaching. It came at Chester. He began by affronting the bishop, Stubbs the historian, to whom he addressed a letter as "The Rev. Dr Stubbs". His lordship deigned not to reply. Then he quarrelled with his local secretary, daughter to another bishop, who disapproved of his views on Tennyson. His first lecture could not be heard on account of a musical meal which was being given next door to six hundred poor of the city. But the Emerson lecture was heard only too plainly, for he quoted two lines of a poem by his author called "The Initial Love":

> And kiss, and couple, and beget,
> By those roving eyeballs bold—

and gave terrific offence. It was more than the cathedral mind could stand, and portions of it left the room. The ladies of Chester were prepared to hear about Emerson, but not what Emerson said, the local secretary forwarded their complaint to headquarters, his impropriety was censured, Tom Hughes his defender was ignored, his fate was sealed. Things do not alter much. I remember, thirty years later, a lecturer upon Euripides at Weybridge having to defend himself against the charge of condoning the conduct of the Bacchae.

It is characteristic of Dickinson that, even when appearing to fail, he should gain something of permanent value. This dingy incursion through the Midlands resulted in two lifelong friendships. One was with Edward Carpenter, the other with Mrs Webb, wife of the rector of Mansfield Woodhouse. Mrs Webb attended his course at Mansfield, and saw through the badness of its matter and manner to the sincerity behind. Though she was twenty-five years his senior, they quickly became intimate, he poured out his difficulties, a correspondence ensued, and after her husband's death she and her daughter moved to Cambridge. Although he was never drawn to women in the passionate sense, all his deepest emotions being towards men, his life would have been empty and comfortless without them. He found in them—

47

that is to say, in a few women—a patience and a nobility undis-
coverable elsewhere, and his tribute to Mrs Webb must be
quoted here as paying tribute not only to her. He speaks of the
illnesses troubling her old age, and then continues:

> But all this left and leaves her as it were unsullied, uncomplaining,
> the most beautiful soul perhaps I have known or shall know, except,
> it may be, my sister Janet and Mrs Moor. She has also a strong and
> sincere mind, which prevents her swallowing any humbug. She is a
> member of the Church of England and the widow of a parson. But
> what she believes now I do not know, nor I think does she. But she
> has "faith" in the sense of courage, love and hope. Those are the
> last great qualities that abide when all other things go, and we can
> but wait our passage to annihilation or whatever else there may be.

3

His failure as an Extension lecturer led to a most extraordinary
reaction. He concluded (which one can understand) that he had
no gift for speaking or teaching. But what is so startling is the
alternative which he adopted. After his failure at Chester he went
for a holiday in Wales. He climbed Snowdon alone. Great
torrents of mist came rolling up over the summit, revealing and
hiding by turns the precipices and valleys below. The scenic
greatness of life—never far off in his outlook—now took a new
form. He still desired to discover reality and help mankind, but
was it only through literature that this double goal could be
reached? In the pinelands of Heidelberg or of Surrey he had
thought so, but was there no other path? Abruptly, and not on
the grounds of felt inclination or capacity, he decided to be a
doctor.

Science always attracted him, and he had, like many men of
letters, hopes from it which are seldom cherished by scientists
themselves. In his later years he tried to follow Eddington and
Jeans and was in close touch with the popularizing work of
Gerald Heard—work, he considered, as valuable as any which
has been done in our day. In 1886 his outlook was cruder, and
he regarded science as a sort of Buddhism; it was to illuminate
and confirm a positive view of the world, and culminate in a
mystic revelation. And, if science led to reality, one branch of
science—medicine—enabled him by a happy coincidence to
help mankind. Two birds of his desire could be killed by one

stone, and in deciding to be a doctor he felt surprised that he had not thought of this before.

On descending from Snowdon, he wrote a long letter to his father (17 April 1886), explaining the position. He says that, although poetry and philosophy seem to him the best in life, he does not find in himself the creative gift which would make him a real artist. He has thought, therefore, of medicine, both for scientific and humanitarian reasons, and has hoped to make enough money by lecturing to support himself while he studies it. But lecturing is unsatisfactory, and prevents him from thinking; so would his father finance him for four years, on "business principles", until he has got his medical degree, when he will pay the money back? The letter—like all he wrote—is both straightforward and considerate; he makes it clear what he wants, and makes it easy for his father to refuse. His father assented, and in the autumn of the year he returned to Cambridge, and began to study for the M.B. degree.

He was instantly seized with panic. Cambridge seemed dead, his friends had gone down, he was no longer in college. He saw that he would never make a doctor, and that the arguments influencing him had been unreal, and he wrote to his father saying that he wanted to abandon the enterprise. Next morning he breakfasted with his contemporary, Headlam (afterwards Sir J. W. Headlam-Morley of the Foreign Office), and told him what he had done. Headlam persuaded him that he had made a mistake, and he wired to his father telling him not to open the letter. Presumably the letter arrived before the wire, and had already been read, but his father never said anything about it, and he entered duly upon the course. It is a queer little display of wobbling, and in his opinion (not in mine) it is typical of his character; he also comments that it shows "the uselessness of taking up definite work merely because one thinks it good. . . . There can have been few people less gifted for scientific research (as distinguished from speculation) than myself; and few less qualified for the observation and manual dexterity that the medical profession requires." This is no doubt true.

He then settled down quietly, and worked hard, but without any feeling of vocation. "I've begun dissecting and it's not so bad as it might be, has even a certain kind of geographical interest," he writes to May: "but I can't arrive at the 'artistic' view of it which the professor and others seem to take; 'it's *beautiful* dissection' is the phrase." Later on: "Corpses are not repulsive,

49

merely dull" or "I don't regard anatomy as serious work."
He informs Ashbee the physiology interests him more, "but then
it's such an infant science and consequently a chaos of incomprehensible and contradictory facts", a true enough description
of physiology fifty years ago. Roger Fry—whom he now began
to know—was also doing medicine, though with neater fingers,
and would sometimes extricate him from the frog or worm with
which he was involved. He passed his first M.B. examination in
1887, his second in 1888. But by that time his fortunes had taken
another and a more appropriate turn, and his career as a doctor
came to a close.

Medicine was certainly the strangest of his incursions into
the realm of matter, but as one looks back at a friend's youth,
or indeed at one's own youth, there is always a good deal which
seems strange. The personality is then freer, because it is inexperienced, and it starts this way and that, down avenues which
will never be explored, without feeling self-conscious. Dickinson
came to realize that his attempt to be a doctor, though mistaken,
was not ridiculous: " I still think . . . that profession is the best,
and does combine the possibilities of that combination of learning
and life which I wanted then and want now, and have very imperfectly achieved as things are."

He gave it up because, contrary to any reasonable expectation,
Plotinus had turned up trumps. Though the fellowships at
King's were then only worth £80 as against their present £300,
there were various advantages attaching, so that he became
financially independent of his father. His father was disappointed
at his change of profession, but as usual never said one word of
blame. From 1887 onward, Dickinson made no more false starts,
but settled down to a life which, in his opinion, was not the best
sort of life but the best which his capacities allowed.

chapter nine

From Mysticism to Politics
1887-1893

I

To the north of the front court of King's rises a precipitous wall of stone and glass: Henry VI's chapel, tending by its very size to nullify itself when it has become familiar and to enter but little into the general consciousness of the college. On the south of the court the chapel is acknowledged by some presentable buildings of the Gothic revival, containing the hall, lecture-rooms, the undergraduates' reading-room, the dons' combination rooms and so on. Westward, the early eighteenth century speaks; Gibbs's Building, or Fellows' Building, almost closes that side of the court: a solid three-storey block, graceful, grave, and grouping with its precipitous and perpendicular neighbour into a harmony peculiar to England. There are compliments outside the rules of etiquette, and perhaps they are the only compliments worth receiving. Gibbs is pierced midway by a cavernous entry, known to initiates as the Jumbo House, in whose sombre recesses are usually to be found a ladder, a hand-cart and a small heap of sand. These too are peculiar to England. The range from them to the soaring chapel buttresses, pinnacled in the intense inane, is the range of the English mind. They are the unexplained, balancing the inexplicable. Above the arch of the Jumbo House rides a fine semicircular window, above that is the chief architectural feature of the block, a classical pediment, topped in its turn by a couple of chimneys and by the flagstaff from which, on days of commemoration, the dark blue flag of the college depends. Most of Dickinson's academic life was spent in various rooms of Gibbs, and he would recall with amazement how he had wanted it pulled down when he was an undergraduate, on the ground that it had no soul.

On the further side of Gibbs a new world opens: the façade of Clare; an enormous lawn sloping towards the Cam; a bridge over the Cam; the trees of Scholars' Piece; the trees of the

Backs; the trees, flowers and tennis courts of Fellows' Garden. Here we return—and indeed to most visitors the whole expedition has been superfluous. Nearly everyone knows what King's College, Cambridge, looks like; it has been depicted and described since curiosity began. But as we return, as we recross the bridge, as we ascend the gentle slope of the lawn, note how the buildings of Gibbs dominate, how they set their seal upon the composite beauty of the scene. It is they, not the chapel, who would reign in the last resort, but they are too moderate and too civilized to declare their power. What colour are they? It is simplest to say "gray" and to leave the initiate in the course of years to memorize the exquisite modulations into black, into white, which have been caused by the weathering of the Portland stone.

There are four staircases in the block, lettered E, F, G, H. Each gives access to six sets. Most of the sets contain three rooms, a large one in front and two small ones behind, looking over the Backs, but this disposition is not invariable.

2

Such was the framework. Although he was to remain in it all his life, he was elected to a fellowship in the first instance for six years only. During this period he is still a recluse, who has not yet realized his teaching powers. He is moving into the open, and, as he does so, four main points may be noted. Firstly, there is the development of his private life—affectionate, emotional, disciplined, idealistic. Secondly, connected with this, is his poetical output. Thirdly, there is a changed attitude towards the world, which leads him away from Plotinus and mysticism and towards Hegel and politics. Fourthly, connected with this last, come his early prose publications.

This period is to be dealt with in the present chapter, and the following letter shall serve as an informal preface to it. To A. J. Grant:

1 All Souls Place, Langham Place, W.
16 July 1887

I am not unaware, O Grant, that you have probably been cursing me; yet I hope not overmuch, being a reasonable man and aware that friendship does not depend on correspondence. I believe I've a good deal to tell you too. The end of term and of a year at Cambridge is always an excitement; even to ancients like me. People dissolve then as at no other time and it becomes evident that there is no good like friendship; which indeed may be termed love; which love, it seems to me, is the one thing to be cherished if there is to be any purport in life; cherished as the fundament of all one's conduct and opinions—much deeper and more important than they. That one should take a diametrically opposite course to other men is to be expected; but that one should cease therefore to love them is "anathema maranatha" —n'est-ce pas? Of which things indeed it is good for the most part to be silent; but also occasionally to speak. I've just returned from Durham where I've been staying with Headlam. I shall miss him awfully. I'm going into his rooms and he'll haunt me like a ghost. He's the best man possible; you'll see his soul in his eyes, if you look; lovely eyes. He has an Oxford brother who appears to have no πνεῦμα and therefore has no eyes; otherwise he is clever and epigrammatic— rather wearisomely so. He is naturally going into the church. You should have seen me going to church at Durham in a top-hat, with prayerbook and hymnbook complete. Headlam took me to Tyne-mouth, and I wrote this.

> Far in the north beside a lonely shore
>   A priory crowned the cliff; its little bell
>   Morning and evening sent a drowsy knell
> Across wide waters; and above the roar
> Of booming tempests oft the wild wind bore
>   Deep misereres seaward, greeted well
>   By pious mariners, who when darkness fell
> Marked the rich light from painted lancets pour.
>
> This was: now, thick with smoke and din, the land,
>   Mile upon mile of brick, is populous,
> Save where three arches, black with traffick, keep
>   A frowning watch to seaward. Men discuss,
> Passing in haste to business, why they stand
> Thus idly eloquent of an age of sleep.

That art is the best thing man has, the reward and crown when his social state is settled, is becoming my conviction. Whether at present art is the thing is another matter. Having got himself comfortable it remains for man to "see the world and behold it is very good"; and that is what the artist does for him. Meantime, however, he has to get himself comfortable—with infinite labour, and destroying all his beauty in the process; at which, I suppose, no wise man will unduly repine.

I've made various plans for myself this long; among others the reading of some Hegel. I don't know if that'll come off; just now I'm a little sceptical of metaphysics, but without more reason than other people. To be sceptical of metaphysics means, as often as not, that one is too lazy to read them; it means that with me at present. I'm going away with my people to Thursley at the foot of Hinde Head, near Tilford (do you remember) for August. Can't go to Cambridge; there's no one up that I know. Or is it really a fact that Berry is going up for August? Tell him to let me know.

Are you enjoying Germany much? I don't feel as if Göttingen is an exciting place. You ought to go to Heidelberg and see Ord. Are you reading Der grosse Goethe at all yet? Or what are you reading in special? I should like to have come to see you; but I'm going to stay and work like a good boy. When do you come back?

I've seen Laurie today. He's been trying (in top-hat and black coat) for an Edinburgh professorship, but is pilled. He has got a post however, at the "People's Palace"; £150 a year. I saw Stevenson at Newcastle. He's coming up to live at Toynbee in October.—It's very wrong of you not to be keener over *Lohengrin*. You must hear *Tannhäuser* before you leave Germany; and go in a duly solemn frame of mind.— Headlam, Ashbee, Fry and I had a most delicious 4 days on the river, rowing from Oxford to London; I think the best time I ever had; a glimpse of the ideal possibilities of life. This summer has been glorious to me; to you too, I hope. England is so lovely it seems idle to go abroad. Even for pictures there are enough in the National Gallery to last one a lifetime. I suppose I don't much deserve for you to write to me; but I would be awfully glad if you would. My love to Berry.

Yours ever,
G. L. Dickinson.

The people mentioned in the above letter are contemporary Kingsmen. Headlam is Headlam-Morley; Arthur Berry, a Senior Wrangler, afterwards became Vice-Provost of the college; Roger Fry, the painter and critic, is now Slade Professor of Fine Arts at Cambridge. The sonnet about Tynemouth was printed with a few variants in the *Cambridge Fortnightly*, a magazine which Fry edited. The letter, as a whole, is the sort of thing which Dickinson turned out when he was feeling easy, and in its unpretentious way it introduces various points which must now be considered: friendship; poetry; intellectual development; prose.

3

Shortly before becoming a Fellow, he had been elected to one of those discussion societies which still flourish at Cambridge and play an appreciable part in its mental life. The characteristics of such societies vary but little. The members are drawn from the older undergraduates and the younger dons, they meet of an evening in one another's rooms, a paper is read, lots are drawn to determine the order of the speeches, the order is observed or ignored, there are developments and digressions, and finally the reader replies to his critics, handing round as he does so some such refreshment as anchovies on toast or walnut cake. Some of the discussions are logical in their tendency, others informative or whimsical, but in all cases formality is avoided, presidents and secretaries are reduced to their minimum, and there is no attempt to be forensic or even parliamentary. The young men seek truth rather than victory, they are willing to abjure an opinion when it is proved untenable, they do not try to score off one another, they do not feel diffidence too high a price to pay for integrity; and according to some observers that is why Cambridge has played, comparatively speaking, so small a part in the control of world affairs. Certainly these societies represent the very antithesis of the rotarian spirit. No one who has once felt their power will ever become a good mixer or a yes-man. Their influence, when it goes wrong, leads to self-consciousness and superciliousness; when it goes right, the mind is sharpened, the judgement is strengthened, and the heart becomes less selfish. There is nothing specially academic about them, they exist in other places where intelligent youths are allowed to gather together unregimented, but in Cambridge they seem to generate a peculiar clean white light of their own which can remain serviceable right on into middle age.

Dickinson's life as a young don was more intense than as an undergraduate, and under this white light he entered upon what may be regarded as the second cycle of his friendships. His intellect and his affections were more closely connected than most men's, and discussion for him was not a cerebral exercise but an agitation which went deep into his being. His severely logical mind did not tolerate humbug or haziness, and in most cases such a mind either atrophies the emotions or functions independently of them. In his case it reinforced them. He was attracted to people in the first instance because they shared or seemed to share his interest in intellectual problems. Other and more important links might be forged, but a mutual desire for truth must precede personal intimacy. Thus he, Roger Fry, J. E. McTaggart and Nathaniel Wedd were originally drawn together by their passion for philosophy, and they were fired by a belief which McTaggart

55

at all events never abandoned: the belief that philosophy explains the universe. It never did that for Dickinson, but it established relationships which lasted till death.

> Since then I have seldom been out of love, if the word love may be used of a feeling continually thwarted on the physical side. That question I leave to casuists and medical men, though without much expectation that they will have anything important to say about it. For emotion, which to me is the determining fact, lies outside their province, and usually outside their competence.

Fry and McTaggart had come up from Clifton together. Goldie's relation with Fry soon became the more profound, and they "lunched and breakfasted every day together" in the academic year 1887–8. Fry went down with a science degree, but determined to become a painter. He lived for a time in the dignified house of his father the judge. Dickinson visited him, but did not at first make a good impression on the establishment: he was unobtrusive and untidy and forgot to bring his white tie. "Have you any further luggage coming, sir?" inquired the footman. More congenial were the expeditions that the friends made together in the country. Dickinson loved England, he felt its scenery to be trembling on the verge of an exquisite mythology which only Shakespeare has evoked and he only incidentally. Despite our vile climate and the increasing vileness of our towns he kept a vision of sunlight, water, hedgerows, flowers, and the names of flowers. These last—though he frequently forgot them—were an earnest of our native poetry, he thought; speedwell and traveller's joy represent something which has scarcely found entrance into our literature, and not at all into our lives.

> It is a lovely place [he writes of the Frys' Somersetshire home]. We sat in the garden and walked about the country. I remember an early morning sunrise, the sun coming up a huge red globe. I remember a hot walk, when Roger, who was afraid of sunstroke, plunged his head into a stagnant and filthy pond. I remember a wood full of foxgloves, which prompted the little poem printed in my book. Another time we walked along the Dorsetshire coast, from Corfe and Lulworth to Weymouth, and back by the valley of the Stour. . . . Then I remember, after a long day's walk, supping out of doors at Weymouth and realizing, what so often I have felt before and since, the perfection of happiness given by physical and emotional well-being—a happiness which the young, and even the older, are apt to interpret, as I did then, as somehow revealing the nature of the universe. Alas, it is but a moment casually permitted to one of the little creatures meaning-

lessly produced in a world indifferent either to their happiness or their misery.

Fry's influence naturally increased Dickinson's interest in pictures. He had not here the same sureness of instinct as in literature and music; he desired to educate himself, and to share his friend's enthusiasms. Difficulties arose, for Fry was constantly developing both his theories and his practices. The chariot of art, as driven by him, has never pursued a straight course in the literary sense of the phrase, and Dickinson often flew out of it at a sudden turn of the road. Fry, though never scornful, was often surprised, for he could not understand why a jolt should have been communicated. He would reason with his fallen companion, and would induce him to remount and admire objects which he disliked or endorse arguments which he mistrusted. Here are two letters recording an early mishap. The first is from All Souls Place (18 April 1891):

> I went to the English Art Club the other day, and I now feel sure that if that's what pictures are I have no sense for them. I suppose colour and tone are really lost on me. . . . I can't do without form, and if it once gets recognized that pictures have nothing to do with form I shall be much relieved, for then I can make up my mind once for all that I don't care a damn for "art", and go no more to exhibitions. But I still cherish a hope that you're going to do some pictures I can like, or else give me the necessary perception for such things. I went with Furness who agrees with all I say, and ten times more.

And he remarks of the work of Steer: "One can only hold one's tongue and pray about it." But his next letter, dated from Cambridge a week later, is humbler in its tone; something persuasive must have arrived from Roger in the interval.

> I gave you my real feelings about the N.E.A.C., but they're too negative to be worth much; just the kind of criticism in fact that I bar in literature. It's quite true that I don't understand the thing because I don't feel it; perhaps you'll make me some day. You know I've learned most things that depend on the eyes from you, besides many more important things. I'm glad to be up here again [the letter goes on], it's cold still but there are daffodils and primroses and undergraduates and all the positive things which it is the one delight of the world to present to one and then add ironically "that isn't the truth nevertheless" and so she negatives it all with winter and death and politics and "social questions" and philosophy. . . .

The New English Art Club was not the last of his troubles. It is true that he learned to require tone, and that he was conceded form, but he was conceded it rather too insistently, and was asked to sacrifice on its rigid altar the one thing for which he did care: subject-matter. He took the "literary" view of art, if by "literary" we may understand poetic. What he wanted in a picture, and what he discovered with mischievous friendliness in Roger's own pictures, was romance: hills, not of this world, where the spirit could walk, people, recognizably human yet transformed— all the trailing garments of Shelley. Thus when the Post-Impressionists came along he should have been sorely tried, but by then he had grown content to pick his own way on foot, and to realize there were tracts he should never explore.

At the beginning of 1892 Fry's work took him to Paris, and they spent many weeks there—rather a dolorous visit. Italy had already been visited with Ashbee, and brought overwhelming delight; there are long paeans, respectably pagan, about its blue skies and its wine: "No words can describe the divine enchantment of this place" from Tivoli, and from Rome "I've been lying on my back with Rome below and the stars above and murmuring waters all around". Paris proved uncongenial, though he praises it to May as "a city, whereas London is a congeries of houses", and compares Haussmann's architecture to Wren's. He did not feel easy there. He was to develop no special sympathy for France, nor indeed for any foreign nation except China.

Roger and I took a room in the Rue de Tournon, close to the Luxembourg. He was studying art and I visiting museums and galleries, attending lectures at the Collège de France, and writing a kind of drama on Mirabeau. This I still have, though I have not the interest or patience to read it through, and I daresay it has no merit. Still, it interested me at the time. I used to write at it in our untidy attic, after we had had our roll and coffee and when Roger had gone out to his work. I should think that few young men ever got less out of Paris than I did. For to get anything out of it, it seems to be essential to approach it by the route of women, and that was no route for me. I am amused, as I look back, to remember a visit to one of the dancing places (was it the Moulin Rouge?) and my boredom for the short time I could stay. And also, how a very ugly old prostitute came up to me once, in some eating place, and began fondling me. I fairly ran away. Paris, to me, at that time, was merely a place where one continued one's own thoughts in more or less discomfort. But, of course, I liked being with Roger.

The "kind of drama on Mirabeau" is often mentioned in his letters at this time. He writes to Fry that "behind all these feverish actors I must get a divine ἀνάγκη, partly from lyrical interludes, partly from giving the irresistible brute force of the populace—which I find is rather difficult to treat". He was hopeful of himself as a poetic chronicler, and had already published *From King to King*. I must be the only person for many years who has read *Mirabeau*. It is partly in prose and partly in verse, and it is less interesting as literature than for its connection with *Revolution and Reaction in Modern France*.

This constant companionship was interrupted when Fry fell in love.

> I still recall the conversation we had, late at night, in the house where he was then living, in Beaufort Street, Chelsea. I was unhappy, yet not very, nor lastingly. For Roger did not cut me off from anything I had had. Later, he became engaged, then married, and I saw less of him, yet still a great deal. All our life we have been friends, and I have indeed a kind of married feeling towards him. Now, when age is coming on, we seem to have less in common in our interests, for he has become more, and I less and less, interested in art. Still, I think our affection will last as long as we do; it rests on an intercourse so long, so continuous, so varied. At Dorking, at Hampstead, in Italy, in Switzerland, I see myself with him, and always happy with him.

He got to know Jack McTaggart at the same time as Fry. He has himself written about McTaggart with respect and affection, so it will be sufficient to quote a passage from the *Recollections*. It was written about 1926, before his friend's death, and it is more vivid than anything in the published memoir, and also more frank about the estrangement necessitated by the war. Since it is chiefly concerned with early memories it finds its proper place here. Note Dickinson's method of depicting character: he begins from within, and then proceeds to the oddities which make up the visible man. Method of the dialogue-writer rather than of the novelist, who hopes, by recording the surface, to indicate the forces beneath it.

> As for McTaggart, if I may digress for a moment about my old friend, at one time the most intimate and most frequented of all, he was, from the philosophic point of view, quite uninterested in the concrete; for he did not believe that philosophy could handle it, except— important exception—at one point. He held then, and I suppose does still, that in the relation of love we come into the closest contact we can attain with Reality; that Reality is an eternally perfect harmony

of pure spirits united by Love. This idea is the key to McTaggart's philosophy, and the real thing that drove him to pursue it. The rest has been a continuous and (I suppose) vain effort to prove it by logic. The concrete and phenomenal world being excluded from philosophy, he was able to submit frankly to his prejudices, as something, so to speak, too low to be taken seriously. But if he did not take them seriously he took them very violently.

When he first came to Cambridge, he was then an unkempt young man, thin, crooked, walking always with a twist of his body towards the wall because, as was credibly affirmed, he was always being kicked at school; and with amazing gray eyes, through which his soul shone. He was a follower of John Stuart Mill, a radical, and an empirical realist. But after a year or two at Cambridge, having discovered Hegel and become an idealist, he became also, for most purposes, a conservative. He has been, ever since, an imperialist, a believer in public schools and universities (of the older type), a lover of all ceremonies and traditions, of feasts, port wine, scarlet robes, professorships, mayors and corporations, bishops, the House of Lords, and in fact everything English except the House of Commons. One of his suggestions for the reform of the Upper House was that those bishops should be added to it who were excluded under present rules. He became, in fact, and is the most curious combination imaginable of Dr Johnson, Hegel and Robert Browning. He was at this time the most intimate friend of Schiller, Fry and myself, the inspirer of our thoughts; witty, profound, sentimental, absurd, everything in turns, at once exasperating and delightful, and never more delighted than when he exasperated.

When I see him now, with all that shut in under so thick a veil, when I consider what he was to us and compare what he now is for younger generations, who hardly take him seriously, I could weep or I could laugh. Yet both attitudes probably are irrelevant. For the same man, I believe, is still there, behind the mask; and sometimes . . . the mask lifts, and astonishes the young men with the vision of something they cannot understand or accept, yet cannot fail to be impressed by. The war broke off my intimacy with him, and I suppose it will never be renewed. But there have been few men to whom I owe so much, few who have been more part of my life; and I salute him here, in words that he perhaps will never read, but that spring from a depth below our estrangement, from that common fountain in which once the springs of our youth were mingled.

Happy in his friendships and his dislikes, McTaggart is said, by those who are qualified to judge him, to have been a great and a lovable man. But to a biographer of Dickinson it is rather the greatness of Dickinson which comes out in the foregoing passage. Few men can so have combined the powers of the head and the heart, and by the use of reason have so fortified the affections to withstand the inevitable shocks which await them. It is sometimes said: "What is the use of education?" Well, here is an instance of what education can do.

A recent letter to their contemporary, G. C. Moore Smith (7 December 1931), says:

> As to Jack's character and performance of course one's judgement depends upon what one thinks is the proper use of the mind. Desmond MacCarthy was insisting last night that its only proper use is to attempt to comprehend the whole universe and that Jack was the last of the great philosophers who pursued that purpose. My own view now is that that route is closed and that presumably the human mind and senses are so limited that men while they are men cannot expect to comprehend it, though they ought never to abandon the aim, pursuing it however by other methods. What lies behind death I do not know but suspect it may be stranger than we are apt to suppose. We are both getting near it now, and it remains true anyhow that "the readiness is all".

The fourth of this group of friends who centred in the discussion society is Nathaniel Wedd. When I was at King's, Wedd taught me classics, and it is to him rather than to Dickinson —indeed to him more than to anyone—that I owe such awakening as has befallen me. It is through him that I can best imagine the honesty and fervour of fifty years back. Wedd was then cynical, aggressive, Mephistophelian, wore a red tie, blasphemed, and taught Dickinson how to swear too—always a desirable accomplishment for a high-minded young don, though fewer steps need be taken about it now.

> He is, I think, one of the ablest men I have known. He became a Fellow and classical tutor at King's, and his teaching was universally admired by his pupils. But he was more than a teacher. He gave up all his time and energies to undergraduates, was at home to them at all hours of the night, stimulated, comforted, amused, and generally maintained the best tradition of King's, that of friendship and intimacy between undergraduates and dons. But he overworked and over-smoked himself, so that in the end he fell seriously ill, and many years of his life have been thus frustrated. During all that time I never saw him cast down, nor did his mind or memory ever seem to weaken. He is now back at King's and in better health than it ever seemed likely he could achieve, though not able to do any teaching.

Some memories still survive of that far distant discussion society of theirs. The paper by Dickinson which made most impression was called "Shall we elect God?" It imagines a meeting of a celestial branch of their group convened for that purpose. The members present are Goethe, Hegel, Turgenev and Victor Hugo. They speak in turn, and each from his own standpoint is doubtful or hostile over the proposed election. They know too little about this God, or do not like what they have heard about him. Just as they are going to vote, there is a knock on the door and God comes in. He wears a hat and cloak, and his face cannot be seen. They must hear him speak before deciding, he says, and he tells them that, however little they think they know him, it is he whom they meet at every turn of their lives. If they go into the street, it is his eyes which peer out at them from the faces of every passer-by, he is all they struggle against, all they believe in, they cannot exclude him if they would, for he is himself the founder of their society. The four members are moved, but unconvinced. "Let us see your face," they say. God agrees and throws off his hat and cloak. They all cry out at once—Goethe "Das Schöne!", Turgenev "La Vérité!", Hugo "L'Idéal!", Hegel "Das Absolut!" This paper of his and another by McTaggart entitled "Violets or Orange Blossom?" were preserved for many years. The peculiar mixture of honesty and idealism which inspired them has now passed away.

One more friend of this period remains to be mentioned: Ferdinand Schiller. He stands apart from the rest and he was to occupy the supreme position in Dickinson's life. Although Schiller belonged to the same set and had strong intellectual powers, he had an even stronger vein of common sense, which led him to take a sardonic view both of philosophic speculations and of schemes to regenerate or improve the world. He was naturally drawn to the business career in which he has since become successful. In the summer of 1888 he had left Cambridge and was preparing to go to Calcutta, and though he and Dickinson had been previously acquainted it is from this moment that they begin to know one another well. Schiller's people were at Gersau, on the Lake of Lucerne. Dickinson, Fry and McTaggart all went to stay there, and the visit seemed in retrospect an idyll of laughter, wit and romance.

His mother was the kindest, humanest, most pagan woman I have ever known. Her husband being in India, she had brought up her sons at home in England. Her devotion to them and to all whom they cared for was her almost exclusive motive for living. I remember as though it were yesterday our first arrival at Gersau, Max (now a K.C.) and Canning (now the pragmatist and don at Oxford) on the tennis court and the dear lady overflowing with gaiety, kindness and shrewdness. There was a tennis court behind the house, a bathing shed in front. Close by was the church with its clanging, pitiless bells. The house is now the Pension Fluhegg. How it lies bathed in sunshine and gaiety in my memory! There was a largish party, and I shared a bedroom with Roger outside. We walked, played tennis, bathed, chaffed for a happy month. Then came the end and Ferdinand, that autumn, left for India.

Five years later he returned on leave, and there was a second visit to Gersau, and the foundation of a relationship which was to be affectionate and permanent, yet disturbing. Devoted to Schiller, but constantly parted from him, and doubtful whether his devotion was returned, Dickinson suffered for many years from a sense of frustration which the sensitive will understand. They corresponded regularly, he writing every week and Schiller once a fortnight. Their letters are pessimistic in different ways. Schiller is despondent about the world, and amusingly bitter over the poor chances it offers to people who want to be decent, or even wealthy. Dickinson, equally despondent, dwells rather upon its hostility to perfect intercourse, and hopes for the "company of pure spirits related to one another by perfect love", which constituted McTaggart's heaven. "I . . . cannot understand," he comments afterwards, "how I thought that this personal passion in transitory individuals could be the key to the universe." Schiller could not understand it at the time. He left India in 1899, for reasons of health, and settled in England, and Dickinson looked forward to being with him constantly. This was not to be; the diversity of their occupations and interests kept them apart and it was not until later that affection and fidelity triumphed over circumstances, and bore fruit. Schiller is implicit in much that Dickinson wrote, particularly in the sonnets and in the character of Philip Audubon, of the dialogues.

Scenically this relationship was set against a background of mountains and mountaineering. In Schiller's company and on his account he climbed the Piz Palu in the Bernina group as well as minor heights, and also walked all one night to the top of the Gemmi Pass. On one occasion (19 August 1902) he did with J. J. Withers a climb which has been recorded in the *Alpine Journal*—the ascent of the south-east face of the Piz Pisoc in the Ofen Pass district. One does not think of him as an athlete, but he had toughness and determination, and delighted in the life of the body provided it was unorganized; he could scramble, ride, boat, swim, and when he could combine any of these exercises with romance he was perfectly happy. Though he deplored the ugliness of Switzerland, its lumpiness, spikiness and woolliness, and often contrasted it with Italian grace, he could not forget the deep emotions and the radiant health vouchsafed there, nor the visions—O that they were true!—where precipices and avalanches seemed to promise an ecstasy unattainable on earth, and

> the valley waters found,
> Far-gleaming to the dim horizon's bound,
> Among the cloudy islands of the Blest
> In that most ancient river Ocean, rest.

It has been necessary to dwell on these early relationships because though he made other friends they never sank so deeply into his life. His nature was not only loving, but tenacious, and it is impossible at any period of his life to conceive of him as apart from Fry, McTaggart and Wedd, or, more particularly, as apart from Ferdinand Schiller. Similarly, though he made various women friends, there were none who could ever take the place of his sisters or of Mrs Webb, or of two who have not yet been mentioned—Mrs Moor and Miss Stawell. It is now, when his mind is developing, that his heart is most sensitive to joy and pain, and his surrender to intimacy most complete. It is now that he writes to Mrs Webb: "I think the one immortal thing we are given in direct experience is love; I don't believe it goes when it seems to; it only gets hidden."

4

Through his emotions we approach his poetry. In his own judgement, he was too much interested in ideas, and too little interested in form, to be a great poet; his diction was facile rather than distinguished, his style was derivative, and he had not the power of transforming little things. But as an expression for what would otherwise have remained unexpressed he valued his poetic craft highly. It is not only in early manhood, when emotional developments were agitating him, that he turned to verse; the impulse recurred—for instance in 1913 when he was in China, and again in 1929.

The tribute to Shelley under the robes and cowl of Savonarola has already been mentioned. His next printed work was *Jacob's Ladder* (1887), a twenty-two page brochure, which he had multiplied in about twenty copies for private circulation. It is a curious experiment, consisting of a prologue and seven sections. The theme is the progress of mankind through the ages, towards some lyrical consummation, "and, as usual, it was the idea, not the form, which interested me". A dying Viking (who exhibits the influence of William Morris), a Greek (M. Arnold), a Roman of the Empire (in the style of Browning), an ecstatic Christian and a tough optimistic evolutionist (Browning again) are followed by the twilight which is passing into dawn. Two ideas (he tells us) were in his mind at the time of writing: the idea of perfectibility in time and the idea of perfection in eternity, and he was not clear how the two were to be reconciled. If, as the nineteenth century thought, the universe is getting better and better, when will it become best? How does progress culminate in heaven? And heaven, the absolute, was necessary at that time to him, as at all times to McTaggart, because without it he could neither explain the strength of human love nor justify its shallowness. It is the experience of most of us that personal relationships are never perfect, but that when they are intense they hint at perfection. A modern young man is inclined to dismiss such hints as unimportant; Dickinson's temperament and upbringing inclined him to take them very seriously. The Rev. Page Roberts shrewdly remarked to his father that *Jacob's Ladder* ran up "rather oddly into personal passion", and indeed it must, for without the personal the universal could not be attained.

> Where we oft had been
> We sauntered by familiar sweeps of lawn
> And silent places waiting for the dawn,
> Where chestnuts arched above, and, rarely heard,
> Sounded the note of night's enchanted bird.

These are the Cambridge Backs, and because of the emotion felt there the ladder can reach heaven. He wrote the poem mostly in the British Museum reading-room, but part of it on a backwater above Henley, lying in a sort of ecstasy throughout a golden summer morning.

Robert Bridges was encouraging, and said that the Greek section "gives promise of poetry of a rare and original character". Dickinson now became less doubtful of his powers, and writes to Mrs Webb (January 1891):

Last Sunday I spent with Robert Bridges the poet. I like him. He was particularly kind to me, and we talked much on poetry, metres, etc., and agreed a good deal, though he's not interested much in some things which are the most interesting to me. He was very encouraging about my poetry and I begin to be surer myself that my faculty is in that direction: certainly, by a negative exhaustive process, it appears demonstrably not to lie anywhere else.

The idea of progress was more successfully expressed in *From King to King* (1891). This, his first book to be offered to the general public, is connected both with his historical studies and with his theory of history. Its theme is the Puritan Revolution, treated in a series of prose and verse scenes, and it illustrates his belief that history should be a form of art, and that it had never been better treated than by Shakespeare. He retained that belief in later years, but when he wrote *From King to King* he held that history should also be a philosophy, and he had spent much time in reading the eighteenth-century and early-nineteenth-century theorists. This did not spoil the freshness and charm of the book. The early summer meadows at Thames Ditton, a foal in the grass, Milton's "Penseroso", a moonlight walk, friends absent and present, are entangled in its charming sequence. Writing to Fry, shortly before its publication, he says:

> It is a kind of satisfaction to me to have got something done at last; we used to defend "being" as opposed to "doing", but I can't now; one must create somehow or other in order to be. Creation's a sort of digestion, and there's all the world to be digested before a single soul can be finished.

And thirty years later, in the *Recollections*:

> I have still a weakness for that little book . . . ; for I believe it was a good idea of handling history, that the moments were well chosen, and the drama succinctly unrolled, from Eliot in the Tower to the execution of Vane. And the words of Mr Pepys introduced at the close of all still strike me as an admirable ironic commentary on the whole. I suppose, however, that the conception was inadequate. Anyhow the book excited no interest.

Those who have read *From King to King* probably share his favourable opinion of it and wish it could be reprinted. He issued an American edition of it in 1907, containing a few alterations, chiefly in the prose scenes.

Mirabeau has already been mentioned, and he was evidently

hoping at that time to develop the poetic chronicle as a form of art. But critics were discouraging. Robert Bridges was disappointed with some further work which was sent to him, and considered it inferior to *Jacob's Ladder*. For one reason or another Dickinson experimented no more in this particular direction. His two acting-plays, which will be mentioned in their place, are of another type, as are the dramatic fantasies which he wrote during and after the war.

But it is in his lyrics and sonnets, rather than in longer poems, that he best expresses the spirit of these early years, their unrest, yearning, rapture, sensitiveness to nature and to man. He had begun to write verses as soon as he emerged from the nightmare of school, and he could dimly remember a poem evoked by the event of his mother's death, and the mood of pleasure, pain, romance, sentimentality, in which it was composed. One of his early efforts was sent by a friend of the family to Christina Rossetti for her opinion. She replies (May 1883) with a long and unfavourable judgement: the poem submitted to her, she writes, "shows talent rather than genius". And he complains of his own work to Fry:

> There's something terribly Tennysonian about it, however, and Tennyson *will not do*; he's only half alive, and that half is diseased. But as Heine says, Modern Literature *is* one vast hospital. What if Walt Whitman isn't a poet, he's got the temper the next great poet will have.

The numerous manuscript poems of this period confirm these discouraging opinions; they are sensitive, sincere and elevated and have a sort of generalized charm, but they lack vitality or distinction or the magic of words.

He did, however, write some poems which satisfied him, and he issued them in 1896 in a small privately printed volume for circulation among his family and his friends. Here are twenty-five "Shakespearean" sonnets written in 1893-4, and some lyrics of the same or of an earlier date. The sonnets are in his opinion "my best poems and . . . have, I think, really some permanent value". I hope that there may be some opportunity of reissuing this volume for the general public. I quote from it now wherever I can. He does, here, attain Parnassus. Personal passion, mountaineering, rowing on the Thames, sunsets in Surrey, foxgloves in Somersetshire, the music of *Tristan*—all the experiences he enjoyed or endured in those sensitive years—are secured by the accident of art against the ravages of time.

> The thing that hath been, is. Those heavenly lights
> That made a marriage of the hills and sky,
> Those azure-shining days and shadowy nights
> With all their golden candles set on high,
> Even in this wintry fit of rain and snow
> Fade not nor fail because the summer's dead. . . .

The beauty and the accomplishment of the 1896 volume have delighted and sustained his friends for many years; and it is surprising that his desire to be a poet, his honesty, his intense feeling, his musical ear and his technical ability did not between them carry him further. But he had not the temperament which creates verses out of nothing and has produced so much worthless yet authentic stuff. He could only write in a mood of high serious-ness, and there are perils in such a mood which he did not avoid. Escaping the dust, he became involved in the clouds. It has, indeed, been objected against him that his poetry is too philosophic and his philosophy too poetical, and that this has endangered his supremacy in either sphere. Probably it has. But there are certain people who cannot be judged in terms of spheres. Their total achievement is greater than the sum of its parts. They triumph through a medium of which they are not consciously aware: through the capacity for visitation accorded in theology to certain angels.

It is convenient to mention at this point a later volume of poems, *A Wild Rose*: ten short studies in unrhymed verse, a form in which he became interested. He wrote them about 1906, when he was stopping with Ashbee at Broadway (the title-poem was published in the *Albany Review*, June 1907), and he showed them to his friend, J. H. Mason, a scholar and a printer, who conducted a printing class under the London County Council. Mason grew to like the poems, and personally printed an edition on large paper as a tribute (1910). He also produced a small-paper edition, as an exercise for his students. One of these poems from *A Wild Rose* ("If as I love my friend . . .") is included among the lyrics of *The Magic Flute*. Another ("Do you name your hope?") was reprinted in the brochure which was issued on behalf of the college after Dickinson died.

Poems by him, signed and unsigned, have appeared in various periodicals. There is a fine one, for instance, in the *Cambridge Magazine* for May 1912, called πάντα κόνις. It is about the wreck of the *Titanic*, and may be compared with Thomas Hardy's "The Convergence of the Twain", which the same catastrophe inspired.

> If I *had* been a poet, I should, I suppose, have *had* to be one. But I had, it would seem, some justification for my experiments in that direction. Anyone who reads this memoir [i.e. the *Recollections*] will quickly perceive that I had no overmastering impulse at all, but a wide range of sensitiveness.

There was one direction in which he did have an overmastering impulse, and here is the place to mention it. His feeling for music went far beyond the sensitiveness of the ordinary cultivated man, and had his specific gift been adequate he might here have achieved the ideal which he vainly pursued through poetry. Mozart and Wagner, the main pillars, show that the edifice was of catholic scope. Once inside it he felt sure of himself, and in a place more real than the other arts provided. Mozart received homage at the end of his life in *The Magic Flute*, Wagner near the beginning of it in the 1896 *Poems*. With them were Gluck and Bach, Beethoven and Schubert. To these six he probably owed even more than to Shelley, Plato, Goethe, because they were not an extension of his life, but a revelation which he would have missed if they had not existed. Music, returning via them to his philosophy, convinced him of transcendental truth, which existed as surely as the reunion of Tristan with Isolde when the final curtain falls, or as the union of passion with peace in the last movement of the Choral Symphony.

On the executive side he was becoming an attractive pianist with a charming touch and marked facility. He played duets not only with O.B. but with a much finer musician, his friend Adolf Behrens, down at Richmond. His range was increasing when it was checked by the loss in muscular control which also affected his handwriting. He never complained of this, but it was a serious blow. Later on rheumatic trouble developed, and he gave up the piano before I knew him well. His sisters remember his Handel in childhood. Munro speaks of the Beethoven and Mozart at Charterhouse, Fry of the Cambridge period; all agree that, for an amateur, his performance was remarkable. There is no doubt that, though he lost the power to play, the fact that he had once had it allowed him to enter more deeply into music, both technically and passionately, and to pass beyond the antechamber of "appreciation" where most of us have to stop.

5

While his emotions deepened and flowered into poetry and music, his intellect developed on practical lines; indeed this period in his life may be labelled "from mysticism to politics", though such labels are rather misleading, for his mysticism always remained in his heart, folded up like a flower before the heat and brightness of a new day. He desired, as the sun rose, to help humanity, and realized that he could not do so without discovering what people are like and how they live. Some young men who have this desire rush about the world in search of what is termed "actuality", but Dickinson, to his own regret, was ill-equipped for field work, and descended into the public arena by the slower route of academic history.

A few years before, he would have been impatient of history, and invoked Mohini or Plotinus instead. But by 1887 he could no longer accept their assumption that the universe is a veil to reality, for the reason that this view, though it may well be correct, offers no scope for action or thought, and ignores the existence of pain. Pain, to Dickinson, was indisputably real. There is no getting round the toothache. He dreaded pain both for himself and for others, he was impatient of any attempt to explain it away, and outraged by any theory which glorified it. His knowledge that people suffer pain, his belief that suffering can be cured, are the two foundation stones of his political life. And, just as he had been attracted to medicine because it heals the individual body, so now he turned to the diseases of the State, and examined the remedies philosophy prescribes. The worst of these diseases—international war—had not yet expanded in his consciousness, it too lay folded up like a flower. He was rather occupied with such problems as forms of government, social distinctions, the distribution of wealth, the franchise, and war in the nineteenth-century sense of that activity. Behind every problem he sought for a solution.

This gradual movement towards practical affairs is coupled with the unexpected name of the German philosopher Hegel.

We have seen from the letter to Grant that his first struggle with Hegel dates back to 1884. Three years later he writes to Fry:

> I've really begun my tussel [*sic*] with Hegel; it's the hardest work I ever had, worse than Plotinus. I don't get in more than a couple of

hours and then collapse into idiocy and physicality. You will wonder doubtless why I bother myself, but it's worth bothering about, for the thing that Hegel professes to do (I haven't the least notion whether he's done it) is the thing I've always wanted done as a preliminary to anything else in thought: i.e. to establish the relation of thought in general to the objective world and what it is thought everywhere is trying to do and what is its necessary movement.

He now began to read the monster systematically under the guidance of McTaggart, to whom Hegel meant "a release from his empiric realism to the idealism he has since pursued". They did so many pages a day, in an English translation, and got through the great and the small *Logic*. It was a curious situation, because, though he followed McTaggart faithfully into the "Hegel of Eternity" and was pleased at any road which seemed to lead into a mystic world, he was also peeping about for a path of his own in the "Hegel of Time".

Our reading, however, seems to me, in retrospect, to have been very unprofitable. We never really discussed the difficulties . . . ; and the whole notion (so preposterous, as it now seems to me) that the world can be deduced from abstract logic, and that, being so deduced, it somehow changes its whole character by merely becoming what is called rational, we accepted as a kind of article of faith.

That was the aspect of Hegel which interested McTaggart.

I was, however, myself really more interested in the applications of the *Logic*, though I was compelled to admit that they were not logical. Nevertheless, I believe that the real merit of Hegel is in that extra-ordinary survey of the life of man, his history, his art, his religion, which brought it all into a seeming concord with the postulated laws of thought. I remember sitting down, with a sort of intoxication, to a book like the *Aesthetics*, and I know not how long it took me to dis-cover that this fascinating rhapsody omits altogether the thing that is specifically art. But in that it resembles most other treatises on aesthetics; and I did not then care about that. I wanted to see Reason progress magnificently through the panorama of life; and so she did, in the crabbed, cunning, imaginative works of that pedantic and poetical enchanter.

What he gained from his "Hegel of Time" was a belief in the understandability of history, and a hope that by understanding the past he might influence the future. He had first found this hope in the political writings of Plato; now it was extended and confirmed. Since the accumulation of facts for their own sake did not interest him, he neither became nor wished to become a professional historian, and only one of his works (*The International Anarchy*) shows any high degree of research. His aim was to interpret rather than to record, and if he did not become viewy and careless, like his admired O.B., the explanation lies in his scrupulous regard for truth.

His political opinions at this time were illogical and harmonious. Was he conservative, liberal or socialist? It would be difficult to say, but it is easy to recognize his voice. By temperament he loved tradition—old houses, old trees, all the feudal charm with which he has surrounded the figure of Lord Cantelupe. Nor was he even insensitive to the joys of jingoism; there are some letters to R. C. Trevelyan during the Diamond Jubilee of 1897 which make painful reading for his steadier admirers; he exclaims how wonderful it is to see the Empire marching past, and he contemplates bicycling down to Spithead to see the Naval Review. He never reached Spithead. It was too far. And even oligarchy did not carry him over the edge. "I unfortunately like anachronisms but do not believe in them," he writes to Grant, and he knew that old houses and old trees, exquisite as they are, breed old men. His conservatism was not mere sentiment, and he could find serious arguments for it. But he found that as a working proposition it would not do, and by the end of the century he had moved to the left, and had reoccupied with stronger forces the position marked out fifteen years before under the influence of Henry George.

For the working classes as then existing he had little enthusiasm, and it was not until much later in his life that he established personal contacts with them. He had been brought up in a Victorian household, he minded h's being dropped, he knew he ought not to mind, still he did mind. And—a more serious aversion—he could not see that the working-class movement was proceeding in a direction which was either good or new. He writes to Fry after the Trades Union Congress at Liverpool: "We're really in a revolution without knowing it, and how dull it is! And all things except 'friendship, wit and love'. As soon as the working classes begin to *get* their bread and butter they show up as a new and equally dreary bourgeoisie." He might have written "an even drearier", for when Labour gets thoroughly respectable, and is stimulated neither by danger nor by art, it does seem to acquire a sausage-and-mashed quality unknown to suburbia. Miss Stawell remembers him once denouncing "a

state of things where we have men enjoying their work, enjoying their play, enjoying their food, and wondering in the discussions of their well-regulated debating societies what in the world Shelley could have meant by 'the desire of the moth for the star' ".
He was lecturing at the moment on the Spencerian ideal of progress, but the stricture applies to modern democracy generally. He feared that there would be a levelling down, instead of a levering up, and that the Many, in the process of making themselves comfortable, would throw away the pearl of great price which has been handed down to them by the Few. Art, literature, music, culture are not external decorations, but age-long secretions in the soul of man, and one of the problems of our revolution is to prevent man from despising or forgetting his own past. Thus, although he came more and more to condemn our economic system and advocate drastic changes, he had no sympathy whatever with the Marxian who rejects Shakespeare and Chekhov on the ground that they wrote for capitalists. Such a view seemed to him childish and self-conscious, and best corrected by an intelligent study of history.

As soon as one has got the general hang of his character—and I do not think it is a difficult one—his apparent political contradictions fall into line. From his main idea he never departed. He wanted a democracy where everyone will be an aristocrat. And all his work as a teacher is directed towards this utopia.

6

His earliest historical work, *From King to King*, has already been mentioned under the heading of poetry. In his own opinion, there is no distinction between the two muses: "dramatic treatment is the only one that really represents truth at all, and most history books are mere materials for books," he tells Mrs Webb. It was, however, followed next year (1892) by a work very different in form: *Revolution and Reaction in Modern France*. This was the outcome of a set of University Extension lectures at Norwich, and it attempted "to see what had become of the Revolution, and to test (or ought I to say, to impose upon history?) my rather vague and tentative theory of progress", and to trace the ideas underlying events down to the establishment of the Third Republic. It was his first attempt to write in prose at length, and "the style I evolve in this book, a series of very short sentences, grouped into paragraphs and unconnected except by the colon, which I misused for the purpose, is not good. But it was sincere, in the sense that I was determined to avoid all mere talk and meaningless empty phrases, such as fill so many text-books of history." Indeed it anticipates in its bareness, though not in its accomplishment, the prose of his latest period, when he frees himself from "literary" apparatus and brings us into direct contact with his mind. It was well received, both in England and France, "mais je crois que vous tirez trop les choses au tragique ou plutôt au romantique", writes the historian James Darme-steter, "et que vous les considérez en poète plus qu'en historien, sans peut-être vous en rendre compte vous-même". In 1927 the book was reprinted with slight modifications in the last chapter.

The next book, published in 1895, is remarkable for its con-servative tendency. It is thus described in the *Recollections*:

> I sat down to study the Parliamentary history of England, from the first Reform bill onwards; still with the idea that the history of the recent past would give guidance for the future. I ploughed through debates, pamphlets, histories, innumerable "dry as dust" stuff, which ultimately turned into the book *The Development of Parliament in the Nineteenth Century*, which was published in the year 1895, but has long been out of print and never reprinted. As may be seen from this book, I was then, in my political opinions, a kind of socialistic Tory. This was due, I suppose, on the one hand, to a contempt for the House of Commons as I imagined it to have become, a contempt really based upon Carlyle; and an absurd belief in the House of Lords, based upon nothing but antagonism to the Commons.

The book argues that the House of Commons can only express the forces which excite the nation, whereas national wisdom is expressed in the House of Lords—which is furthermore necessary as a rallying-point for the Empire.

> If I was not then a fully convinced socialist, I saw at least that the question of labour and capital would overshadow all others in the future. Of foreign politics and war I was not then thinking. This is expressed in the book, which was at any rate genuine and sincere. Its weakness was that it was written from a place so remote from the actualities of politics; and from that point of view the annoyance or contempt of such practical radicals or socialists as attended to it was probably justified. Here I am concerned with it only as an indication of my attitude at this time. I had had, since my early youth, the double impulse, both to deal with contemporary problems and to maintain

detachment and impartiality. Perhaps this is really impossible. But the impulse kept me, through all my Cambridge life, in a state of tension and unrest.

In 1906 *The Development of Parliament* was translated into French, and Dickinson wrote a new preface for it, which is interesting as showing the growth of his political opinions. He says that further study of democracy, particularly in the United States, has convinced him that it is a menace to the poor rather than to the rich, because the rich have the intelligence and the leisure to manipulate the political machine, whereas the poor are too inexperienced and too much occupied in the struggle for existence. He notes, furthermore, that it is the Cabinet, rather than the House of Commons, which governs; also that the governing classes tend to experiment in the direction of socialism, and that a revolution may be obviated or mitigated thereby. On these points he disassociates himself from the opinions expressed in the English original published eleven years before.

Neither the original nor the French translation attracted much notice, and the failure seems to have suggested to Dickinson that his life had become too secluded. "Not wholly from the world withdrawn Nor wholly to its service sworn" was his motto for himself, "very bad verse, but very true psychologically", and he was always faced by the problem of using Cambridge without being used up by it, a problem which in the long run he surmounted triumphantly. His immediate move was in the direction of academic teaching, and though the progress of a don from his own rooms to his lecture-room is not spectacular it may have important developments. When he had lectured before it had been either in a missionary spirit or because he needed money. Now that his mind and his heart had developed, teaching became a pleasure to him. This change, and its consequences, form the subject of the next chapter.

The chapter now ending has emphasized Cambridge, architecturally, emotionally and intellectually, and has said little about his home life. He remained in very close touch with his sisters, and the marriage of Arthur in 1888 served if anything to emphasize this. Most of his vacations were spent at All Souls Place, where his father continued to work as a portrait-painter, and where Hettie and Janet kept a little school. He met quantities of young people there of various types, was frivolous and domestic, took part in the musical evenings, was charming to the girls of all ages, and then would vanish to his room at the top of the house. This home life is not easy to convey in a memoir, it was so light and so quiet, but it belongs to his permanent background and must never be forgotten. Though its social ease never quite penetrated him to the core, it did act as a partial solvent and stop him from becoming eccentric. A friend of the Dickinson family, Miss Townsend, well remarks: "No one could be so intellectually unselfish as Goldie quite without effort. He came from a home where an analogous and perfectly successful effort had become second nature."

chapter ten

The Socratic Method
1893-1914

In the autumn of 1892 the question of the renewal of his fellowship came up before the governing body of the college. A committee had been appointed to report, and expressed the opinion that his studies were "likely to be of material service in the promotion of Historical and Political Science". They quoted the favourable critique of Lord Acton on *Revolution and Reaction*, and they recommended that his fellowship, which ran out in the following spring, should be renewed for five years. However, when the motion to renew was proposed in the college meeting it was defeated by one vote. The news was brought to him by his friend Laurie. He was playing the piano at the time, was "more excited than distressed" and began to wonder what he should do now that he was thrown on his own resources and obliged to make his way in London. He did not speculate for long, for that same afternoon the college held a second meeting and made him librarian, a sinecure post to which a fellowship was attached. He held the librarianship till 1896, and was then appointed college lecturer in Political Science, also with a fellowship. This he held till 1920, when he was given a pension fellowship, tenable for life.

This chapter covers events between the renewal of his fellowship and the outbreak of the war, with the exception of his visits to America and the East and their implications, which will be considered separately. The outstanding event is his emergence as a teacher. He becomes more and more anxious to stimulate, and less interested in learning and artistic expression for their own sakes. His studies, his political opinions, his lecturing, his published works, his capacity for friendship, his interest in the young—all flow into a single channel, which might be called educational if the word were not so misused, and "maieutic" if the word were not a little pedantic. Though he does not remind one of Socrates personally, though he had neither the nagging qualities which wore down the sophists, nor the physical high spirits, nor the toughness to fight at Potidaea, nor the desire to fight there, yet Socrates is his master. It is as a teacher who was constantly being taught that he must be regarded during these twenty-one years.

A letter to May, dating from the threshold of this period, will serve as an informal preface to it, as did the letter to Grant in the case of the period preceding. While quoting in full I have missed out most of the underlinings, because like the stresses in his talk they are faint, the pen travelling lightly beneath the word, and only emphasizing half of it.

King's College, Cambridge
10 March 1889

Writing the date reminds me of your birthday, for which I send all possible good wishes and greetings—and would send a present if I had one! Isn't this spring weather delicious? At least it is here—snowdrops and crocuses and aconite everywhere, and that delicious sense of beginning, which is so much better than fruition.

"And then and then came Spring and Rose-in-hand
My thread-bare Penitence apieces tore",

which is a sentiment of Omar Khayyam I quite understand. Fred was here last Sunday, that perhaps was partly why I didn't write, and also I was busy with papers. I'm not pleased with my lectures, but I don't quite know how they ought to be; they're certainly not interesting enough, and I should be very angry with myself if I were in the audience.

I'm growing magnificent ideas of what a university *ought* to be; it ought to lead thought, as it did in the Reformation, and not skulk behind and talk of vested rights. And there never were places with such chances as Oxford and Cambridge. I don't want them popularized, I want them to educate leaders, and let there be other universities to educate the rest. So we ought to teach politics somehow through history, which has always been O.B.'s idea, and like all his ideas is good. We do teach people how to live, how to make friendships, etc., but I don't think we teach them, as a rule, how to think, i.e. how to apply their knowledge to here and now. All this is "ideal", and one gets ashamed of what's ideal, but it may become practical. I shall probably come to London next Thursday week, or thereabouts. The Choral Symphony must have been fine. We had Mozart's Requiem on Thursday in chapel; music different to anything else of his. Great as Beethoven, I think. Best love. I heard of you from Miss Johnson. Isn't she nice? A. Berry was up yesterday, and Lennie ——(?) gets nicer and nicer.

78

Lennie's surname is indecipherable, but that he got nicer and nicer there is little doubt: most of the people who constantly saw Goldie did that, though he did not realize why.

2

He ceased to be a bad lecturer and became a good one as soon as he ceased to "lecture" and began to speculate aloud. In his University Extension days he had tried to convey facts, to impose opinions and to arouse emotions, but he modified considerably on all these three points. As for facts, he soon realized that they are best learned from textbooks and that the lecturer who ladles them out to an audience who gobbles them down is only carrying on the educational traditions of the Misses Woodman's morning classes for the sons of gentlemen. As for opinions: the formation of these was indeed his chief aim, but his method became more tentative as his grasp on reality tightened. He believed that his own opinions were right or he would not have held them, but he never dictated them or desired that they should be accepted; instead, he encouraged clear thinking and decent feeling and hoped that on such a soil right opinions would flourish. And as for arousing emotion: he neither aimed at this nor did he achieve it in any crude sense. The seriousness of the theme provided its own emotion. Knowledge of the past will help us to control the future, and unless we can control the future our happiness, private and public, is at the mercy of chance. Thus a subject like the History of Political Theory, which is on the face of it academic, became arresting and disquieting under his treatment, because he made his audience feel they might influence Fate. For instance, the dilemma of Jeremy Bentham—how can a selfish statesman provide an unselfish policy?—appeared as real to his audience as it had been when Bentham formulated it.

Dickinson had the external framework necessary for a lecturer: he was accurate, well-informed, polite, dignified, clear, punctual. But it was the light within which impressed his audiences—no will-of-the-wisp of the Coleridge variety, but a light which for all its spontaneity shone steadily and guided to a goal. His voice and his expression are not easily conveyed, because they were not dramatic; it was no mission of his to vibrate with emotion, or to point out the choice before us with his forefinger, or to stamp upon international anarchy with his foot. He left such achievements to orators. What did come across was a modulation in the tones and a light upon the face, which showed that the whole man was alive and was working at a distance to bring help. This helpfulness was present at all times, but it was unusually moving when it shone through the formality of a lecture framework.

His official subject at King's was Political Science, then locally known by the title of Analytical and Deductive Politics, and he continued in it two terms a year from his appointment in 1896 to 1920, when he resigned the lectureship. He was, during precisely the same period, lecturing at the London School of Economics, and some reference must now be made to his activity there. It has not the glamour of the Cambridge connection, and it is not so generally known, but it was important to his audiences and to himself.

The London School of Economics and Political Science was founded in 1895, chiefly owing to the efforts of the Sidney Webbs. Dickinson's early socialism had brought him into contact with Fabianism, and he had already arranged for visits to Cambridge from Webb, Hubert Bland, Olivier, Bernard Shaw and others then belonging to the group. The visits had caused some excitement. Webb had argued with McTaggart, neither side scoring a victory. Bland had talked football to the young men. Shaw had lectured brilliantly, also telling a story about an Irish uncle who thought he was in heaven and hung from the ceiling in a basket dressed in gauze. Asked on behalf of Dr Westcott what his moral basis was, Shaw had replied to Dickinson on a post-card: "Ask the old boy what his is, and tell him mine's the same." So, though Dickinson's temperament was far from Fabian and his methods anything but statistical, it was natural that he should be invited to teach at the newly established School. His connection began in 1896. In 1911 he was put on the permanent staff as lecturer in Political Science; in 1920 he resigned. His lectures at the School were, so far as their subjects and general outlook went, a repetition of the courses delivered at Cambridge. Here is a complete list. He began with "The English Civil Service". He followed this by courses on "The Machinery of Administration in England", "The Use of Political Terms", "The Structure of the Modern State", "Popular Government", "The British Empire and Other Composite States", "Some Theories of the Basis of Political Obligation", "The Government of the British Empire", "The Structure of the Modern State", "The Functions of the Modern State", "The Central Government of England comparatively treated". This brings us to the year 1902, when he began to deliver the most noteworthy of his courses, on "The History of Political Ideas", and repeated it with constant changes until 1920. In 1924 he returned to the School to give one short course on "The Causes of the War of 1914"—one of the pieces of work preliminary to *The International Anarchy*.

Since the London School of Economics is non-residential, there was little opportunity for social intercourse. He travelled up, gave his lecture in the afternoon or evening, held an informal class in connection with it, and then went back. But even such an arrangement as this leaves a mark when it continues for twenty-four years. Besides doing good there, he enlarged his experience, for he met students who were not as well off as their Cambridge contemporaries, and were less exclusively the products of public schools, and he also became acquainted with Indians and Chinese.

The titles of some of his Cambridge courses were: "Modern France" (1892), "The Transition to Democracy in Modern England" (1894–6), "The Machinery of Administration under Democracy" (1897), "The Theory of Law and Government" (1897–9), "Analytical and Deductive Politics" (1900 onwards). When he looks back at his lecturing both there and at London his summary is as follows:

My business was to enlarge and concretize my subject, which became, in fact, a general discussion of modern political problems. I came in time, I believe, to lecture well, in the academic way. I spoke always from notes, added continually from year to year, to my matter, as was natural in a subject so continually developing, not to say bulging and protruding outside all skins of general theory. I was interested myself, and I think I interested my pupils, most of them. At any rate my audience always continued to the end without any defalcations to speak of, and varied round about a hundred in the later years. I had a quite definite idea of what I wanted to do in lectures—to stimulate the students' interest so that they should feel they were dealing with a live subject, which was going to be of interest and practical importance to them all their life. I used not to conceal my own opinions, but also not to preach them unfairly, having, in fact, in many important questions, a very open mind. I lectured in this way for some twenty-five years, never losing my own freshness and interest. Whether I produced any result, or what, who can say? The parable of the sower applies to all such work; and a single teacher is rather a light makeweight against family and social interests and preoccupations. Still, I expect I helped to wake up some minds. What more can a teacher do, or what better?

Most people would say that he was a really great lecturer of his type. That type, as he is careful to point out, was the academic. Neither his matter nor his manner could move masses of people, and he believed indeed that it is impossible to touch men to any fineness when they are gathered into anything so clumsy as a mass. Towards the end he was a triumphantly successful broadcaster; he had the opportunity of addressing numbers of individuals who remained individuals, an opportunity which no speaker has yet had since the beginning of the world; and he was extending his audience in this sense when he died. But except at an election (for instance, at Scarborough in 1909), he never addressed a crowd. His hatred of crowd psychology was so great that he could scarcely bear to discuss it, much less to utilize it; in fact it was too great, and limited his utility; when two or three hundred were gathered together, he felt too sure it was in the name of the Devil. And it must be remembered that he believed in the Devil—that is to say in the existence of evil; it was one of the points on which he differed from his more youthful audiences.

After his death one of his former London students contributed this impression of him to the *Journal of Education*:

> We were an odd-job lot at those evening classes! Clerks and students and teachers, young and old, men and women of all sorts and conditions; but he interested us all and aroused us in a truly wonderful way. . . . He had no physical advantages except a charming smile and a very sensitive mouth. His voice was always husky though very pleasant to listen to, and he had none of the arts of the orator. But there was a distinction about his whole individuality that arrested attention and in some curious way kept his large class of not highly intellectual students, such as he lectured to in Cambridge, spellbound. I think, perhaps, we never knew what to expect and we never quite grasped his point of view. . . . He seemed now to be an aristocrat, now a thorough-going democrat, so that often his class was left gasping. You went away to *think*—and that was, I suppose, what he wanted.

A sympathetic impression of his lecturing at Cambridge is to be found in Osbert Burdett's *The Art of Living*.

Lecturing, as he conceived it, was a thoughtful conversation. No reply was anticipated, but the speaker had to keep the naturalness and good manners of talk. So that the transition from the lecture-hall to the class, in which his pupils did talk, was easy and welcome, and the transition from the class to luncheon or to a ride, where his pupils could both talk to him and lecture him, was easier still. He broke up the illiberal distinction between lessons and leisure which has done so much to cramp human development; hard work lay at one end of the scale, amusement at the other, but both required intelligence and sensitiveness, and were aspects of education. So continuously did he believe in education that he seldom used the word; it was the air breathed by the spirit of man, and if the air a man is breathing is resolved into its components the result may be stimulating to experts, but the man himself dies.

Besides the classes held in connection with the lectures, he took the third and fourth year History men at King's in essays. The sort of subjects he set were: Church and State, Machiavelli, Toleration, Malthus, Wells's *Utopia*. When the essays came to be corrected it became apparent that, like all genuine educationists, he did not teach for teaching's sake. He roped people in to get ideas on some problem which puzzled him and so would talk more about the problem itself than about their treatment of it. This disconcerted his weaker pupils, who wanted to be shown where they went wrong, but his indifference to their heresies was counterbalanced by his severity over their style. "It hasn't come yet," he would say. He knew very well when sentences went wrong, had no patience with the "mot injuste", which often seems so marvellous to the young, and came down, perhaps rather too heavily, on the side of limpidity and logic. How good is his own prose style? He was at that time disciplining it and paring away "beauties", so that it might respond better to the movements of his thought.

From his classes and essay-talks we slide onwards into social intercourse and hospitality, and this is the moment when I want to introduce myself.

I first met him in 1898. A friend of his father's and of my aunt's had asked him to be kind, so he invited me to lunch. We had Winchester cutlets, a sort of elongated rissole to which he was then addicted, but I can remember nothing about the conversation, and probably there was none. Impressions get so mixed; but I recall him as sadder and older than he appeared to be fifteen years later. He knew nothing about me—there was nothing to know—and I had never heard of him. His rooms were on staircase H of Gibbs, ground floor—the staircase nearest the chapel (see illustration facing page 136)—and we sat alone in the large front room silently eating the cutlets and drinking the reddish-brown sauce in which they lay. The food was less good than it became in later years, the host shyer, the guest shyer still, and I departed unprepossessing and unprepossessed. A few weeks later I asked him to lend me a play which had a great vogue among my fellow freshmen. I forget its name. He handed it to me gloomily, and asked when I brought it back what I thought of it. I replied nervously that I was afraid I didn't think it so very good. His face lit up. "No, of course it's no good," he said. This lighting up of the face was a thing to watch for. It meant that he had seen something which must vaguely be called "life", and it brought life to anyone who saw it. It was part of what—vaguely again—must be called his charm. Charm, in most men and nearly all women, is a decoration. It genuinely belongs to them, as a good complexion may, but it lies on the surface and can vanish. Charm in Dickinson was structural. It penetrated and upheld everything he did, it remained into old age, and I saw it first that afternoon at the end of last century, when he was only thirty-five, and when I kindled him by managing to be honest over a trifle. The "lighting up" really belonged to a greater occasion than this—to the entrance into the room of a friend. Then he would emerge from his inner life with a smile, which made him for the moment indescribably beautiful.

He photographed well, so that I need not try to describe his features. The complexion was not good, the head bowed a little forward from the shoulders when he walked, though the shoulders themselves, like the body generally, were shapely and strong. The hands were large. The clothes, except during the American visits, erred on the dowdy side—dark blue serges, shirts of indistinction, podgy ties. I dress like that myself, except for illogical flashinesses, and once when I invited him to accompany me into one of these he replied that it is hopeless to dress well unless one's personal appearance corresponds. This made me realize that he was at all events not contented with his own appearance. I did not understand why. There was a beauty about him which cannot be given that patronizing label "spiritual", a beauty which, though it had nothing to do with handsomeness, did belong to the physical, so that his presence was appropriate amid gorgeous scenery or exquisite flowers. The portrait of him on the frontispiece by Roger Fry features a sumptuous costume, which is not typical, but it is satisfactory that he should have been obliged to wear it once.

I did not see much of him while I was an undergraduate, and when in my fourth year I turned from classics to history and planned to go to him for essays I was dished by Oscar Browning, who said: "You're not coming to me at all, you must come to me." So once a fortnight I read aloud about Wallenstein or Louis XIV to the handkerchief which covered O.B.'s face, and Dickinson's power to teach remained unknown to me, except as far as I have heard of it from others. I belonged to his "Discussion Society", however. He had founded it in 1900 as the result of some popular lectures on philosophy which had been delivered by McTaggart. It was a blend between the type of society described on page 55 and the tuitional type presided over by a don. Dickinson presided, but there was freedom for the rank and file. The papers I forget, with the exception of one on Sex, read by George Barger (now Professor of Chemistry at Edinburgh). Sex was not mentioned at Cambridge in those days—that is to say, not in the small circle I knew—and there were some high anticipations about Barger's paper, and some care on Dickinson's part to ensure that only serious-minded youths should attend. The paper was statistical, the discussion stilted, the evening interminable, yet I recall it as an example of his sensitiveness and tact; he knew just how large a stone it is wise to drop into the pond.

The above trifles may show how consistent his influence was, and how it could penetrate unpromising material. "I think of him," writes Dominick Spring-Rice, "at the queer society he ran in which you drew lots as to your turn for speaking and had to tell what you believed was the truth; standing, at the end, in front of the fireplace, rubbing himself and saying clearly for each of us what in our muddled way we could not say clearly for ourselves." Teaching, to him, was a process which transcended any formula and went on at all times, and it could not be distinguished, in the final analysis, from being taught. By the end of his life he had become so wise that he was able to learn from the young. His affection for them and his desire to help them were joined with a much rarer quality: respect. "Maxima debetur pueris reverentia"? No, certainly not. It was not that type of respect. It was a recogntion that the young may instruct the old.

Financially his lectureships enabled him to live and to write books, and since the college considerately let him confine his teaching to the two winter terms he was left with the Summer

Term and the Long Vacation for creative work, an arrangement "which no commission would ever approve. It slipped through under the freedom of the old Cambridge." Before coming to the books themselves we must glance at his general attitude towards the university, the university for which he entertained such high and unusual hopes, as the letter quoted at the beginning of this chapter testifies.

3

His love of Cambridge was touched with fear. He only trusted her in so far as she is the city of youth. For him the undergraduate is the true owner of the university, and the dons exist for the purpose of inducting him into his kingdom. Having taken his degree there, he passes out into life, bringing with him standards of conduct and memories of affection and beauty which cannot be elsewhere obtained. Cambridge did this much for Dickinson, and she did it through him for dozens, perhaps hundreds, of young men who now mourn his memory. "An unspoilt youth of twenty with his mind just waking up and his feelings all fresh and open to good is the most beautiful thing this world produces," he writes to Mrs Webb, and Cambridge shared with ancient Athens the maieutic power which brings such minds into the light. The Cephissus flows with the Cam through this city, by the great lawn of King's under the bridge of Clare, towards plane trees which have turned into the chestnuts of Jesus. Ancient and modern unite through the magic of youth.

But there was another Cambridge which filled him with dismay and which he connected less with the scenery than with the weather: the Cambridge of the organizing and the researching don. Stuffy yet raw, parochial yet colourless—what a city was this! What a hole! Schoolmasters paraded its streets, specialists riddled its walls, governesses, married to either, held their lugubrious courts in its suburbs. Here the east wind blows for ever and the mist never lifts off the mud. Yes, he dreaded the increasing fuss and rush of university business, not for selfish reasons but because it tended to neglect the needs of the individual undergraduate and to keep him in the position of a child, children being more easily managed. And he mistrusted research even more, although it is in itself so admirable and so necessary, because research atrophies the mind and renders it incapable of human intercourse: "the spectacle of learning gets more depressing to me every year," he tells Mrs Webb. "I care only for fruitful and vital handling of the eternal commonplaces or else for a new insight that will really help someone to internal freedom." If the schoolmaster teaches wrongly, the specialist cannot teach at all, and between the two of them what room is left for Socrates?

There is something to be said against his views, as he realized, and there is a third Cambridge whose existence he forgot— the agglomeration conveniently known as "the varsity" which takes pass-degrees, roars round football fields, sits down in the middle of Hammersmith Broadway after the boat race, and covers actresses with soot. Silly and idle young men did not come his way, no more did hearties and toughs unless they had intellectual leanings. This was due partly to his own constitution and partly to that of King's, which only admits men who are reading for honours and does not duck an intellectual in the fountain oftener than once in twenty years, apologizing elaborately to him afterwards. In its exquisite enclosure a false idea can be gained of enclosures outside, though not of the infinite verities. Dickinson, pacing up and down with his arms behind him, kept in touch in his own fashion with the world, but he could never slap it on the back or stand it a drink. And he loathed its brutality and bullying—with them there could be no compromise; his objection to rowdiness was not its noise but its inability to flourish without a victim.

Essentially a college man, he did not take much part in university affairs. The chief occasion was in 1903, when at the invitation of Professor Marshall he helped to form the new Economics Tripos. Economics had hitherto been inadequately included in the History course. Realizing its importance in modern life, he sought separate recognition. What interested him, though, was not economics proper, not the laws of supply and demand, not the mathematics of wealth, but the reaction of men to material surroundings and their attempts to improve them. He held that the study of recent history and of political institutions could help them here, and it was as an advocate of his special subject, Political Science, that he joined forces with Professor Marshall. He became a member of the "Economics and Political Science Syndicate" which was appointed to report to the Senate. In the ensuing debate he made a short and effective speech, in reply to the pure historians. He regretted that everyone could not know everything, and especially that historians could not know the whole of history, but pointed out that there is a profitable alternative in the analytical method, which studies causes and effects among coexistent phenomena. When the new tripos was established, he became the first Secretary of the Economics Board.

His other university activities are not important. When it came to a vote at the Senate House he was on the side of freedom, but freedom is a word variously applied. We find him, for instance, in 1898 voting against recognizing a Roman Catholic lodging-house as a hostel, on the ground that any institution recognized by the University ought to be free to all creeds. Henry Sidgwick and others of his friends voted for recognition, on the ground that Roman Catholics ought to be free to have a hostel. In 1902 he voted for the abolition of compulsory Greek ("disliking the word 'compulsory'," comments one of his classical friends, "and not seeing 'Greek' came after it"). And he assisted in the unchaining of women, but without enthusiasm. His suicidal sense of fairness left him no alternative here. If women wanted a degree or a vote or anything else which men monopolized, it was his duty to help them to get it, even if they overwhelmed him afterwards. There were a few women to whom he was devoted and a few to whom he would have confidently entrusted the destiny of mankind, but he was not a really creditable feminist. He did think that men on the whole are superior. "Oh dear, what is to happen to them?" he once murmured sadly as a stream of aspiring and uninspiring spinsters flowed round the front court of King's; "I don't know and they don't know." And then in still lower tones as if his bookshelves might overhear him: "Oh dear! What they want is a husband!" These were his unregenerate thoughts. At other times he remembered the cruelty and parsimony of the Victorian girl's upbringing, and felt that no restitution could be too generous, and there exist among his manuscripts a few pages of a fantasy about Héloïse and a Chorus of Cats which is conceived in this spirit of atonement.

One other academic activity must be recorded, and it is a surprising one: on 14 March 1900 he rejoined the Cambridge University Officers' Training Corps. He did this not because he wanted to crush Kruger, but because he hoped to avert conscription. He is said to have been no more efficient as a soldier than he had been twenty years before, and on 22

January 1902 he resigned. The episode is significant: at no time was he a thoroughgoing pacifist.

4

The first of his maieutic books is *The Greek View of Life* (1896). He had been brought up on Latin and Greek, in a stupid and wasteful way, and it was not until he had got away from the classics that he saw what they meant. Now that he had studied modern conditions and begun to teach politics intelligently, he realized that the ancients are modern, and that Athens in particular had expressed our problems with a lucidity beyond our power. Nor was this all. Greek literature combined beauty and depth, wisdom and wit, gaiety and insight; it was the greatest literature the world had yet produced, its drawback being that it could only be read by people who had sweated at it for years, and by most of them imperfectly. Translations are the only hope, and while he admitted that most readable translations—e.g. Butcher and Lang's *Odyssey* and Gilbert Murray's Euripides—get the colouring all wrong, he preferred them to nothing at all. *The Greek View of Life* might be called an introduction to translations. It is an attempt to show the non-expert the character and environment of hidden treasures and to leave him among them. The idea came to Dickinson "in our dining-room at All Souls Place, in the old armchair, now long vanished from my life—who bought it, I wonder? Does it still exist?" and he began to carry it out at Kandersteg, "and it consoled me there through some bad times". He looked back on the book as the most useful he had written, and its large circulation in England (it is now in its seventeenth edition) and in the States was a satisfaction to him; "I still feel that I have got hold of . . . the central thing, the thing that makes Greek of permanent value to civilization." Some of us feel that he got hold of it more satisfactorily in the book of his old age, *After Two Thousand Years*; he had by then wider experience and greater mastery of style. But *The Greek View of Life* is the more ordered survey and has found favour with educationists.

Three years after publishing it he went to Greece itself. It was a happy visit with perfect companions: Wedd; Robin Mayor (afterwards a high official in the Education Office); A. M. Daniel (afterwards Director of the National Gallery); and C. P. Sanger.

I had been depressed and worried. But from the moment of landing at the Piraeus life renewed itself in perpetual interest and delight. The Acropolis at Athens revealed to me the meaning of the architectural mouldings I had seen parodied all over Europe. It was like hearing music at last played in tune, after a long perversion by slight discords.

Then he remembers "far too faintly" the line of the sea against Marathon, the Sunium column rising from a sea of red poppies over the sea of blue waves, the plain of Eleusis, the Delphi charioteer. And then comes a passage which carries us on from Greece to another stage in his Socratic activity.

But above all I recall an evening spent at Mistra, above Sparta. We rode through the little village, for such it now is, hidden among orange groves, and then up the slope of Taygetus to that deserted medieval town of whose very existence I was unaware. There we stayed the night in a monastery inhabited by a single monk, strolled under the full moon round the deserted streets and churches, and heard from below the chant of the frogs, the "brekekekex koax koax" of Aristophanes. It was here on this night that there occurred to me the idea of writing a dialogue on Good, which I carried out in the following year or so.

Mistra might symbolize the synthesis at which Dickinson, like Goethe, aimed, and it is appropriate that it should have inspired him to write the first of his dialogues. He often spoke of that moonlit scene where, as in the pine woods above Heidelberg, Classic and Medieval seemed to unite and herald the Modern, where Faust reigned with Helen and Euphorion was born. He visited Mistra again, thirty years later; the hour was the afternoon, the hills seemed lower, the wild romance had gone, yet how beautiful the place still was, and how solitary! And how exquisite did Greece as a whole remain! How the Mediterranean stimulated his feelings and perceptions as it stimulated Goethe's when he first saw Italy and tore himself away under a sense of duty to return to work in the unfriendly North!

The dialogue form, to which he turned after this visit to Greece, exactly suited his genius. It allowed him to assemble opinions and, so to speak, to tint them. The personages through whom he converses are never coloured vividly; whether they are taken from public figures, like Cantilupe and Remenham, or from his friends, like Audubon and Coryat, or made up entirely, as Wilson appears to be, they are quieter and paler than their equivalents in the world of fiction. He had not the novelist's eccentricity, which permits a sudden swerve from the main course. Whether such eccentricity makes a book more "like life" is arguable; he, with his generous admiration for methods differing from his own, often praised it. His own method, working from within, allowed no vagaries, not even the development of a character under the stress of talk. His business was the argument, human and humanly held, but not allowing irresponsive interludes. Plato and Berkeley were his models, and, like them, he would sacrifice dramatic excitement for consistency and dignity. It is significant that none of his disputants is a female, unless we may include the Queen of the Night, and she is the despair rather than the life of the argument. The instincts and passions could be discussed, and they were discussed with insight and frankness; but they could not be illustrated, any more than the interlocutors could walk away from their chairs. Thus, from the opening of *The Meaning of Good* down to the sombre conversation in the Hermitage of Jesus in *The Magic Flute*, and the Elysian encounter of *After Two Thousand Years*, his people are always sedentary, and the appeal to reason, however much they may ignore it, hangs like a sword over their heads. An essay on "Dialogue as a Literary Form", which he wrote at the end of his life for the Royal Society of Literature, may be consulted in this connection.

The Meaning of Good was written partly at Thursley, where he was stopping with Roger Fry, and partly in lodgings at Westcott. By now he had established his lifelong friendship with Miss Melian Stawell, formerly a student of Newnham, and he corresponds frequently with her about his work. They discuss alternative titles, such as "A Dialogue concerning Good", or "Many that Say", and she persuades him to print a sonnet from the 1896 *Poems* as a preface. The dialogue did not displease him in retrospect, though he felt that there were too many characters, and that much of it was frigid. From the philosophical point of view:

> What I believe to be true, in my own book, is the tension of experience, the quest of Good, the perpetual dissatisfaction, and the knowledge therefrom derived. When I say this is "true", I mean that it is true of those who count in such matters, of Goethe, let us say. What is more questionable is the mysticism which still haunted me, as it haunted Plato, and which appears in the concluding myth. . . . One thing further is perhaps worth noticing in this book, that, while I was still influenced by McTaggart's idea of an eternal perfection of spirits related to one another by love, I also suspected that this might be an illusion, or (perhaps I should say) an imperfect parable. For my

myth, though it does not go beyond that conception, yet suggests that there *is* a beyond.

Just at this time another philosopher had risen to power in Cambridge, in the person of his friend G. E. Moore. It would be too much to say that Moore dethroned McTaggart, who was essentially undethronable, but he did carry the younger men by storm, and cause Lytton Strachey to exclaim, "The age of reason has come!" Dickinson, while not going so far as that, felt uneasy. Moore's steady questioning as to What *is* good? What *is* true? had already torn some large holes in the McTaggartian heaven. More care—I speak as a complete outsider here—more care had evidently to be taken as to what one said and how one said it, and intuition seemed less than ever enough. Two years before, in a letter to R. C. Trevelyan (8 August 1898), Dickinson is already complaining of the strain:

> I'm fagged to death—result of a metaphysical talk with Moore. What a brain that fellow has! It desiccates mine! Dries up my lakes and seas and leaves me an arid tract of sand. Not that *he* is arid—anything but: he's merely the sun. One ought to put up a parasol—I do try to, one of humour, but it has so many rents in it. Oh dear! Surely I once had some rivers? I wish you were here to water me. All poets water. They are the rain. Metaphysics are the sun: between them they fertilize the soil.
>
> Yours so far as there is anything of me,
> G. L. D.

Moore's *Principia Ethica* came out while *The Meaning of Good* was in proof, and Dickinson, on reading it, discovered that he had been guilty in his dialogue of a new philosophic error which Moore had discovered and had named "the naturalistic fallacy", "a phrase which always amuses me, for it suggests some kind of unnatural vice. I tried to dodge this error in my book at the last moment, but I expect it is there, and also that it doesn't much matter. Moore has probably long ago altered his position, on this as on other points." On which note of gay defiance the Naturalistic Fallacy may be left. The dialogue came out in 1901. I remember the enthusiasm, the attractive blue cloth of the binding, the lightness of the volume, the solidity of the contents, and my great friend and fellow undergraduate, H. O. Meredith (now Professor of Economics at Belfast), reading as he stalked along King's Parade and chanting, "You shall never take away from me my Meaning of Good . . .". This must be the moment when Dickinson won a name in his own university.

Four years later he published a second dialogue, which won him a name in the outside world. This was *A Modern Symposium.* It is dedicated to a Cambridge discussion society, and it represents in a glorified form the sort of evening he loved— an evening of contrasted opinions, stated fairly, sincerely and good-temperedly. The personages are supposed to be members of "The Seekers", a club which he had actually tried to found, and they build together, before the morning breaks, a dome of many-coloured glass through which eternity shines. It is again the harmony of Plato and Shelley—Goethe perhaps harmonizing. Plato contributes most. Dickinson always needs a form which will allow him to express the views of others without judging them by his own, and having experienced in *The Meaning of Good* the difficulty of the dialogue proper he turns here to the particular form of it used by Plato in the *Symposium.* Set speeches take the place of conversation and argument. The thirteen speakers of his choice can state their positions without fear of interruption all through the calm of an English summer night, and their rhetoric can pass into poetry when they wish. When the dawn comes and they vanish into mist or sunlight they leave a strong impression of actuality behind, and it is no wonder that the book has been admired not only by utopians but by men of affairs.

> But still it does not solve the problem, which is perhaps insoluble, of making the bridge between speculation and art, and all that side of life, and what is called practical politics. For practical politics involves fighting, and the object of such a book as mine (as it was Plato's object long ago) is to raise the mind above the fighting attitude.
>
> There lies here obscurely the great problem of the relation of ideals to passion and interests, which I do not seem able clearly to formulate. ... It seems to be impossible to go into active life of any kind without also being ready to kill, to lie and to cheat.

And following this line of thought he considers the case of the man who will think his *Modern Symposium* and all his books either pernicious or futile.

> I am conscious, in all I have written and thought, of complete dis-interestedness in the pursuit of truth. But it does not seem to follow that the other kind of man need therefore regard me with particular respect. "What have you done?" he will say, with Kipling. And if I reply "No particular harm", he will say "No, and no particular

good". "Neither have you," I might reply, "I see nothing but harm."
And somewhere about there the imaginary debate would end. We
have not, in fact, either the knowledge or the standards to deal with
the subject.

He had to write *A Modern Symposium* twice before it satisfied
him. It was finished at Baslow in Derbyshire. His father, now
very old, was deeply moved by it, and, in a conversation reported
by Miss Stawell, told her that it was like "a re-statement of the
incarnation, a vision of the divine that is growing in men and
more than we can comprehend". Goldie was impressed by this
unexpected sympathy, and said to Miss Stawell a few days afterwards: "Isn't it curious that of all my friends it is my old father
who has understood best what I wanted most to say?" He added:
"Of course in old age the body fails and the mind is hampered,
but it seems to me the soul goes on and goes further." His father
was perhaps thinking of the final speech, where Geoffrey Vivian
(who is George Meredith) pours new wine into the nineteenth-
century bottles of evolution, yet not more than they can hold. The
episode is interesting as suggesting that Dickinson never broke
from his family tradition, only remodelled it and re-expressed it.

Following as it did on the *Letters from John Chinaman* and his first
American tour, *A Modern Symposium* brought him some notoriety,
and there is no doubt that he could have become a prominent
figure if he had cared to improve his position. But he was bad at
improving positions. Each time he wrote or spoke he went straight
back into the inner world, and had no sense of those subtle
movements of the surface which indicate the drift of popularity.
Some writers, and they are not necessarily worldly or corrupt,
have a natural instinct for self-advertisement. Dickinson lacked
this. He had not the little touch of swagger which draws a crowd,
nor the counter-attraction of faroucheness. When he was taken
up for a little by "society" he found the people he met agreeable,
easy, amusing, sympathetic, quick. But he had nothing in
common with them. He sat in their flickering aviary like a
little dusky bird on a perch, and, being wise, like a bird of
passage. So with the greater public. Although he never did anything to affront it, he never kept his hand on its pulse, and by the
time the war came it had already begun to move away. He began
to recover it at the very end, through broadcasting, and many
then heard of him for the first time whom one would have
expected to know him well. To a biographer, the movements of
fashion's barometer are interesting, so let me emphasize the very

high level touched by the mercury about 1905. It looked then as if Mr G. L. Dickinson would easily beat Pater and Gobineau, and even creep up towards Voltaire and Mr Bernard Shaw. Such competition was not to be.

In 1908 appeared *Justice and Liberty*, the last of the trilogy of dialogues. It is more closely connected with his teaching work than the others, and tries to set out the fundamental political truths in which he believed, and upon which he was lecturing in Cambridge and London. He wrote it with difficulty, and felt that it must be difficult to read and repellent, in spite of his effort to introduce Platonic charm. Perhaps he was disappointed with it. It was his last experiment in the Socratic method for twenty-two years.

The Greek View of Life and the three dialogues are all closely connected with his main activity during this period: an educational activity. He was always giving out, and chiefly nourishing himself in order that he might give out. He had become aware of other people, and realized that whether we like it or not we are members one with another, and this had led him to concentrate upon politics. He was at one time a sort of Tory-Socialist, during the period covered by this chapter he was a Liberal, and in consequence of the war he became Labour, and remained so till the end of his life. But politics, as he understood them, are not based upon party. They represent the attempt of Man to adapt himself to his environment and to control his future. Knowledge of the past may help him here, and both as a writer and a lecturer Dickinson had this in view. Art and philosophy were subordinated, and the problems of personal salvation and survival after death, which obsess so many introspective people, now occupied less of his time. We must first get the house straight, then fill it with beautiful things—such was on the whole his attitude in these years, though he was sensible enough to know that unless we have a certain amount of beautiful things lying about we shall not think it worth while to get the house straight. Which is what distinguished him from the Fabians.

At the beginning of the century he was concerned in founding a monthly magazine, the *Independent Review*. The first number appeared in October 1903. Edward Jenks was the editor; Dickinson, F. W. Hirst, C. F. G. Masterman, G. M. Trevelyan and Wedd were the members of the editorial council; Roger Fry designed the cover. The main aim of the review was political. It was founded to combat the aggressive imperialism and the

Protection campaign of Joe Chamberlain; and to advocate sanity in foreign affairs and a constructive policy at home. It was not so much a Liberal review as an appeal to Liberalism from the Left to be its better self—one of those appeals which have continued until the extinction of the Liberal Party. Dickinson thus defends the opening number of his review against the freelancing of Ashbee (letter of 9 November 1903):

> If Liberals, as you say, are not "constructive", that perhaps is due to the fact that they believe in liberty; which means that they think all legislation can do is to give the utmost scope to individuals to develop the best in them. That I confess is my own point of view. But I believe to do that will mean gradual revolution in all the fundamentals of society, law of property, law of contract, law of marriage. Yet all that revolution would be abortive unless people have ideals for which they individually care, and which are of the spirit, and not mere megalomania. I find in Joe and his followers no trace of such ideals. And I should be very much astonished, I confess, to find them in colonials.

He did not contribute much to the *Independent* on politics. His article in the first number was on "Ecclesiasticism", and directed against the argument that, though religion may not be true, it is necessary to society. Other articles are: "Religion and Revelation", "Euthanasia", "Faith and Knowledge", "How Long Halt Ye?" Another article, entitled "Motoring", is a desperate outcry against speed and materialism, and has a magnificent descriptive passage about Hampton Court—one of the finest bits of "writing" he ever did. The religious and philosophic articles were afterwards included in two little volumes—*Religion: A Criticism and a Forecast* (1905) and *Religion and Immortality* (1911).

The *Independent Review* did not make much difference to the councils of the nation, but it struck a note which was new at that time, and had a great influence on a number of individuals—young people for the most part. We were being offered something which we wanted. Those who were Liberals felt that the heavy, stocky body of their party was about to grow wings and leave the ground. Those who were not Liberals were equally filled with hope: they saw avenues opening into literature, philosophy, human relationships, and the road of the future passing through not insurmountable dangers to a possible utopia. Can you imagine decency touched with poetry? It was thus that the *Independent* appeared to us—a light rather than a fire, but a light that penetrated the emotions. Credit must be given to Jenks, an able and a pernickety editor, and to his colleagues, but the inspiration was Dickinson's. The first number lies on the table as I write: as fresh and attractive to hold as when I bought it on a bookstall at St Pancras thirty years back, and thought the new age had begun.

5

There is another side of him which finds expression during this period. It is what he calls the religious side, though I am inclined to use the words more cautiously than he himself uses them. When a man is modest, gentle, unselfish and generally decent, and confesses, as he did, to possessing and valuing certain instincts, there is a disposition among people who have formalized such instincts to annex him as one of themselves. They want him —and no wonder. Christians often said he was a Christian, and when he went to India he was hailed as a devotee of Krishna. If these tributes are regarded as foreign decorations, conferred on a distinguished alien, they will pass, but they are not issued by his spiritual country. All the creeds, he writes, are guesses and bad ones. And he not only rejected authority and mistrusted ritual. He condemned the specifically religious virtue of humility. He effaced himself—never abased himself. He was also suspicious of martyrdom, believing it to be a method of casting out the devil by Beelzebub. Only Socrates (he writes in *After Two Thousand Years*) has managed to remain human and humorous through martyrdom, and has escaped "not only from hypocrisy and hatred, but also from the righteous indignation that clouds even the noblest souls". His opinions on sex ran contrary to Christian ethics. He also believed that we have the right to take our own lives, and the duty of taking the lives of those whom we love if they desire us to do so, and if by doing so we can save them unbearable pain. He was a great heretic though a quiet one. And, if his religious feelings are to be incarnated in one figure, Socrates and no one else is that figure.

"For my own part I've always had a curious feeling that I should be at my best in old age. I believe it depends on whether one gets religion," he writes to May. The letter is dated 1903 (when his actual age was forty), and six years later he is writing to her again and defining more clearly what "getting religion" is. The occasion is their father's death, and the breaking up of the home which the three sisters had made for the family at All Souls Place.

97

There is no remedy that I know for any trouble centering about oneself except a complete and disinterested absorption in interests outside oneself. And that sometimes seems beyond one's power. My notion of religion is the attitude which can say "Well, what does it matter what I am or what happens to me in this extraordinary interesting world." But it is not an easy attitude to get or keep hold of.

This was not his whole notion of religion; and what definition of religion does cover all that we attach to the word in our varying moods? He was not only concerned with "this interesting world" but with whatever may be outside its walls, and he suspected that there is a key to our prison, though we shall never hold it in hands of flesh and blood. Though the intellect is our best friend, there are regions whither it cannot guide us. He touches on this in a letter to Mrs Moor. Mrs Moor was a friend of his family, who though many years his senior had become a close personal friend of his own. He is writing to her (27 July 1904) about the launching of her children on the world, and by the characteristic avenue of sympathy he approaches the unseen.

I can only dimly conjecture what goes on inside you. You have your reserves. And, du reste, how little one knows of anyone. "Quel [sic] solitude que l'âme humaine." But to penetrate that solitude seems the thing most worth while, if one could. In any future world in which we might meet I think it will be you who will have to look out for me, rather than vice versa. I'm sure the "brainy" people will be at a discount there compared to the religious ones!

Three days earlier he had written a "brainy" letter to Miss Stawell in which the relations between the intellect and religious intuition are more carefully analysed. Miss Stawell had sent him her paper on Christianity and Hellenism. After discussing it, and agreeing with her that "Huxley's idea of nature being 'just' (of all things!) makes one foam at the mouth", he tackles the question as to whether it is possible to have an "experience of God", and he concludes that if such an experience were established, after the requisite critical tests, it would be a part of knowledge, and not something unique.

I mean as much a part of knowledge as the perception of beauty, which you instance. People may lack that perception. And they may lack a perception of God (if there is such a perception). But the things would appear to be strictly on a level. Only unfortunately, God is a word full of the most diverse and confused associations, and therefore a very difficult one to use without great danger of sophistication. E.g.

98

people have edifying feelings under the stars, and call it a perception of God. And that carries with it a whole illegitimate theology, as that he is at once omnipotent and good, and other such things, which may be shown to be contradicted by all experience. I mean, that the clarifying process would have to insist rigidly on the exact character of the alleged perception, or apprehension, and on the relating it to all others. Much as we do when a man says he saw a ghost. I daresay you agree. But then the result of such a process I should call a result of knowledge. And that's why I say religion doesn't give us knowledge. What gives us knowledge is knowledge.

He wanted knowledge to extend as far as it can. He had the religious temperament, but he hated all the religious weapons, and thought that much evil can be traced to their use. In the above letter, his caution over the word "God" is significant. "God" and "Jesus" and "Krishna" trail so many associations and are coloured by so many earthly passions that it is difficult not to be carried away by them, and he was more reluctant than his women friends to be carried away. He saw at the end of those famous short words, which boom like a gong out of darkest night —he saw not light, but more darkness, mass psychology, crowd cruelty. To be carried away? Yes, but in which direction? Away from the truth or towards it? We cannot know, because the tests of knowledge do not apply. Towards kindness or towards unkindness? That we can know, and the sinister record of religious idealism in the past made him scrutinize his intuitions carefully, and stick to the intellect, which anyhow sheds less blood.

One may almost say of him that he held nineteenth-century opinions in a twentieth-century way. For him, as for the Victorians, life was a pilgrimage, not an adventure, but he journeyed without donning their palmer's weeds. It is significant that though he felt the questions of personal immortality and the existence of God to be so important he never got fussed over them. The struggles and shames of the previous generation, with its "Do I believe?", "Couldn't I believe for my family's sake?", "What will the servants say when they find out I'm an agnostic?", did not trouble him after he was mature. One can contrast him, here, with another academic speculator, Henry Sidgwick. Sidgwick wanted to believe in God, and his inability to do so caused him a constant strain. Dickinson, equally conscientious, was somehow freer and less glum. It would never have occurred to him as it did to Sidgwick to compose his own funeral service. As soon as it came to the question of his own death, his own fate, he turned easy and modern, and one of the reasons that attracted the young to him was that he never gave them the sense of nursing a private destiny. He was not only selfless here, he believed in the imagination—believed in the sense that he was interpenetrated by it, and so was not personally mortified either by the victories or by the defeats of reason. "Sidgwick was the Cambridge spirit at its best, and therefore with its limitations most clearly and tragically apparent," he writes to Mrs Moor. "He felt, as he said, that he was put like a soldier to hold just that position. I have the same intellectual position. Only I feel increasingly that *all* intellectual positions 'hang in a void of nescience'. And in the void and the dark strange wonderful things brush me. Well—"

It is difficult for most of us to realize both the importance and the unimportance of reason. But it is a difficulty which the profounder humanists have managed to solve.

His most considered pronouncement on religious subjects was made in America. During his second visit there (1909) he delivered the Ingersoll Lecture at Harvard. According to the terms of the lectureship he had to deal with immortality and he chose as his theme "Is Immortality Desirable?" He came to the conclusion that it is—if we can have a continuity of experience after death and an opportunity for developing those impulses towards good which seem so significant on earth. In that sense, not in any other, Dickinson wished to be immortal, and whether immortality is possible in any sense he did not know. He hoped. He had no faith. But he was concerned to point out that no conclusive argument against immortality has been brought forward so far. The lecture is reprinted in *Religion and Immortality*. The dryness of the reasoning and the heat of the emotion are held together by the simplicity and honesty of the style. Only a man who was at once imaginative and devoid of self-consciousness could have delivered it. It is his classic utterance on this particular problem.

As a footnote to these more academic studies comes his interest in psychical research. This had begun when he was an undergraduate and Colonel Olcott handed round the turban. Now it links up with his general attitude. He valued all evidence about the unseen, and séances, planchettes and the rest had to be tested in case they revealed anything of value. Consequently he formally joined the Society for Psychical Research in 1890, and was a member of its Council from 1904 to 1920, also attending its

Jubilee celebration. In later life his interest declined. His attitude was of course always sceptical, but he did believe that there was an unexplained residuum in the phenomena which must be carefully examined, whatever religious orthodoxy may feel or scientific orthodoxy think. He did not expect to discover the supernatural, because whatever is discovered becomes natural; no, he hoped to increase the sum of ordinary knowledge.

An example of his method shall be given. In 1906 he came across the case of a lady whom he calls "Miss C." and investigated it with other observers. Miss C., when she was in the hypnotic state, professed that she had previously lived in the reign of Richard II. This was mixed up with a good deal of tosh about planes and going up into the blue, and would not have interested Dickinson but for its wealth of historical detail. As far as he tested them by the documents all the details were correct. Miss C. alleged that her chief friend at the court was a certain Blanche Poynings, and Blanche proved to be a historical personage, and —what was so intriguing—a personage of no importance. All the events of the reign were described from the standpoint of this obscure woman, whose character came out vividly as a fussy self-important matron. Miss C., who was truthful and reliable, declared in her waking state that she had never studied history and had read no historical novel of the period. Dickinson began to wonder whether she really had not lived in the reign of Richard II and might not still be visiting Blanche Poynings there. The explanation was distasteful but it had to be contemplated until a better turned up, it could not just be labelled "unscientific". Fortunately he solved the mystery. He was at tea with the C.s, and Miss C. began to use a planchette. Nothing occurred until she was questioned about Blanche Poynings, when the planchette wrote out the words, "Countess Maud". *Countess Maud* proved to be a book which she had read when she was twelve and had forgotten. Blanche Poynings occurred there in passing—a pious, dull person, who owed all her liveliness to the workings of Miss C.'s subconsciousness. Dickinson published this piece of research in the *Proceedings* of the Society for August 1911, under the title of "A Case of Emergence of a Latent Memory under Hypnosis". It illustrates his seriousness and the high value he places on the creative imagination. Some of the meetings of the Cambridge branch of the S.P.R. were held in his rooms. I attended one of them and remember a funny scene before a mixed audience when a young man who had been hypnotized was told that the room was a flowery glade with a stream down the middle of the carpet. "How beautiful," he said in mincing tones, as he gathered a nose-gay of books. "I think I'll have a bathe," and he began to take off all his clothes. He had to be restored to the waking state as quickly as possible, and conceivably he had never left it.

With psychical research, that dustbin of the spirit, this imperfect survey of Dickinson's religious outfit must close. Like all sensitive people, he behaved differently with his different friends, and owing to my limitations we kept to personal matters, literature and gossip when we talked. But I could see that everything linked up, that friendship had to do with politics, and philosophy with both, and that if he too had his limitations he was, within those limitations, complete. Of most of us this cannot be said. We do not link up within us such gifts as we have. With him, one had the experience of contact with a person who had allowed no internal barriers to survive, so that on whatever side one touched him there was the same impression of unity—an impression which he himself received from his master Goethe.

6

The chief event in his home life during these years was the death of his father, which occurred in the winter of 1908. It came as a terrible blow to his sisters, and particularly to Janet, who had been a devoted nurse. He himself lay crippled with sciatica in the next room, and went to and fro with difficulty during the last hours. Janet "somehow typifies for me everything best in women—the things they have and men haven't," he writes to Mrs Webb. The letter continues:

> But looking back and seeing him a little in focus, I see what a really remarkable man he was—so many-sided, so human, and, in spite of much worldly success, so fundamentally unworldly. I feel as if I never knew him properly—that is so often the case with near relations. He had a very complete and happy life—gathered the best of all earth had to give—and always kept his horizon open too. To see him dying... was to me like seeing a machine run down. He wasn't there. Is he anywhere or anything? I somehow think he is; but our thoughts are mere inarticulateness, after all, in face of the fact of death.

The absence of intimacy between himself and his father was always a regret to him, especially since he could assign no definite reason for it. It was an inhibition, perhaps dating back to the tuck-shop catastrophe at Beomonds. He always spoke of him with affection and admiration, and he was, in every external sense, a devoted son. He now became more and more the support of his sisters, and the actual though not the titular head of the family. All business arrangements devolved on him, and he developed an aptitude for practical affairs and for the handling of money, which is not uncommon among unpractical men. The house at All Souls Place was vacated and finally sold. Hettie had married a Mr Lowes, a distant connection, and had gone to live in Northumberland. May and Janet took a charming little house in Edwardes Square. They often came to Cambridge and there were pleasant travels abroad—for instance in 1910, when they ascended Etna while it was in eruption, and in 1911, when they went to the Italian Lakes; I joined them there and I remember a long walk with him, westward from Iseo, and his remark that it was only in upland country such as this that humanity would survive in the event of a great war.

His personal interest continued to centre in Cambridge, though his two greatest friends seldom came there, Fry being often abroad and Schiller usually at Esher. About the time of his father's death he got to know O. P. Eckhard, who was then up at King's. With Eckhard, with his mother, and with others of his family, he remained in touch until the end of his life—indeed there can seldom have been a life where so little was lost. Much had to be sublimated, but that was a process which he expected, and which he furthered as well as he could. When he looked back, he could say with truth that his personal relationships had been enduring, though he was sometimes appalled by their austerity. They were rooted in his idealistic philosophy. And philosophy for him was not only a subject of study, it was the source of all conduct, as it was for his ideal man, the Platonic Socrates.

chapter eleven

America, India, China

I

He had spent the summer of 1901 in lodgings at Betchworth. There was a long garden sloping down to the river Mole, where he sat and worked through the exquisite English weather. Far away raged the Boer War, disturbing him but slightly. Nearer at hand, also unseen, someone kept singing out of the solitude and the greenery, singing the words of a popular song:

> There is not any other
> To take the place of mother.

The peace, the gentleness, the sentimentality, made his heart ache, for he was about to venture on his first American tour.

He was ostensibly going to visit his brother Arthur, who had been transferred to New York in the course of his accountancy business, as senior partner in the firm of Price Waterhouse. He intended to cover expenses by lecturing at universities and elsewhere. "The White Man's Burden" was the title of one of the courses he was preparing; it dealt with India, with the problem of native races generally, with the South African crisis. In 1901 there was no escaping from Kipling, and "The White Man's Burden" was the obvious title for all coloured problems and implied no cynicism. The alternative course, "Self-Government with British Empire", followed the lines of his academic teaching; it dealt with the English in America, with the British Commonwealth and with Imperial Federation. But neither the visit to his brother nor the lecturing was the real motive of his expedition. He went because he feared that he was falling into a rut at Cambridge, and acquiring the oddities of the unmarried don—those oddities which purport to enrich the personality yet often suck all the juices out of it. America was a drastic prophylactic. She worked, and on his return Mrs Schiller complimented him on his improved appearance and manner. He became more self-confident, lost his shyness, and could talk to all sorts of people without displaying or causing discomfort. More than that America did not do and was not asked to do.

"My enterprise looked a gigantic one for a small skinless creature to embark upon. However, once in it, it went easily enough." He sailed (25 August) on a transport from Tilbury with about two hundred fellow passengers and ninety stallions. The voyage was steady and dull, the Atlantic unattractive, and for the first time since school he was thrown into continuous contact with "ordinary" people. They proved to be alien rather than alarming.

> I have three others in my state room [he writes to May], of whom one is the most amusing inconceivable little cad I have ever seen. England had the honour of producing him, but he has early changed his nationality to America. He looks about 17 but professes a rich experience of men and things, having run away from school at 14 and taken up his abode with a music-hall actress. His language is the choicest I've ever heard and I've had a great deal of experience in that particular respect. His insufferable cheek is only equalled by his incapacity. He got up to perform at an entertainment we had, and half recited half sang a music-hall song fortunately inaudible to most of the company. I heard only "D'ye follow me? You do?" and the word damn. The funny thing is I rather like the little beast.

At his table he was the only male, and successfully coped with six American ladies at once. He also experienced the organized merriment which forms so large a part of ocean life:

> At the "entertainment" [the letter continues] a certain "Colonel" recited a poem composed by himself. The moral was that if you don't say your prayers your child will get run over by a dray.
> But the interesting point was not the moral but the "style". It was a sort of newspaper-paragraph telegram English hitched into rhyme, but ignorant of the fact that verse also involves rhythm. We were all much affected and I had the cheek to ask him to send me a copy. I do want one for reasons. He's a dear good "Colonel", owner of the stallions, and the "poem" represents a genuine feeling—or would do if it were a poem. . . . In conclusion I may say very honestly I have not met one single person on this boat who has intellect. They may have every other virtue. But I suppose most people don't have or require intellect. Intelligence no doubt they have.

He was only in America for three months, and the detailed diary which he kept is a collection of reminders rather than an account of his impressions. After visiting his brother and founding a durable friendship with his two little nieces, he went straight across to San Francisco. He felt romantic as the train drew out of New York and reminded himself that the country he saw had been recently inhabited by Red Indians. But he was unable to sustain such feelings for more than a few miles, and after a week he arrived something of a wreck. His lectures at Berkeley were on the British Empire, and were very well received. Thrown upon his own resources, he found he could get on with people well, met administrators, businessmen, missionaries in Chinatown, Chinese; "but I experienced then, what is a common phenomenon with me, the sense that all the time I was acting a part, and that the essential me was looking on, with detachment and some disapproval, at the performing animal."

When this course of lectures was over he went to the Yosemite valley and wandered about there alone. One day (26 September), high up above the Yosemite Falls, he had one of the experiences which befell him about half a dozen times in his life. "Mystic" is too specialized and pretentious a word for the experience. The language of every day can adequately describe it. It represents a heightening of normal consciousness rather than a revelation. In the Yosemite, as at Heidelberg, Frensham Ponds, Snowdon, Mistra, his inner life showed itself more clearly. Writing in his diary that same evening, he only says: "Saw no one all day. Had idea of a book on America and things in general—sort of a 'free Rhapsody', analytic—synthetic—critical—dithyrambic —above all clean cut and intellectual." Twenty-five years later, the *Recollections* describe the experience again, and the "book on America" now appears as part of a larger scheme, and as a symbol of the expansion of his mind.

> I felt convinced that my business was to discover and illuminate the fundamental notions that should guide modern civilization. That sounds pretentious enough, and I suppose it was; but not consciously, to me. Only, I did not realize the magnitude of the task nor the pitifully little I could hope to achieve. But the aim was, and is, mine and I cling to it still, for what is left of my life.

Of course this aim was not a new one; what is remarkable is its reinforcement by the means of grand scenery, and American scenery. America had already become an inspiration as well as an irritant.

On his way back from California, he stopped at Strong City, Kansas, to see his old friend "Plump" Hughes, who was ranching there; Pip and Plump had both been with him at the Misses Woodman's school, and Tom Hughes their father had tried to protect him at Chester. Then more lecturing at Boston and elsewhere; invitations from Goldwin Smith, Cabot Lodge and other celebrities; Niagara—which obsessed him as an epitome of the continent. He found the Falls neither attractive nor beautiful. They gave him the sense of tremendous power and bulk, but these were the very things he was learning to hate. For the question always arose, "Is this force good?" and nature gave him no answer or not a hopeful one.

Sometimes America was the Yosemite and elevated him. At other times she was Niagara and repelled him. It is as Niagara that she usually appears in the 1901 tour. To C. R. Ashbee:

Pittsburgh
20 October [1901]

... The two things rubbed into me in this country are (1) that the future of the world lies with America, (2) that radically and essentially America is a barbarous country. ... The "life of the spirit"—the one and only thing which justifies and dignifies the life of men on earth—is, not accidentally or temporarily, but inevitably and eternally killed in this country. All that man has achieved in this region, from Buddha to Goethe, is just non-existent for Americans—they have, in their own phrase, "no use for it"! (I don't count the purely adventitious fringe of cultured people who cling to the skirts of Europe, and are despised and hated by true Americans.) And this American spirit, alias the "Chicago spirit", is to dominate the world! Don't reply with the usual excuse that the country is "young" etc. It was much better when it was younger still! This is its adult age, its deliberate choice now it has broken loose from Eastern traditions. It is a country without leisure, manners, morals, beauty, or religion—a country whose ideal is mere activity, without any reference to the quality of it; a country which holds competition and strife to be the only life worth living.

This diatribe—which suggests the speech of Ellis in *A Modern Symposium*—would have been modified by him in later years. Perhaps even at the time he writes more violently than he feels, in order to get a rise out of Ashbee. Perhaps he was feeling tired. Fatigue, in his own opinion, explains a good deal of his sourness against America. He was thankful to get away. He escaped to his own country on New Year's Eve. Never had he felt more British,

There is not any other
To take the place of mother.

At Niagara he had received the first copies of *John Chinaman*. We shall see that this book, under the title of *Letters from a Chinese Official*, was soon to make a great stir in the States, partly owing to the naïveté of William Jennings Bryan, who mistook its author for Chinese, and wrote *Letters to a Chinese Official* (1906) as a reply to it. *A Modern Symposium* was also to succeed. So that by the time Dickinson paid his second visit to America in 1909 he had become a celebrity, and he was inundated with lecturing engagements, and entertained on an enormous and exhausting scale.

The diary of this second tour (April–August) is a whirlpool of little entries—speeches to the Twentieth-Century Club at Brooklyn on New Evidences of Survival, to the University of Wisconsin on the Aesthetic, the Intellectual, the Religious Ideal, to a public dinner on the Tariff, to schoolgirls on Democracy and Art; delivering the Ingersoll Lecture on Immortality at Harvard. This alternates with meeting Coolidge and Eliot Norton, seeing Niagara again and Mrs Gardner's house, picnicking on a golf course, sampling Colorado Springs. Long Island: "See Jolly Trixy the world's fattest girl she weighs 685 pounds, Holy Smoke, she's fat she's awful fat." He has stuck Jolly Trixy's lilac-coloured advert at the end of his diary with the comment "Inter alia!"

The letters written on the second tour repeat, inter alia, the previous note of irritability, but they are more sympathetic. Here is an example of the change. To O. P. Eckhard:

> University Club, Madison, Wis.
> 6 May 1909

> I find I can always rise (or fall) to these occasions. My lectures seem to me always to go well, that is I always feel I've "got" the audience in the first two minutes, and I believe one can't be mistaken over that. I talk quite simply, always in my head, and am sometimes surprised to hear my subconscious self turning out epigrams and exhortations which weren't in the programme at all. . . .
> This is rather an interesting place, about the antithesis of Cambridge. It's a "state" university, and the university helps the state to assess its taxes and value its property, and even has a bureau of classified information for legislators. Whether, in the midst of this, anything like culture survives I can't judge. I'm inclined to think, after all I've now seen here, that Oxford and Cambridge really now are the last refuges of that. And that perhaps we ought to realize that, and concentrate on that aspect of things. Three Canadians the other night besought me almost with tears to resist all reforms in our ancient universities.

They said, in their picturesque language, that they had "got us skinned alive" in all applications of science, but they knew in their hearts that we have the one thing they won't get by all their efforts: disinterested intellectual culture. Certainly America is only drawing interest (hundred per cent) on the capital of European ideas. And if we cease to generate the ideas . . . ? I feel that all I have said about America is true; but I omitted a good deal—perhaps all—that is most important. Their candour, good temper, immediate and fearless experimentation, sense for fact etc. is the positive pole of their incapacity for discussions and ideas. They *bore* me as it is impossible to be bored in Europe, but that is because *any* fact interests them, and *no* idea except as it can be shown to be in direct relation to fact. That makes a type of conversation particularly *assommant*. But I don't think it implies a bad type of character. Of course I confess myself terribly flattered by the way they read my books, though that seems incompatible with what I have just said. All the economists here take my *Justice and Liberty* quite seriously.

So, half charmed, half critical and wholly fatigued, he flounders through an experience which was familiar to other foreign lecturers but which is particularly humorous in his case, for one contrasts it with the calm of Cambridge, the slipping into the train for the London School of Economics, All Souls Place, slipping back, rowing down the Thames, bicycling with Fry, going to Greece with Mayor and Wedd. "Good Lord, what a life!" he exclaims to May, and though he is pleased at being appreciated more effusively than in England he wonders how much lies behind the uniform cordiality of Americans. In one way he merited their praise, for he never talked nonsense to them in the dishonouring and dishonourable way which was quite common at the time, and he never talked down to them. He gave them his best. In particular the Ingersoll Lecture ranks with his finest and most careful work.

His real objection to the country was the absence of personal relationships as conceived in Cambridge discussion societies and indeed in England generally. So much cordiality, so little intimacy, such gleaming teeth, so little tenderness, such mixing, so little fusion! Co-education, as exhibited at the University of Wisconsin at Madison, fairly made him shudder. The young men there went "girling" or "fussing" and the young women said "Our fussers are coming tonight" and the indecent game didn't even culminate in sexual acts. He sympathized with the Scotchman who wanted less chastity and more delicacy. Human intercourse, whatever its type, seemed sterile, all faces (except the

Negroes') seemed devoid of emotion and thought. This—not the
absence of culture—intimidated him. Culture can wait, but how
can any civilization grow out of people who can't or daren't be
intimate with one another? There just isn't the soil.

Fortunately he made one great American friend who, if he
didn't solve the problem, complicated it, which was a relief.
Just as he had found Mrs Webb when Extension-lecturing as
a youth, so in this later and more triumphant scramble he
managed to discover Russell Loines. His friendship with Russell
Loines—whom he had first met when returning from the 1901
tour—made all the difference in 1909. He had here an American
with whom he felt at home and who gave him a home. He stopped
with Loines on Staten Island, where Rupert Brooke was afterwards to be entertained at his introduction, and went with him
for a short tour in the Adirondacks. Loines was more than a host:
he helped to make the continent less like Niagara. His death in
1922 was a great loss to Dickinson, and incidentally impover-
ishes his biography, for he would have given some inside information which I lack. I should like to have known what
general impression Goldie made upon the Americans he met. Did
he seem to them better or worse than the other cultured lecturers
from the old world who were in circulation at the time? Did his
candour strike them as offensive, his fairmindedness as feeble?
Or, like Mrs Webb and Loines, did they see through to the light
within and realize its kinship with earth and heaven? These
questions cannot now be answered. The moment of his American
notoriety has passed. Niagara continues. But, sharing his optimism about America, I would like to think that his influence still
persists there, though the newspapers have ceased to quote his
name and the friends who treasured it most are dead.

On getting back to England he contributed some articles to
the *English Review*, and republished them, rather reluctantly,
as the first section of *Appearances* (1914). His feelings about
America had changed after the election of Wilson and were to
become still more favourable, and he regretted his earlier note of
exasperation. However, the articles made a good pendant to the
letters about the East, which form the bulk of the book, so he
admitted them and he emphasizes that, however critical he is of
the West, it is there rather than on the East that he fixes his hopes.

Another result of the American tours was a four-act play,
Business. I will give a short résumé of it since it has not been
printed. He got the idea partly from Ida M. Tarbell's *History*

of the Standard Oil Company and partly from his personal impressions of Chicago, Pittsburgh, etc. *Business* deals with the efforts of William Rackham, a petroleum king, to crush his rivals and establish a monopoly. Circumstances bring him up against the owner of a petroleum refinery, his old love, Mrs Bond. He ruins her, firstly by corrupting one of her employees, and secondly by taking advantage of her private difficulties, for her son has forged a note to pay his gambling debts, and it has to be redeemed. Here is the world of Rockefeller: only money counts, human relations are eviscerated, religion is distorted into something false and insipid. Into it drifts an inhabitant from another world—a picture by Giorgione—and the contest between the two makes the spiritual plot of the play. Money can buy a Giorgione, but cannot measure it; that has to be done on a different pair of scales. When Rackham is murdered by the employee, to whom he refused a job on the ground that he could not be trusted, he leaves Mrs Bond an enormous legacy, on condition that she enters his combine. She refuses, and her son will be arrested, but the situation is saved by the connoisseur from Europe who owns the Giorgione. Realizing that cash will now be of practical use, he sells the picture to Rackham's widow, who fancies that the nude figure with a star on its forehead symbolizes petroleum. "What's money for except to be used?" he remarks; "I might be a rich man if I liked. I shall be, perhaps, when I'm degraded enough. Art's a very profitable thing if you make a business of it." And he redeems the forged note, and presumably marries Mrs Bond. *Business* was produced by the Stage Society, on 19 and 20 March 1911, the author's name being given as John Goldie. The part of Mrs Bond was taken by Kate Rorke. Before Rackham is murdered, he reads out to his wife his forthcoming address to "Christian young men of business"—a document for which Dickinson had historical evidence.

He heard conflicting opinions about the play and cherished a casual printed remark of Shaw's referring to him, among others, as a playwright of promise. "I had the personal experience (only too common, I suppose!) of finding my own play very interesting and moving on the stage. But I am pretty sure that was not the general opinion. However, I was satisfied, and thought of writing other plays." He did, as a matter of fact, finish two just before the war. One of them was on the subject of Lassalle and Helene von Racowitza. The Stage Society rejected it, but the manager of the Little Theatre professed enthusiasm and was to produce it in the autumn of 1914. Then came the war, the manager lost both the typescript copies, and Dickinson was left with only two acts of the final version and felt "no impulse to try to reconstruct the rest from memory". The manuscript of *Lassalle* exists in composite form, but I have not succeeded in getting a clear estimate of it in this condition. His own view of it was favourable. His third play, a fantasy called *Peace and War*, has fortunately survived intact, and will be considered later.

Neither *Business* nor the chapters of *Appearances* offer that imaginative pronouncement on America of which he had a vision in the Yosemite valley. Other activities claimed him. America survived as a distant prospect, which at the time of the Peace Conference included a rising sun, and which never excluded the stars.

2

On 11 October 1912 I hung over the edge of a ship at Port Said—my first glimpse of the East or of Dickinson in a sun-helmet. He bobbed far below me in a little boat, looking dishevelled and tired. He had been stopping at Cairo, and he was joining R. C. Trevelyan and myself to visit India. G. H. Luce was also with us on his way to a job in Burma.

Dickinson was among the earliest holders of an Albert Kahn Travelling Fellowship. Kahn, a French Jew of imagination and disinterested genius, believed that acquaintance with other countries may help international peace and had founded fellowships to the value of £660 each for this purpose. He was a Bergsonian, and his fellows were the extreme forward point of the "élan vital", and bore a grave philosophic responsibility. Dickinson, no Bergsonian, was an excellent choice. He was both open-minded and well-grounded—an unusual combination. His Report, which he presented to the Kahn Trustees in 1913, is within its limits a masterpiece. (Reprinted in 1914 as *An Essay on the Civilisations of India, China and Japan.*) The normal itinerary of a Kahn Fellow included America, but since he had already been there twice it was arranged that he should confine himself to the East.

We hated the boat, but the voyage to Bombay was fascinating. I have been that way since, but have never again seen such colours in the sea, so many flying fish, dolphins and sharks, such sunsets, such flights of birds and of butterflies (the last-named meeting us when we were still two days from the Indian coast). On board were many Anglo-Indians, as they were then called. These I have often seen again. The contrast between their clan and our clique was amusing. We were dubbed "The Professors" or "The Salon", and there was the same little nip of frost in these jests as in the title of "The Three Graces" which had been fastened on Dickinson and his school friends at Charterhouse. They recognized that we were gentlemen, sahibs even, yet there was a barrier. No doubt we did look queer, and once when we were all four in a row at our tea a young officer opposite could not keep grave. We played chess on Sundays, compared Dostoyevsky with Tolstoy publicly, argued over the shape of the Earth at the breakfast-table, balanced on bollards instead of playing deck games, and discovered another young officer, a very different one, Kenneth Searight, who pursued romance and poetry in a solitary deckchair. We kept diaries. "The extent of the heat may be judged from the fact that, on descending to my cabin, a tube of Kolynos was found in a semi-liquid condition" is a sentence which Dickinson gave me to put in mine. He said it was the ideal diarist style. I transcribe it here not for that reason but because nonsense is too seldom recorded. Wit and humour get put into a biography, foolery is missed out. It is so evanescent, it needs a gesture or a smile to fix it, and these cannot be transcribed. Dickinson could be ever so gay and ridiculous, laughing and talking at once, making everyone laugh, shooting out little glints of nonsense like flying fish. If one could convey the little glints, the sea and the sky would take care of themselves. The last time I saw him (outside a hospital) was in my garden, which was overdone with pink sweet-williams. He murmured: "I don't like pink. I did speak to God about it; however, some people do, and anyhow it can't be helped." Here again it is futile to transcribe nonsense. One needs the gentle voice, the innocent and unsuccessful flowers. . . .

We went on shore at Bombay in a native boat, rowed by ugly men with beautiful skins, who reminded us of the stupider apostles. Then we parted for a time, Dickinson and Bob Trevelyan going off with a deplorable servant called Samuel, whom they shared, and who wailed "This is no proper arrangement" as soon as he had to do any work. They took turns at controlling Samuel. From the moment he landed, Dickinson's tour became strenuous. In three months he not only saw the most important sights of India, but presented many introductions, official and non-official, English, Hindu, and Mohammedan, and also did some speaking. His anxiety to learn, his great conversational powers, his intelligence and gentleness, his interest in religion, his readiness to enter into every point of view, made him popular with Indians of various types. But as a rule he was not very happy with them, and though he was stronger socially than he had been on his American tours he still longed, vainly, to be alone. For the English he felt either strong sympathy or strong aversion, and in either case he pitied them for having such an uncongenial job.

> For the hardworked and conscientious Anglo-Indians I met I felt a sympathy tinged with a kind of despair. For it seemed almost that the more conscientiously they did their work, the further they were from the native sympathy and mind. But that too may be illusion. I am, however, pretty sure that the irony that brought the English into contact with the Indians is only equalled by that which brought them into contact with the Irish. The barrier, on both sides, of incomprehension is almost impassable. I feel this incomprehension very strongly myself. Indian art, Indian religion, Indian society is alien and unsympathetic to me. I have no sense of superiority about it, but one of estrangement. What indeed is there or can there be in common between the tradition of Greece and that of India?

Our paths in India crossed several times, and I will add a few personal memories, mostly of a light character. I can see him cowering under the great sandstone portal of a temple, repelled by the monstrosity of its forms. I can hear him apologizing for keeping an elephant waiting under the Fort at Gwalior and receiving the monumental reply "Elephants sometimes wait four hours". I attend an address which he gives to orthodox Hindus at Lahore, under the misconception that they belong to the Brahmo Somaj; the audience is polite and sad. I watch him receive the good news of the election of President Wilson, also at Lahore. And there are two memories which dominate. The first is Peshawar, where we went to stop with Kenneth Searight. We were escorted up the Khyber as far as Ali Masjid, and there Dickinson sat by the edge of the track, watching the caravans pour past him out of Central Asia, and registering this new proof of the restlessness of the world. We dined at the mess that evening —the Royal West Kents. He was instantly beloved. The young officers were charming to him, and looked so fine in their gay jackets that militarism became permissible. They called him "The Don", and said "I say, will he put you in a book?" to one another. They made him swallow prairie oysters. They got rather drunk, in exquisite style, while Bob Trevelyan sported with them, and Dickinson and the C.O. sat apart, a couple of benign but contrasted uncles. Looking back to that jolly evening, I see him then for the first time as a solid figure, who has won his own place in the world, and holds it firmly. This is the time when I begin to use him as a touchstone, and to condemn those who fail to appreciate him.

My second memory is of Chhatarpur, a remote native state in the Bundelkhand Agency which has since figured in J. R. Ackerley's *Hindoo Holiday*. We lived for nearly a fortnight at Chhatarpur in the Guest House on the top of a little hill. Monkeys played with their children on the slopes, the city lay below, lovely at all times, but loveliest in the early morning, when the spires of the Jain temples pierced up through the gray and white mists and the trees looked like cushions of clouds. Down in the city, struggling to meet us, dwelt our host, the Maharajah, and a constant stream of notes, counter-notes, landaus, motor-cars and horsemen passed up and down the hill. The Maharajah was a tiny and fantastic figure, incompetent, *rusé*, exasperating, endearing. He lived for philosophy and love, and he hoped that the two were one. He is dead now. "Tell me, Mr Dickinson, where is God? Can Herbert Spencer lead me to him, or should I prefer George Henry Lewes? Oh, when will Krishna come and be my friend? Oh, Mr Dickinson!" I found these questions grotesque, but Dickinson attuned them to his own Platonism, and there was instant sympathy. When he was well enough (for Chhatarpur disarranged his digestion) he sat with the Maharajah in the palace courtyard, under an umbrella as big as a tent, and spoke with him as one seeker with another. Sometimes the chaplain from the military cantonment joined them, a friendly bounder who shouted "Come, Maharajah, why don't you eat beef? Do you good", and we winced with horror and the Maharajah smiled into his sleeve, and the Private Secretary said afterwards: "The padre sahib is a very nice man indeed, he has no interest whatever in religion, and that is suitable for a clergyman." Or the Political Agent would come, a more sinister figure, and try to interfere with the Maharajah's private affairs. Or there would be religious plays—the Birth of Krishna, etc.—enacted in the evening. Or Dickinson and his host drove out to another palace, Mau, a lovely ruin on a lake, and arrived there when their car did not break down ("See, Mr Dickinson, that balcony—did Hamlet climb up there to visit Juliet?"), and they meditated over the lotuses, upon which a nymph, the daughter of the lotus who fed upon lotuses, had once walked, and they saw the myriads of water-fowl cloud the setting sun, and the Maharajah offered Dickinson his palace of Mau for ever, forgetting that he had given it to me only two days before. For we were all philosophers. But Dickinson was philosopher in chief, and here the Maharajah showed his sense. If India ever came near winning, it was at Chhatarpur.

China, not India, won, and on Tuesday, 12 December our paths divided finally, and my friends set off in the direction of the Far East. The stars were cantankerous, and no day could be found by the court astrologers which favoured both them and myself, who was stepping westward. The Maharajah was distressed, but he could scarcely hesitate where the safety of Mr Dickinson was concerned. "Mr Forster, I am very sorry, but. . . ." So I lost my train connections, my servant got no food, and when I arrived at Bhopal armed with a distinguished introduction to its Begum she omitted to receive me. The other two proceeded safely, as did Samuel.

He came to feel that the main cleavage in civilization lies not between East and West but between India and the rest of the world. His further course was to Benares (where Trevelyan had to read *The Oxford Book of English Verse* to exorcize Hinduism), to Calcutta (where they enjoyed the hospitality of the Tagores), to Madras, Southern India, Ceylon. Here are extracts from letters both written on 20 January 1913 from camp near Madras, to illustrate his later impressions. To Mrs Moor:

> We're in the real jungle, forest around us for miles, and I'm so happy! I sit alone in a dry river bed and watch things and listen. Monkeys are jumping by in the trees. And though I don't see tigers I hear they do pass at night and leave trails. The butterflies are exquisitely beautiful. Unfortunately there are other flies, at this moment tormenting me. But you can't have everything; or, rather, you must have everything! A wasp has been depositing paralysed spiders in a hole in one of the tables, laid her eggs, and carefully sealed it up with wax. What a thing nature is! How do the spiders feel? Let's hope they're unconscious! In the face of these things, most religious talk seems "tosh". If there's a God, or gods, they're beyond my ken. I think perhaps, after all, the Hindus took in more of the facts in their religion than most people have done. But they too are children, like the rest of us.

To H. O. Meredith:

Anglo-Indian society is the devil—it's worse than America. We eschew it all we can. It's the women more than the men that are at fault. There they are, without their children, with no duties, no charities, with empty minds and hearts, trying to fill them by playing tennis and despising the natives. . . .

There is no solution of the problem of governing India. Our presence is a curse both to them and to us. Our going will be worse. I believe that is the last word. And *why* can't the races meet? Simply because the Indians *bore* the English. *That* is the simple adamantine fact.

I disagree with the last paragraph. Perhaps he was overtired, perhaps temperamentally averse, but he never found in Indian society either the happiness or the peacefulness which have made my own visits to the country so wonderful. He has recorded some of his impressions in the Kahn Report, in *Appearances*, and in articles written at the time for the *Manchester Guardian* over the signature of "Don". At the end of his life, he wrote a significant letter to an Indian correspondent (page 190). As to his main conclusion, it is that India is the home of religion; a conventional conclusion, but he reached it by his own route. It was a revelation to him that men could take such constant and passionate interest in the unseen, and less of a revelation that neither their conduct nor their art seemed to benefit thereby.

3

If Dickinson visited America in the hope of self-development and India from reasons of curiosity, it was in a very different spirit that he approached China. He came to her as a lover, who had worshipped from afar for years. In a life which contained much disillusionment, China never failed him. She stood firm as the one decent civilization, and when he mourned over her it was not because she had disappointed him but because he had lived to see her destroyed by the violence and vulgarity of Europe. In his last years, her fate seemed to epitomize mankind's. If China could have been saved, he would have been persuaded that humanism is indestructible. His was an impersonal love; no private relationship coloured it, although he became friendly with many individual Chinese. It rested upon natural sympathy and intellectual affinity. He once amused the students at a summer school by saying: "I am speaking to you about China, not because I know anything about the subject nor because I once visited the country,

but because, in a previous existence, I actually was a Chinaman!"
And when one looks at the portrait of him in his Chinese cap
(page 169), or indeed as a boy (page 9), one realizes a physical
as well as a spiritual kinship. The Hellenist, the disciple of
Shelley and of Goethe, is precipitated, with a slight alteration of
focus, into a Confucian plane.

The first link in the connection was fortuitous. At the beginning
of the century, previous to his first American visit, he was in a
restless state of mind "such as usually, in my case as in those of
greater men, precedes composition". He wanted to make some
fundamental criticism of western civilization, which should be
read by the general public, and should have some kind of artistic
form. He experimented in various ways, and tried to utilize one
of Swift's myths in the form of "Letters from a Houyhnhnm".
The gulf between his temperament and Swift's was too wide, and
the medium proved unsuitable. Roger Fry then suggested that he
should try a Chinese setting; China was in the foreground
politically, owing to the Boxer riots and the European expeditions
to suppress them, and he had read Giles's *Gems of Chinese Literature*
and *La Cité chinoise* by Eugène Simon. The suggestion bore fruit,
the painful period of incubation ended, and at the same time as
he was writing *The Meaning of Good* he produced the first four
"Letters from John Chinaman" and sent them to the *Saturday
Review*, where they appeared anonymously.

A comedy then developed. He intended no deception, knowing that there was good precedent for that kind of form in
literature, and not supposing anyone would be taken in. A correspondent of the *Saturday Review* pointed out that the letters could
not really be by a Chinese and there the matter seemed to end. He
added some more letters, and after he had sailed for America the
little volume, soon to be famous, was published by his friend R.
Brimley Johnson, with a grotesque picture of a Chinaman on the
cover. "I didn't think much more about the book, for I was well
accustomed to being ignored."

The presentation copies of this edition followed him over the
Atlantic to Niagara of all places, and when he was lying in bed
in the hotel there his brother Arthur entered in a state of great
animation,

> saying that he had been reading the book, and that it was "wonderful".
> He did not know it was mine, and felt a natural disappointment
> when I revealed the fact. For who can think as much of the opinions
> of a friend or relative as they do of those of an unknown author?

They know too much about him! I remember being much excited and pleased at the moment.

But the book would, I suppose, have fallen as dead as my others, if George Trevelyan had not quoted it in an article in the *Nineteenth Century*, which excited some attention. People then began to speculate as to whether it was really by a Chinaman, and a good many copies were sold. It then penetrated to America, and there everybody seems to have accepted naïvely its Chinese origin. It was atttributed to the then Chinese ambassador; and Mr Bryan, the famous politician, thought it worth while to write a special reply to it, in which he observed, among other things, that clearly the author had never seen the inside of a Christian home. Before publishing his book, he ascertained that the author was really an Englishman, and he said as much in his preface. But he thought his book none the less worth publication, and it is not for me to dispute that it may have been.

Unlike much that he wrote, the *Letters from John Chinaman* appeared at the right psychological moment. The reaction from the Boer War and from economic imperialism was just gathering force, and Englishmen were sensitive about aggression and exploitation to a greater degree than they would have been a few years before, and to a degree which became impossible for them after the Great War. For a short time his words travelled far beyond his usual liberal and academic surroundings, and, by their power and beauty, moved people to think of the flaw in European civilization. For that, and not the wrongs of China, is his theme. "I still think this book well written and its contents true and important." There is said to be a translation of it into Gujarati by Gandhi. When this was reported to him he displayed no pleasure but characteristically remarked that he had written for the West, not for the East.

Besides being topical, *John Chinaman* is famous for the beauty of its prose, and particularly for the sumptuous yet delicate passage beginning "A rose in a moonlit garden . . .", a passage which has been quoted by Logan Pearsall Smith in his anthology. Here is oratory—so winged with poetry that the words nearly leave the earth, but they just remain on it, and rightly, for their purpose is persuasion. All that is delicate and noble challenges all that is brutal and vulgar, and he employs for the contest neither appeals to the empyrean nor arguments of force, but the subtlest of all weapons, good taste. To Mrs Moor he writes (9 February 1902):

My little J.C. book is approved by many people whose approval I value, and that gives me satisfaction. I am just beginning to realize that I have a certain faculty of appealing to what I call the "life of the spirit", and that I have no other faculty. So I may as well do what I can in that line for the future, and let others, more competent, run the affairs of the nation. Only I can't illuminate the spirit—my own or anyone else's—without bringing an immense amount of the fuel of contemporary issues, worries, and controversies. G. Trevelyan sent J.C. to Meredith—and he says it is "excellent" and "might be thought timely, were the ears of England open". A most Meredithian phrase.

Though he never affected scholarship, and learned no Chinese, he now began to attract educated Orientals who were visiting England, particularly students. An Anglo-Chinese society was formed at Cambridge—largely recruited, it is said, by Chinese from Singapore who knew less about China than he did, but the interchange of ideas flourished under his auspices. The Chinese amused and charmed him in a way in which Indians did not. "Clearly I'm Chinese and not Indian, though I believe I was Indian from the age of twenty to twenty-five and would have become an ascetic with the smallest encouragement," he tells R. C. Trevelyan. And, as the time of his Kahn Fellowship tour approached, it was chiefly for China that he prepared himself. To O. P. Eckhard:

King's College
12 June 1912

We had an Anglo-Chinese dinner on Monday. The secretary of the Chinese legation, Mr Kwei, was there. He sat next me and talked the whole time, and I hardly understood a single word. It was like a nightmare. One thing however I grasped after half an hour's explanation. He applied to my *Letters of John Chinaman* what I understood is a Chinese proverb: In another's wine cup I make my own complaint. This I think explains itself, and is quite true in its application. Mr Kwei got drunk before the end; he began to embrace me, and I thought he would never have finished shaking hands. The net result is that I hope I shall get much assistance in my travels to China.

When we parted at Chhatarpur as already described, he went via Ceylon to Singapore, made a trip to Java and Sumatra, and then proceeded from Singapore to Hong Kong and Canton. As soon as he was among people whose features and physique were Mongolian, he felt happy. At Canton, Bob Trevelyan left him, and hurried back to Cumberland, in order to be in time for the Trinity Lake Hunt, an annual event to which he was romantically addicted. Dickinson found Trevelyan a delightful companion, yet he probably gained by being left alone on the threshold of China. He was thrown on his own resources, and was obliged to look at a country about which he had hitherto only read, written and dreamed. Canton he loved. Then came Shanghai and politics and an interview with Sun Yat-sen; he was too sensitive to be a good interviewer, and "didn't get much out of him". Then a solitary voyage of ten days on the Yangtse, in pouring rain, which kept him in his cabin and obliged him to play many games of patience. Then a long railway journey to Peking.

At Peking he stopped several weeks, seeing much both of English and Chinese, and it would be possible, from his diary and letters home, to construct a complete account of his movements. But the movements of a tourist's body are not worth recording unless they generate movements inside his mind. Here are two typical reactions. The first is a rhapsody in free verse, such as often occurred to him while in the Far East. As soon as he got clear of heavy India little poems began to flit and glint as though winged by some new spirit in the depths of him. This particular poem records a visit to the Temple of Agriculture at Peking.

A Temple

What do they hide?
The cypress Avenue and the coral wall,
The green and amber roof, what do they hide?

A wooden plough and an altar consecrate to earth.

An emperor once held the plough,
An emperor made sacrifice.

The coral wall is falling now, falling the amber roof,
The cypresses decay, the altar crumbles;
Crumbles the altar consecrate to Earth;
But Earth abides.

On the day previous, he had been taken to visit a very different type of temple. He writes of it to a friend:

Oh, but the most amusing thing I want to tell you, I went to a Chinese banquet, at which "sing-song-girls" were introduced. They are in fact superior, accomplished and expensive tarts, rather pretty, and I shall suppose attractive to the normal man. But imagine me behaving as is expected on such occasions, with one of them on my knee at one time, and smoking the same cigarette; really it was rather funny, though very embarrassing. And though the girls are to be had, I gather it is only if they like you, and for large money. Some of them were wearing pearls and diamonds. We adjourned to their house—I suppose really a superior brothel—and had a second feast of Chinese dishes, very trying to a weak stomach. Most people seemed to leave without anything happening. They were all very "respectable" commercial Chinese.

One compares this banquet with the restaurant in Paris many years back, where in even greater discomfort he had met a French lady. And one contrasts it with the "girling" and "fussing" which had so revolted him in the mixed University of Wisconsin. What seemed important to him in sexual as in other relationships was the quality of the emotion aroused. He disliked vulgarity more than frivolity, more indeed than anything, and at all events these Chinese were never vulgar; they showed a well-bred combination of reticence and frankness in their levity as in the more serious intercourse of life. They understood personal relationships in the sense in which he and Cambridge understood them and America has failed to understand them, and that is why Chinese civilization did not disappoint him, nor vary greatly from his preliminary vision.

Peking
8 June 1913

Dear Forster,

> (Hand this on to Bob, if he inquires for news. I can *not* write to everyone—at least not in an interesting way. I get bored with repeating myself. But I was glad of Bob's letter and will probably write later—from Japan.)
> Yours of the 22 May. (That, I think, is the business method.)

China is a land of human beings. India, as it glimmers in a remote past, is supernatural, uncanny, terrifying, sublime, horrible, monotonous, full of mountains and abysses, all heights and depths, and for ever incomprehensible. But China! So gay, friendly, beautiful, sane, hellenic, choice, human. Dirty? Yes. Peking, the last day or two, is all but impossible even in a rickshaw—pools, lakes, of liquid mud. One understands the importance of the sedan chair, and the wall side, 150 years ago in Europe. Poor? Yes. But never were poor people so happy (I speak with all the superficiality you care to credit me with). A Chinese home in Peking is beyond description exquisite: its courtyard, with trees and flowering shrubs, its little rooms and hall, paper-windowed, perfect in proportion and design, its gaily painted wooden cloisters. And you approach them by a slum. A level, rational people—a kind of English *with* sensitiveness and imagination. An immense background, I admit, of ghosts and devils—just to add spice to life—one prays to them, when things go a bit wrong; otherwise one laughs at them. No reaches into the infinite; but a clear, non-restricted perception of the beautiful and the exquisite in the Real. But the hand of the Powers, or rather the foot, is on her throat, I don't know whether she can pull through. Said one of them to me: "The Powers put their foot on China and say 'Get up, you brute!' 'I'll get up,' says China, 'when you take away your foot!' 'No! You get up, and I'll take away my foot!' " The same gentleman remarked: "British rule in India is excellent—at water closets." This, of course, is *technically* incorrect. He was mad, but a madman of genius. He called at 3, and talked till 7.30, when I had to dismiss him—remarking, at intervals, "But I came to hear you talk"—whereupon he was swept away even more on the flood. Yes, China is much as I imagined it. I thought I was idealizing, but I now doubt it. Of course, Lama priests are sturdy beggars and Buddhist priests aren't much better. Then the country! Round Peking, it's Italy. You go out to the hills, and wander from monastery to monastery, each more exquisitely placed than the last. Happy people who have travelled in the interior tell even more wonderful tales. Hunan, Rose tells me, is a land of beautiful mountains, fields of flowers, and farmers tilling their own land who are also scholars and gentlemen. He told one of them about intensive methods of cultivating rice. And when they parted the Chinaman said: "You, a stranger, have come to us and honoured and delighted us with your talk. I shall consecrate to you a corner of my farm, and try the experiment you suggest." Then they are the *only* democratic people—in their manners as well as their institutions—perfectly self-respecting, perfectly courteous and friendly, and altogether declining to be hustled into doing anything they think unreasonable. If such a people could be lifted onto a higher economic level, without losing these qualities, we should have the best society this planet admits of. Whereas I believe *everything* in India will have to be, and ought to be, swept away—except their beautiful dress and their beautiful brown bodies—there they *do* score off the ugly but fascinating Chinese. But their caste! And their whole quality of mind. No, it's all wrong. C'est magnifique—mais ce n'est pas la vie, any more than the Middle Ages were. I'm rather surprised at all this that has tumbled out of my pen. I suppose the "Subconscious" has been working it up, unbe-known to me. Take it for what it's worth, and not too solemnly. It has truth in it—a little scintilla of that dry flint. Well, you did well in India. Does it seem like a dream, now you're home? I must get on to Japan before long, but plans are difficult to make. If you write, best address at 11 Edwardes Square. *Shall* you write a book on India? *I* shall *not*. I shall write a book of essays called "East and West", gracefully alluding, in a remote way, to facts.

G. L. D.

He does not mention in this letter that he had lately had a serious accident. He had gone out one morning riding on a pony, been thrown, and fractured the base of his skull. He was carried back in a dazed state to his hotel, bleeding from nose and ears, and the consequences would have been serious but for the promptness and skill of his friend Yetts, who was at that time Acting Physician to the British Legation; he is now Professor of Chinese Art and Archaeology in the University of London. Yetts received him into his own house, performed a slight operation, and he made a rapid recovery. In a week he was writing again, and before a month elapsed he was strong enough to make an expedition which may be regarded as the soul of his visit to China.

This was a pilgrimage to the home of Confucius. Leaving Peking with Dr Yetts on 17 June, he climbed, two days later, the sacred mountain of T'ai Shan. It was dusk when they reached the top. They slept in a temple, saw the full moon rise and the sunrise, and spent the next day wandering about. Moved by the beauty, freshness and antiquity of the mountain, he experienced once more the enhanced sensibility that came to him through scenery. Mistra had turned him to dialogue, the Yosemite had inspired him with the idea of interpreting America. On T'ai Shan his feelings were definitely religious. He desired to worship, like the thousands of pilgrims who had preceded him. To worship whom or what? He discusses this in *Appearances*. Writing to Mrs Webb at the time he says:

> The cuckoos calling to one another across ranges and ranges of hills, bare and gray, green in the sun. And me lying on top of the most sacred mountain in China, where for four thousand years God has been worshipped, according to Chinese legend; where certainly Confucius came, and emperor after emperor, and streams of pilgrims, year after year. A path lined with cypresses and flight after flight of rock-stairs brings you to the top. And there we slept in the temple with images of Taoist gods watching us and saw the full moon over the plain, and the sunrise. And I have had one of the great days that come now and again. I wish I could communicate it to you. But it evaporates in words, so I got this down to show I was thinking of you.

The same day he writes another verse rhapsody; the most touching of the series.

On T'ai Shan

Not for the young alone,
Cuckoo, voice of the spring,
Not for the young alone that liquid note:
But for all whom the years have freed
From the prison of youth and age,
To the one Life freed that is not old nor young,
The Life that on this spot
Thousands of years have adored,
Thousands of years and millions of men, as I now
    stand and adore,
While you, cuckoo, sing.

He descended from this altitude into rain and realism. They went on to Ch'ü-fou, where Confucius had been born, and where his descendant, the 76th Duke, still lived on a domain secured to him by the Chinese government. Their visit to the Duke had been officially arranged through the British Legation, but he slept, as so often happens in the East. His secretary asked them very politely to do their sight-seeing first, and Dickinson in his naïveté would have consented, but Dr Yetts saw they would "lose face" and he sent a message that they regretted missing the Duke and would retire. A friend of mine, only a year ago, found himself in an analogous position with an English Duke who had invited him to tea, and he sent a similar message, but his Duke sat tight. The Confucian Duke was more trammelled by etiquette. He knew that if the visitors went away in this fashion he himself would "lose face", and he immediately appeared fully dressed with his entourage—a handsomish rip of a man. An interview ensued, carried on amid much linguistic difficulty. How old was Mr Dickinson, why was he not married, why had he no beard, etc.? Then followed a symbolic incident: the offering of a copy of *John Chinaman*. What did the representative of Confucius make of the austere little volume? Not much. An attempt was made to explain to him that the writer was a distinguished western sage, and he was understood to inquire what present he might give the sage in return. Asked for a set of rubbings of the Confucian portraits and inscriptions, he agreed graciously, and after an interminable interval produced some raspberryade. The visitors then took their leave and Dickinson had his first and last experience of a Chinese inn. It was not too terrible, there were no vermin, and he felt happy. A great deal of time was spent in calling on and being called on by "the mandarin, whose attentions and courtesy were rather overwhelming in our humble shed", and who showed them over the temples and the great cemetery of the K'ung clan. The Duke's present has not yet arrived.

Homage paid to Confucius, he went on to Japan, going via Kobe to Kyoto. Japan was more of a treat than China, and he writes long happy letters home about its cleanliness and charm, and the gaiety and beauty of its people: "I really begin to look with horror on our civilization. I suppose I shall recant and settle down into it again. Anyhow I'm fit for no other." But it is China which dominates his memories. A collision had of course occurred between the ideals which he had been fostering for the last twelve years and the actualities, which included decay and mud. But the collision was not at all a severe one, and the picture given in *John Chinaman* continued, in its essentials, to satisfy him. Politeness, gaiety, imagination, good taste—these he found or thought he found. Dishonesty, dirt, immorality—these were disconcerting, but they did not strike at the root of civilization, like the commercialism of the West. As he climbed T'ai Shan and passed "the pavilion of the phoenixes", "the fountain of the white cranes", "the tower of the quickening spirit", and reached on the summit a gate called "the portal of the clouds", he must have seen the full flowering of that fancy in names which budded so shyly in England: speedwell, travellers' joy. And as he looked at the exquisite calligraphy on the mountain rocks and at the pavilions set up where the views are loveliest, he reflected what the West will do to T'ai Shan when it gets hold of it: funiculars and advertisements. If vulgarity brought peace to China it might perhaps be bearable, might not be too high a price to pay for the destruction of good manners and beauty. But no: with vulgarity comes organized violence, commercialism is followed by aggressive imperialism, the body as well as the spirit must be destroyed wholesale. With these melancholy thoughts, which the events of the following year were to intensify, he returned to England by the Trans-Siberian in the autumn of 1913. India had been impressive, Japan delightful, but China retained his heart.

During the war his interests became mainly European. After the Armistice and the establishment of the League of Nations he began to think of the beloved country again, and it is in connection with her, and with her alone, that his name has ever been the subject of discussion in the British Parliament. When the first Labour government was in power it appointed a committee to decide how the Boxer indemnity should be spent, and Dickinson, among others, consented to serve. The money was to be spent in the interests of the Chinese; and the phrase can be interpreted in various ways: it has in fact been interpreted as meaning that we ought to build military railways. He had other views; he had read much about the country, he had visited it, he had many Chinese friends, his qualifications seemed obvious. However, when the Conservatives came in they turned him and Bertrand Russell out and made two new appointments in their places. Since the Bill had not yet been passed, they were technically within their rights; still, it is, I believe, without precedent that one government should thus alter the composition of a committee established by its predecessor. On 17 December 1924, Mr (now Lord) Ponsonby asked in the House of Commons "what is the reason for cancelling the invitations . . . to serve on the Committee to be set up under the China Indemnity Bill?" The debate continued as follows:

> *Mr Austen Chamberlain.* The reason is that, on reconsideration, it was found that the composition of the Committee—the numbers of which it is important to keep small—was not sufficiently representative, and, in particular, that it included no member with practical experience of educational organization in China.
> *Mr Ponsonby.* Considering that these gentlemen were both very well qualified for the post which had been offered them, was this decision really only because of their association with the Labour Party?
> *Mr Chamberlain.* I am not anxious to discuss the qualifications of these gentlemen unless the Hon. Gentleman forces me to do so. I have given a sufficient reason, in my opinion, for altering the composition of the Committee.
> *Mr Riley.* Have any other persons who were appointed to serve on the Committee been excluded . . . ?
> *Mr Chamberlain.* No.
> *Mr Stephen.* Is this an instance of the class war?
> *Mr Buchanan.* I beg to give notice that I intend to ask leave to move the adjournment of the House on this question.

The Speaker ruled this out of order, and nothing was done. The Government was evidently determined to exclude Russell and Dickinson because they would have spent the money in the

Chinese rather than in the British interest, but it is surprising that it could not effect its purpose less clumsily. Dickinson's friends felt some indignation at the way in which he was treated, but he himself remained unaffectedly serene. Incapable of snubbing others, he was incapable of resenting a snub. He had offered his help and been rejected, and he passed on to other work.

In his later years when he was feeling the draught, which was often, he wore a little Chinese cap. The first of this series of caps was given him by his friend Hsu. Foreign trimmings do not as a rule suit the Britisher, but the little cap seemed natural and harmonious in his case even when it broke the line of tufted heads which compose the High Table at King's. The black silk of which it was made, the tiny red button crowning it, were a familiar and delightful sight in Hall, the best talk was in its neighbourhood and the talk never a monologue, it bobbed about Cambridge and reached London, it would be lost, found, trodden under foot, renewed. Never was a man less suitable than Goldie to become the subject of a legend: his whole career was a protest against that particularly silly form of fame. But if the legend-mongers ever do work him up it is on his mandarin's cap that they will concentrate, and perhaps they will relate how Confucius placed it on his brows in return for a copy of *John Chinaman*.

chapter twelve

The War and the League
1914-1926

For lo, what comes!
This blessèd isle with all its congregation
Of friendships made and making, this Elysium,
Whose willow-glassing streams and flowered fields
Invite to love and contemplation, this,
Which like a spirit sings in the cuckoo's voice,
Breaks into war, whose issue, win who may,
Is but defeat!

From King to King (1891)

I

Dickinson's feelings when the war broke out are best conveyed by an analogy: they resembled the feelings which arise when a promise has been broken by a person whom one loves. One knows all the time that the promise will not be kept, perhaps cannot be kept, yet the shock is none the less mortal. Though all his observations had convinced him that men do not live by reason, he hoped that they would be converted in the hour of trial, that conciliation would take the place of arrogance and trustfulness of fear, that the lion would lie down with the leopard from motives of self-interest if not at the dictates of religion, and that a youth would lead them. He had studied the English Civil War and the French Revolution and the contemporary Boer War and the disintegration of China, and in the case of China there had been the first shudderings of personal horror. But that modern Europe, including his own country, should fall into the Devil's trap—that he never believed, however much he may have maintained its possibility in argument. The shock broke something in him which was never mended, and when at the close of his life he again functioned he had evolved a new apparatus, not repaired the old.

How difficult it is to write about the sufferings of any one person under the war! One of the evil things about war is that it provokes a sort of competition in grief, and perhaps some readers will say with a sneer that Dickinson was only a sheltered don who went through no physical hardships and lost no dear friends. This is true, and he realized it, but it is also true that he was, in Shelley's words,

> a nerve o'er which do creep
> The else unfelt oppressions of this earth,

and that if his suffering is rejected as meaningless we can ignore the accounts of Jesus Christ weeping over the fate of mankind. There are two sorts of grief. There is a resentful querulous grief which throws the sufferer in on himself and makes him petty and tedious. There is a grief which expands towards the universal and generates action. Dickinson, like most of us, expressed both sorts of grief during the war, and did not avoid personal irritability and melancholy. But his desire to help others dominated.

He was at Cambridge during the final days of peace. On the evening of the Sunday he bicycled alone by Barton and Haslingfield, looking from a railway bridge at the sunlit meadows and the stream and trying to realize the unrealizable. Then he went by Hereford to Chipping Campden, where the Ashbees were still happily installed, and there he contributed to the *Nation* the first of his many war writings. It is called "The Holy War"; it is about the sacredness of reason, and it asks those who have loved reason in the past to defend her in her hour of need.

> The perfect weather continued, and the dumb impotent feeling of the gulf between nature, the past, all beautiful true and gracious things and beliefs, and this black horror of inconceivability that nevertheless was true. I had felt nothing like it since my mother's death; but this was infinitely worse. I was fifty-two; there was for me no question of enlisting, though I think I should have enlisted if I had been younger, for I was not a "conscientious objector", though I had no illusions about the war, nor anything but despair in my heart. I did, in fact, for a time oscillate as to whether I should enter the Friends Ambulance Corps under my friend P. H. Baker, but I decided finally, and probably rightly, that so far as there was anything I could do it must be of a different kind.
>
> I devoted myself, as far as there was any opportunity for such work, to propaganda for a league of nations.

The work which he achieved in this direction will be discussed later. As to his personal equipment for it, he was at a disadvantage, for the reason that, though he sympathized with pacifism, he did not think that the taking of life is, *per se*, wrong. He could not take up a religious attitude about bloodshed. He was condemned to the agonizing task of convincing the world by argument—agonizing, because he was fully aware of facts. He knew that he was unimportant, that he would be ignored by statesmen and soldiers, that he would be accused of weakening the national effort, that the young men whom he wanted to save did not for the moment want to be saved, but, war-mad, rushed to mutual immolation with the young men of Germany. All this he knew, and yet he could not put on the armour of "peace at any price" which protects its wearers not indeed from physical martyrdom but from many shafts which assail the spirit. He could only have come through if he was a strong man. And the more I consider his character the more I am impressed by its strength. He was morally wiry. To regard him as a wistful sufferer is to see only half of him, less than half. . . .

No doubt he needed sympathy and agreement. We all did. The difference of a hair could cause irritation in those nerve-racked years, and it was not only the sedentary who succumbed, but right up in the trenches the same poison seems to have been at work, dividing man from man in the so-called hour of national union. And since he could not keep his views to himself, for by their nature they had to be imparted, he often found himself severed from his friends. People who romanticized the Allied cause, people who romanticized the Germans, people who took the war lightly, all became alien to him; so of course did orthodox Christians, nor, though he admired the Sermon on the Mount, could he feel that that way was his. Here are some examples of his isolation. To Mrs Ashbee:

King's
4 November 1914

. . . I don't think however that I ought to write to you about the war. If you feel that there is a cause for it, other than mere folly and crime, you are more fortunate than I am, and I don't want to interfere. And again, if you can get some mystic consolation out of it, as some do, you are more fortunate. It would be easier to bear, and probably one would get the perspective better, if one were a young man who could serve, or had trained oneself for some function that might be useful now. But if one's whole life has been given up to trying to establish reason, and suddenly the gulf opens and one finds the world is ruled by force, and wishes to be so, one feels forlorn indeed, and more than forlorn. . . . I don't think I could stomach Cramb. I have read enough elsewhere of that revolting view of life. It cannot be answered. Those things lie too deep for argument. One is one kind of man, or the other.

The name of Professor Cramb has long since returned to its original obscurity. At that uncritical moment it was on everyone's lips. Dickinson elsewhere identifies it with the view that "peace is only a lamentable interval before the next war" as opposed to the view that "war is an evil and a crime, to be got rid of".

A few days later he writes again to Mrs Ashbee:

> No, my dear Janet, I did not mean to accuse you of being of the Cramb school. It requires a male to be led into such preposterous idealism. Nor have I any quarrel with your view of the causes, other than to note that we are here to resist, not to acquiesce, in these cosmic horrors. I don't mind what people *think* about the war so long as they are going to come down on the side of *working* to put an end to war. Do you prefer Oscar strenuous and dead, to Oscar charming and alive? But I don't want to enter into controversy with you. I am glad to know how you feel. And have too much respect for your judgement and experience not to think there must be truth in anything you feel.

He encountered another example of war idealism in Rupert Brooke. He had known Brooke at King's not as an isolated god-like figure but as one in a group of brilliant young men; Ferenc Békássy was another of them, who died on the Hungarian side. The following note, dated 28 October 1914, was written to him by Brooke from the Royal Naval Barracks, Chatham.

> I looked in at Edwardes Square one morning two or three days after I got back from the Antwerp affair. But you'd just gone to Cambridge. I was sorry to miss you. I hope you don't think me very reactionary and callous for taking up this function of England. There shouldn't be war—but what's to be done but fight Prussia? I've seen the half million refugees in the night outside Antwerp; and I want, more than before, to go on, till Prussia's destroyed. I wish everyone I knew were fighting.

A friendly manly note, but Dickinson must have found it difficult to answer. Apart from its implied invitation to himself, it emphasized the notion of the anthropomorphic State, the very notion which his own Holy War had to combat. Many of his friends, both young and old, felt as Brooke did, indeed most of them went that way. And in the opposite direction went the "pro-Germans", the little group who from gallantry, perversity or exasperation reversed the patriotic engine and made it function backwards. Here too he felt isolated. For instance, in the summer of 1915 he stopped with the Ponsonbys, who were extreme pacifists from his point of view, and who also differed from him in thinking that the war might have been avoided. They argued that Germany was not wholly responsible, with which he agreed, but they emphasized this so much that he showed up as pro-French in comparison. His fellow guest, Vernon Lee, became exasperated by his fairmindedness and complained to her hostess that he was "wrinkled with scruples", and he for his part sat silent when she poured forth fantastic diatribes against the Allies. Here too he must have recognized the anthropomorphic fallacy. Rupert Brooke and Vernon Lee had both abandoned the pursuit of reason, and the fact that they could respectively act nobly and were prepared to suffer for their faiths did not make his own course the less clear. He was condemned to follow the intellect in a world which had become emotional.

The line taken by orthodox Christianity in the war ought not to have surprised him, but did. He lets himself go on the subject in some letters to Leonard Elmhirst. Elmhirst, who had recently been at Cambridge, was at that time an earnest Christian, working with the Y.M.C.A. in France; he is now director of an important experimental community in Devonshire. Writing to him under the date of 6 May 1916, Dickinson says:

> I can well believe that your work with the troops is uphill. You will find, perhaps have found, that the fact of being officially connected with any religious organization cuts you off from all the decent English. They will not take their religion that way, and personally I think they are right. The Christian Churches will not I believe ever recover any influence nor do they deserve to. The greatest crisis in history has found them without counsel or policy or guidance, merely re-echoing the passions of the worst crowd. Civilization is perishing, and they look on passive and helpless. Not from such comes the inspiration men are waiting for. If there is to be a religion in the future it will grow up outside the churches and persecuted by them—as indeed is now the case at home. I write all this hastily and crudely, and perhaps unwisely.

In a previous letter to Elmhirst he says that the essential teaching of Christ now seems to him "sheer common sense and sanity, not the paradox I used to think it", but that he is still a follower of Socrates. He adds: "I don't think Socrates and Jesus Christ are enemies. Perhaps they are merely supplementary"; compare his remark to another friend: "I think Jesus acted quite rightly before Pilate, though not prudently, just as Socrates did when he refused to escape from prison. Remarkable men in their great moments are like that. The rest of us do what we can and wriggle out if we can." He felt, like many actual Christians, that Christ had been betrayed by the spirit of nationalism, and when he saw religion becoming frankly tribal, and the army chaplain taking no nonsense from the saint, he believed that it would never recover its spiritual kingdom.

One more of these specimen extracts shall be quoted. He could not take the war lightly and quietly, even for a week-end. His moral earnestness forbade him, just as his intellect forbade him to seek the solace either of patriotism or anti-patriotism or religion. This way and that, he was excluded from comfort. To H. O. Meredith:

> King's College, Cambridge
> 13 February 1918

My dear Hugh,

> It is of course true that I have shirked seeing you of late. That's because my nerves are all to pieces, and I find it hard to speak and behave with the necessary self-control. And anything is better, between friends, than constrained silences about what one's mind is full of, or futile talks. Of course if you *want* to talk, I will. But I put it to you that since we feel so differently it is not likely to lead to much. I am not referring of course to mere differences of opinion about political measures, but you take the war lightly and I take it as an unendurable tragic horror. We are neither of us to blame for this. But it makes it difficult to enter into sympathy pro tem. I'm not "drifting apart" at all for my own part, only lying low—wisely I think.

Except for two visits, to Holland and to America, he remained in England during the war, and as much as possible in London. There he had the sympathy of his sisters, and could sometimes see the friend from whom he was never alienated—Roger Fry. Cambridge only increased his sadness. All that he had cared for and worked for had vanished, and a grim obscene power took its place. I saw that obscenity for a moment myself, during a passing visit in 1915. It took the harmless form of some young Welsh soldiers. A solitary undergraduate in a cap and gown came round the corner upon them, and the soldiers naturally burst out laughing. They had never seen anything so absurd, so outlandish. What could the creature be? To me the creature was the tradition I had been educated in, and that it should be laughed at in its own home appalled me. My trivial experience symbolizes Dickinson's feelings. He saw the tradition he had loved derided by militarism, and by the hangers-on of militarism. No one defended it or even seemed to regret it, it had become a wraith which the next puff of gas would drive away.

To me, the worse kind of disillusionment was that connected with universities and historians. Hardly a voice was raised from those places and persons to maintain the light of truth. Like the rest, moved by passion, by fear, by the need to be in the swim, those who should have been the leaders of truth followed the crowd down the steep place. In a moment, as it were, I found myself isolated among my own people. When I say isolated, I do not mean in any sense persecuted. I suffered nothing in Cambridge except a complete want of sympathy. But I learned, once for all, that students, those whose business it would seem to be to keep the light of truth burning in a storm, are like other men, blindly patriotic, savagely violent, cowardly or false, when public opinion once begins to run strongly. The younger dons, and even the older ones, disappeared into war work. All discussion, all pursuit of truth ceased, as in a moment. To win the war, or to hide safely among the winners, became the only preoccupation. Abroad was heard only the sound of guns. At home only the ceaseless patter of a propaganda utterly indifferent to truth.

In 1916 Bertrand Russell was dismissed from his lectureship at Trinity because he had engaged in peace propaganda and been convicted under the Defence of the Realm Act. Dickinson felt this acutely, as a letter in the *Nation* shows, and the breach between him and McTaggart and others of his friends grew wider. He was disinclined to speak of such matters and I have never gathered a precise account of them, but his general drift towards loneliness is only too plain. It happened everywhere. It happened most obviously in the city which had once seemed the impregnable stronghold of friendship and truth. The *Recollections* continue:

I was still carrying on my work at Cambridge, lecturing twice a week in term. But my class was naturally composed almost entirely of women. Cambridge had become a hospital and a camp. In my college there was almost nobody left but a few dons and the nurses who were quartered in the building by the river. My sense of alienation from common opinion, my melancholy, and my clear sense of fact (for so I must call it) caused me to retire altogether from such life as there was in the place. I lived and ate alone, when I was in Cambridge, and saw almost nobody. The long winter evenings still linger with me.

135

Shut into my room, I seemed for a time to have shut out the world. My dim reading lamp, the rich red wallpaper, the flickering fire, were my background. It was there I used to think about [Oscar Eckhard].

Roger Fry remarks of him: "He had been far too optimistic and naïve in his conception of human nature before the war —he had no notion of how much a primitive and pre-logical mentality still survived in civilized man." I think that he had the notion, but refused to face its consequences. He had shirked the horrors of crowd psychology, and Cambridge was now compelling him to view them in surroundings where he thought they could not occur. But he never abandoned his fundamental hope for humanity. He fought, all through the war, for the spirit of reason in human affairs.

2

It is possible that Dickinson invented the phrase "League of Nations"; it is certain that he was the first person in this country to formulate the idea. In the opening fortnight of the war, while he was at Hereford, he jotted down on a piece of paper two schemes for such a league, and when he returned to London he went round to a few people who might be interested, and formed a group. He claimed no credit for this priority and effaced himself as soon as the idea became fashionable. At the time it was suspect, and the general opinion was voiced by his brother Arthur, who writes to him that "the only organization now called for is an anti-German league". The secretary of Dickinson's group was Richard Cross, an able Yorkshire lawyer, who drafted the scheme, and without whom "I doubt whether we should ever have come, so to speak, to a point". Other prominent members were his namesake W. H. Dickinson (now Lord Dickinson) and J. A. Hobson. Arthur Ponsonby also attended, but was opposed to the proposed sanction of force, which figured among the group's recommendations. Graham Wallas, though in general sympathy, was more concerned to press international cooperation in general than their particular scheme for preventing war. Two of the meetings of the committee were attended by Lord Bryce, and, since he was the first person of public eminence to countenance the organization, it is known as the Bryce Group. It ought to be called the Lowes Dickinson Group.

The Bryce Group is only one of the tiny streams which finally

Gibbs's Building,
showing stair-
cases G and H.
His earlier rooms
were on the
ground floor to
the right, his later
over the archway.
Photo by
permission of
Country Life

Age 58. At Brighstone, Isle of Wight. *Photo by courtesy of Peter Savary*

fell into the Lake of Geneva, but its course is interesting, both to a biographer of Dickinson and to the League historian. It did much to shape the Covenant of the League, one clause of which (that defining the disputes generally suitable to arbitration) was directly taken from its proposals. And it did still more to shape public opinion. In 1915 news of it reached the original members of the American League to Enforce Peace and encouraged them to persevere at a critical moment. The two societies kept in touch during the war, to their mutual benefit. Their respective proposals, together with the proposals of other groups, will be found in *The Framework of a Lasting Peace*, edited by L. S. Woolf.

Dickinson's activities soon took him abroad. Foreign travel into neutral countries had not yet been blocked, and in the spring of 1915 he attended on behalf of the Bryce Group a small international meeting of pacifists at the Hague. Writing to Ponsonby, just before sailing, he says:

11 Edwardes Square, Kensington
2 April 1915

Dear Ponsonby,

Thanks for your letter and enclosure. I'm sorry your constituents are so intransigent. I never realized before how war makes men mad. During the Boer War I took no part in political controversy and hardly realized the atmosphere. One could easily despair; but that is always a silly and feeble thing to do. In fact one's voice, I think, has value beyond the intrinsic, so comforting it is to find in print any expression of decent feeling and sound judgement. What disappoints me most is the collapse of Labour as a force for good. With the exception of the I.L.P., which I gather is numerically weak, the working men lie down and let the *Times* have it all its own way. I'm afraid our working class is the most ignorant and stupid in Europe, at any rate where foreign affairs are concerned. Ilbert's letter is interesting. What he says about Prussia and Russia is more than probable, granting a continuance of the old diplomatic game.

Nearly everyone who has replied about our proposals is in general and platonic agreement, but there aren't many useful suggestions. Our worst enemies are really men like Brailsford and Hobson, who go for a federation. They won't get that: but they may easily help to prevent our getting what we ask for. Always "le mieux est l'ennemi du bien", and so men fall back frankly on the simply bad.

My kind remembrance to Mrs Ponsonby. I go to Holland on Sunday night. I fear I shall be the only Englishman there.

G. L. Dickinson.

He was right in thinking he would be the only Englishman, though a Member of Parliament, J. A. Baker, turned up at the end. Germans and Austrians attended, also several neutrals. At this meeting the Society for a Durable Peace was founded, in whose "minimum programme" was a resolution in favour of a League of Nations, which he drafted. He brought the Society into general accord with the Bryce Group. No further international meetings were possible, for the belligerent powers began to tighten their regulations, and prevented a meeting at Berne, but a number of papers were published, three volumes of which have been collected.

> On my return I was confronted by a statement in the press that Mr Baker and myself had gone to the Hague with the approval and under the commission of Sir Edward Grey. This, of course, was quite untrue. But on my return I had an interview with Sir Edward, explained what we had done, and showed him our resolutions. He expressed no objection to these, but of course I foresaw that the kind of peace we wanted would become impossible by the mere fact that there had been a war. For that matter, I myself always knew that I was engaged on a forlorn hope, but saw nothing else on which I could engage with conviction.

The main object of the Bryce Group was research and study. Meanwhile another group came into existence for the purposes of propaganda, and Dickinson joined this also. Presently the two groups were coordinated, and on 3 May 1915 the League of Nations Society was formally constituted. Various alternative titles for the Society were discussed, such as "World Union of States", "Union of Nations", but it adopted the phrase which was soon to be so familiar. W. H. Dickinson was the chairman of the committee, a membership of several thousand was built up, Lord Shaw was finally secured as president. In connection with its propaganda Dickinson went to America on a lecturing tour.

He had thought of this tour as early as 12 February when he had gone with Ashbee and Laurence Housman to talk to Sir Edward Grey about it. As in the case of the Hague expedition, Grey expressed no disapproval, and seemed content that the idea of the League should spread, though the time had not yet come for official protection. He did not sail until January 1916. It was his third and last visit. He was coming now not to spread culture or study conditions, but to plead for civilization, and the knowledge that the Old World had failed made him more tolerant of the New. He travelled out with Ashbee, also an enthusiast for a League. They carried on board with them the wreckage of a still more utopian scheme in the shape of the members of the Henry Ford Peace Expedition, who had just been over to Europe to ask the war to stop. The war had made no reply, and they were returning to their native shores, minus Henry Ford and not greatly abashed. Their conceit, crudity and superficiality were typical of the America Dickinson knew, but so was their idealism; they were children with the hope of children.

The diary of this tour consists of a few pages of scribble, recording his journeys and lecture engagements. From the beginning of February to the end of April he seldom slept twice in the same place. Keeping in touch with the American League to Enforce Peace he made a tour of universities and other institutions in the East and the Middle West as far as Kansas and Minneapolis. He found the upper classes sympathetic to England and anxious to enter the war, especially in the East. In the Middle West there was no idea of taking part and a general sense that it was another of the fool enterprises of Europe. To H. O. Meredith:

Minneapolis
31 March 1916

I expect to leave this country on April 15, and be "home"(!) some ten days later, barring a merciful target. You wouldn't be interested in what I have been doing here. But touring the colleges and universities has at any rate kept me from over much brooding. I like the Americans much better than I ever did before. They are, at any rate, human and kindly, and if they're uncultured and crude, at least they haven't got a false culture. However, it looks as if they will be in the bloody business directly, and then of course they will be as violent as Europe is. The college professors are much more tolerant and free-minded than the similar herd in England. And they are human beings, which most of ours aren't. Of course they have no influence to speak of. Colleges are an investment to Americans, and educate only as a means of getting on. And in this country if you're going to get on you must have a college education, and almost anybody can get it. They work their way through, at incredibly little cost. Perhaps after all I shall end my life in this country. No place in Europe will be endurable after the war. However, I may as well keep off all that.

From the *Recollections*:

The comparative sanity of America at that time, the mere contact with people who were not war-mad, was a refreshment to me. But how superficial and transitory that state of feeling was, was shown a year later, when America came into the war, and, according to all accounts, precisely the Middle West was the most intolerant and savage part of the country. The intolerance and cruelty of England was bad enough during the war. But anything that happened here pales into insignificance before what happened there. A modern democracy is a mere cloud of dust, and blows any way the wind blows.

On returning to England he continued to work with the League of Nations Society, which made steady progress among humble and unimportant folk, and brought together the very few men and women in England who thought of anything beyond winning the war. He lectured in little schoolrooms, generally to small audiences—meetings too obscure to excite opposition or attract notice. He was in touch with another body, definitely suspect by the authorities, the Union of Democratic Control, which, under his friend E. D. Morel, became involved in an attack on allied propaganda. Dickinson and the Society he represented held that such an attack, though justifiable, was unwise, and that though the Allies, as well as Germany, were to blame for the origin of the war, it was quite useless to say so at the present juncture. He writes to Morel (25 February 1918) "My deliberate policy is to say all I can without provoking a reasonable reader. This may be bad propaganda. But it is me, and I can no other."

Caution is relative, and in 1917 a new body came into existence which regarded the League of Nations Society with much the same wariness as the Society itself regarded the Union of Democratic Control. This was the League of Free Nations Association. Its members were for the most part good haters of Germany and people of importance and influence, who had plenty of money behind them and knew how to run a campaign. The idea of a League was becoming reputable chiefly owing to President Wilson, and it was possible to support it without loss of public credit. And Wilson's advocacy—so intricate are the threads—was due to that American League to Enforce Peace which the Bryce Group had encouraged two years before. This way and that, Dickinson saw his deeds coming back to him.

He and his fellow workers of the League of Nations Society had now to decide a most puzzling question: should they or should they not join forces with the League of Free Nations Association? The Association was willing to have them on conditions, but did not wish to be compromised by their pacificism. It desired to form a provisional League of Nations amongst the Allies at once before the war was concluded. Dickinson was

strongly opposed to this, since it would make the ultimate in-
clusion of Germany more difficult, and might even alienate
neutrals. There was a good deal of "to and fro" as he calls it,
and some mutual suspicion. The problem was finally solved in a
truly English fashion—over food. The executives of either organization appointed representatives to dine at the National Liberal
Club. The Society sent its Chairman W. H. Dickinson, G. L. D.,
J. A. Hobson and L. S. Woolf. The Association sent C. A.
McCurdy, Gilbert Murray, Wickham Steed, H. G. Wells. The
dinner was a success, the representatives liked one another, and
discovered no real obstacles to fusion. Rules were drafted and the
present League of Nations Union was formed under the presid-
ency of Sir Edward Grey. It represents the union of two smaller
streams—the Society and the Association; the Society derives in
its turn from the Bryce Group, and the Bryce Group starts right
back in the uplands of 1914, on the half-sheet of paper which
Dickinson drafted in the first fortnight of the war.

It is unnecessary to describe the negotiations for the union in
detail. Here are two letters which give the general atmosphere.
The first is to Mrs R. C. Trevelyan, who feared that the Society
was selling its soul, a fear shared by other supporters, notably by
J. A. Hobson and Lord Parmoor.

12 October 1918

Dear Bessie,

This business of amalgamation has been and is a great worry, but I
think suspicion on both sides has played an undue part in it. It is
quite clear that either the L.N.S. must amalgamate, or it can play
no effective part at all. For the other association knows how to carry
on propaganda, and we do not. After seeing and discussing at length
with the representatives of the other society, I think that really they
want what we want; certainly some of them do, especially Murray
and Wells; and I think even McCurdy. Their literature is bad, from
my point of view, and they have committed themselves to the policy
of the "league now", which has been turned down by Wilson, and
yesterday by Grey, who is to be our president. I think, as things are
now, that policy, though they may continue to run it (partly out of
obstinacy) is damned and done. On practically every point Grey said
the right thing, and I think we must trust to him and to "our"
element in the new society to keep things fairly straight. I hope therefore you will not look with too jealous an eye on the amalgamation,
though of course I understand your fears. It was a splendid manifesto
yesterday. Even the overflow meeting overflowed. I am still playing
the game [i.e. chess on postcards] with Bob. He seems very happy at

present. What about you? Are you? Are you staying on at Shiffolds? So glad Julian is happy. What a relief for you. But I fear you must be feeling very lonely. I almost dare hope for the end now, but we have so often been cheated of it.

G. L. D.

The second letter is to H. G. Wells, with whom he became very friendly as a result of these negotiations. He had a warm admiration for the *Outline of History* and Wells's work generally, and considered him one of the most important educational influences of our time. He is here commenting on a draft agreement which Wells has forwarded:

King's College, Cambridge
25 October 1918

Dear Wells,

I am here at present, and shall not have an opportunity, until next week, of consulting those of my colleagues who take exception to the paragraph in question, in its present form. If we are to arrive at an agreed draft, in this way, I must reserve a final opinion until I have talked to them. Meantime, as far as I am concerned, there is only one sentence in your draft to which I should take serious exception. It is the sentence "and make reparation and amends for the crime of the great war". I have two objections to this, which I do not think obstructive or unreasonable. First, it does not seem to me a matter for a league of nations society to prescribe punishment for the past. We are concerned with guarantees for the future, such as are sufficiently indicated in the rest of the draft. Secondly, the sentence is too vague and comprehensive. I should approve, if it were practicable (as it may be), the setting up of an impartial court of international justice, to try those accused of definite offences against the laws of war. Such a court, of course, would have to receive charges from *any* belligerent government against nationals of *any* other. But I strongly object to even the appearance of countenancing the kind of indiscriminate revenge against German towns and women and children which I have heard advocated by individuals, and which appear to be contemplated by many organs of our press. I expect you agree with me about this, and I should be glad if you could secure the deletion of that clause.

Mr Keen has also drafted an alternative paragraph, and he will perhaps wish to submit his draft after consultation with others to your committee or to whatever sub-committee you may have appointed.

I think it should be noted (though you may think this criticism rather academic) that the phrase "peoples whose collective will is embodied in the decisions of their government" quite obviously and definitely excludes Japan (whose constitution, in letter and in practice, is as autocratic and militarist as the constitution of Germany was until the recent changes). It would, I suppose, also exclude China, and I am strongly of opinion that China should be a member of the League. These difficulties however are inherent in any limitation such as Wilson himself has put forward, and we must hope that consistency will not be pushed too far. It is, of course, the fact that at present no one is thinking of anything except Germany, and that public opinion will exact the kind of statement embodied in the draft.

You see then that I have only one strong objection to your draft, but that I wish to be free, after consultation, to submit for your consideration an alternative draft, if that should be desired by other of my colleagues. No delay, beyond a day or two, will be involved. I find myself, so far as I can judge from our meetings, in very close agreement with you, personally, on what I regard as the fundamental points, and I am very glad that this should be so.

Yours very truly,
G. LOWES DICKINSON.

I suppose I am right in understanding that the passage at the beginning of the original paragraph about forming the league now is definitely dropped out? That was the point of my opposition, and I understand that policy to be definitely repudiated by Wilson and also by Grey.

There are of course awkwardnesses of expression in the draft which you yourself could amend better than anyone.

When the League of Nations Union was formed, he became a member of its executive council, but presently resigned. The idea was now well launched, he disliked committee work, and his taint of "pacifism" kept him in the background of an organization which was and indeed had to be respectable. He lectured when asked to do so. He received no recognition for his work and did not desire any. But those who had worked with him knew what he had achieved. At the time of his death his namesake Lord Dickinson wrote to his representatives:

He and I worked in very close cooperation during the period when he was laying the foundation stone of the League of Nations. I well remember his coming to my chambers in September or October 1914 to take counsel how the war might be made to serve the purposes of peace, and a little later he set up his committee for studying the question of a League to which Lord Bryce gave his name as President. Lowes Dickinson did the main part of the work of that Committee and it was due to his industry and courage that the scheme took shape which ultimately became the Covenant of the League. Too little was known of this, for he was modesty personified and when others took the work over he quietly dropped out of sight. But, nevertheless, the League of Nations owes its birth very largely to his idealism.

3

Dickinson's war writings date and were intended to date. He was never much tempted to address posterity, and on subjects such as war and peace his sole aim was to form contemporary opinion. With the possible exception of *The Choice before Us* all that he wrote between 1914 and 1918 is likely to be forgotten.

Two pamphlets, *The War and the Way Out* (1914) and *After the War* (March 1915) come first on the list of publications. The first-named attacks the "governmental" theory of Bernhardi and his school: that states are the only realities and that they are natural enemies of one another. The second exposes the futility of crushing Germany, and discusses the formation of an international league to establish and maintain peace. Disassociating himself with regret from the extreme pacifists, he admits that such a league will require the sanction of force. The two pamphlets appeared (substantially) in the *Atlantic Monthly* in America, and they were reissued there as a single pamphlet.

The European Anarchy (1916) heralds both in its title and its scheme his great work *The International Anarchy*, which was published ten years later. *The European Anarchy* is a short historical survey of the events which immediately led to the war; like all his writings of this period, it ends with practical suggestions and advocacy of an international league.

The Choice before Us (1917) is a more considerable work than its three forerunners. The longer Dickinson thought on the problems of the war and the League, the more copious and persuasive became his writings. His range of illustration increased; so did his power of re-statement. He will put the same argument again and again in a slightly different light, which, in the world of propaganda, is the only method which drives an argument home. Statement is useless, repetition useless. Even today *The Choice before Us* impresses the reader by its subtle variations. A man, not an automaton, is speaking of militarism and of internationalism, its two contrasted themes; of a league of nations; of the necessary sanction of force; of the necessity of democratic control of foreign policy. It was written at a moment of tension, just before the occurrence of two events which cheered him up for a little: the Russian Revolution and the entry into the war of the United States. The title suggests that mankind has come to the parting of the ways, and a sort of religious solemnity is achieved. A friend of mine read this book at an impressionable moment (he was just leaving school) and he was converted by it to opinions which he has never lost.

An Introduction to *Problems of the International Settlement* (1918), an Introduction to *Documents etc. Relating to Peace Proposals* (1919), and *War: Its Nature, Causes and Cure* (1923) may be mentioned here. And he became a prolific journalist, as the bibliography at the end of this book will show. The *Manchester Guardian*, under C. P. Scott, was his most influential mouthpiece. He contributed constantly to the *Nation*, then under H. W. Massingham's brave and brilliant editorship, and attended its weekly lunches. He was on the editorial board of the *Cambridge Magazine*, where he could express himself more freely than elsewhere, if to smaller audiences, and he often wrote for *War and Peace*, afterwards the *International Review*. In America the *Atlantic Monthly*, the *New Republic* and the (New York) *Nation* welcomed him.

It would be interesting to know how bad a bad mark stood against his name at the War Office as a result of all this activity, but censorship in England, then as now, worked as much as possible by suppression and as little as possible through open prohibition. He had reason to believe that *The European Anarchy* and other writings were prevented from reaching the troops, but he could not be sure. He did know that his name was on a list (31 March 1917) of people whose works were forbidden to be exported to Norway, where they would have come before the Nobel Committee of the Norwegian Parliament. This suggests that the censorship flung its net wide. A net with a characteristic rent in it, for the list humorously assigns him the initials of his patriotic brother Arthur instead of his own.

Attacks in the press were not infrequent. The *Daily Mail* did its duty, and on one occasion the *Morning Post* consecrated a leading article to him. He had been speaking at an educational conference on the educational basis of internationalism, and had roused the newspaper's wrath; the article notes with satisfaction that animals fight with one another, deduces from this the necessity for modern scientific warfare, calls for a "national school of English history" and concludes: "The writing of history has been left too much to gentlemen like Mr Dickinson, who have been so carefully screened from the present that they do not understand the past."

Dickinson replied in the following letter (15 January 1918):

My attention has been called to an article in which you comment at length upon your reporter's account of an address delivered by me at the Educational Conference. It would serve no useful purpose, even if space allowed, for me to enter into controversy with you upon the fundamental issues which divide me from you. But perhaps you will give me the opportunity of stating, to those of your readers who may have any interest in my views, that your comments are a mere travesty of anything I have ever felt, thought, or said.

As a rule he never replied to personal attacks. If they were on trivial points he felt them to be negligible, and if they were connected with important public issues he was anxious not to complicate the argument.

4

As soon as the war ended, Dickinson's spirits improved. The people whom he most loved were back, and the League of Nations seemed making a good start at Geneva. I stopped with him at Lyme Regis in the spring of 1919. We had not met for three years, so there was much to say. He was looking older and worn, but he was gay and chirpy, we took long walks, bowed to Jane Austen, played chess at the same level of badness and piquet under conflicting rules. He is said to have been the world's worst bridge player. May one allude to improper jokes in a memoir? Several were made. The world seemed settling down into its lost armchair for a moment's rest. My memories of Lyme Regis are rather vague, and one is apt to drill one's memories into a consistency facts do not justify. Still the impression is happiness, hopefulness, clouds lifting. The re-appearance of the *Athenaeum* under Middleton Murry's editorship was one of the things which cheered us up. Here at last was a paper which it was a pleasure to read and an honour to write for, and which linked up literature and life.

Perhaps this is the year when I went to a dinner of old Kingsmen, and the Dean of St Paul's proposed his health and rallied him with somewhat bilish gaiety on being a prig. Anyhow this is the place to record his reply. The Dean said that he admired Mr Dickinson's English style but was dismayed to find at the end of one of his dialogues that a character, whose priggishness had sorely tried him, was intended to voice the author's own opinions. The sally was not quite a happy one, but Dickinson put everything right when he rose to give thanks: he recorded the days he and the Dean had spent together at Cambridge, and particularly their games of tennis "when words, sir, would fall from your lips which did not lead me to suppose you would reach your present position". There was laughter which the Dean did not endorse. Here, too, is the place in which I would like to insert another scrap—though it is a scrap behind his back. The scene is Cambridge itself, the period early post-war. "Why don't you fellows chuck Lowes Dickinson into the Cam?" growls an adjacent schoolmaster to a friend of mine who had had a distinguished military career. They are bicycling together peacefully, and my friend shouts "More likely to chuck in you" with such violence that the adjacent schoolmaster almost falls off. I am glad that he did not quite fall—it would have been subtly unsuitable—just as I am glad that the words which did fall from the Dean of St Paul's will never be known.

While we were at Lyme Regis he was working on *The Magic Flute*, the most original of all his books if not the most perfect. It came out in 1920. It repays a debt. He tries to express in it all he owes to Mozart—"Marsyas to Apollo" the dedication says— and he mingled in his gratitude problems of which Mozart never dreamed. The slight pantomime of Tamino and Pamina is exalted into a mythology of Wagnerian scope. Can Mozart bear so much? Can the Fire be our war and the Water the doubts of the twentieth-century spirit? Can the castle of Sarastro symbolize the modern mind? It seemed to me that Marsyas had bitten off more than Apollo could chew, but Dickinson would never admit that. Anyhow, what a lovely book! May one make a direct appeal in a memoir? I intend to. I urge anyone who has not yet read *The Magic Flute* to read it. It is the writer's chief incursion into the kingdom of Ariel which had been shown to him when he was an unhappy child at school. Forty years in the world of matter had weighed him down but had neither broken nor tarnished his wings. These remained; and if an image in the style of Blake were permissible here it would picture the "soul of Dickinson" as unable to fly, because it had laboured too long in the service of humanity, yet knowing more about flight than those happier beings who rise easily upwards until they are lost to us and to one another in the blue. *The Magic Flute* has its faults. Read it and forget your own.

This seems the best place to introduce an account of an excellent verse play, called *War and Peace: A Dramatic Fantasia*. It is earlier in date than *The Magic Flute*, for it was written before the war started, but the two works are emotionally related. *War and Peace* was never published, and it is too topical to interest an audience of today, but it has invention, wit, action, colour, and it displays very movingly the feelings which Dickinson was soon to express in more permanent form. It opens with a prologue before the Gate of Heaven, and with the arrival of Violence and Futurist in an aeroplane. They wake up Peter, and learning from him that the Family is away induce him to let out War, a mighty monster with a dirty loafer inside it. Scarcely have they gone when Reason and Cynic arrive on a second aeroplane and demand Peace. Hitherto the Father has refused to release Peace, and the Son has restrained War, and since the Holy Ghost does not vote there has been an impasse in heaven and neither war nor peace upon earth. Peter lets out Peace to equalize matters, and the first act of the drama then opens in the Fair of the World, with the nations of the twentieth century trafficking. Violence has arranged War in a box at the back, and provided him with placards such as "Yellow Peril", "French Menace", "Entente Cordiale", "Indian Unrest", "Ulster Will Fight", which are exhibited as the action proceeds, and accelerate it. Violence takes various forms—Salisbury, Carson, Larkin, a Militant Suffragette—but just as the dance of death is at its height, and War bursts out of his box, the second aeroplane arrives, and Reason enters.

The next act is a brilliant debate, with the nations as audience. Reason and Violence summon their respective witnesses. Reason's first witness is Economist, who pops up in cap and gown with a barometer. He can only register, he never concludes. Violence summons Tariff Reform, habited as an Archdeacon, and the two argue. They are not convincing, and the bewilderment of the audience is increased when both Shakespeares are called up. For there is a Shakespeare on either side, one for war, one against, and each quoting from *Henry V*. Then Reason evokes Shelley, but no one can hear what he says; India and Hibernia catch murmurs, and Italy and France dream of their past, Ulster hears nothing, John Bull nothing. Reason then soliloquizes:

> What shall I do? I speak in my own tongue,
> The mathematical, and they laugh at me!
> I speak in verse, they say they cannot hear!
> Most that's in Man's below me. Yes. But something
> Must be above me! Something! What, and where?

He unwisely seeks the support of science, whereupon a pair of sociologists jump up. The first, who is on the side of Violence, is dressed as a priest, and urges the human race to procreate, lest, by control of population, they fall into the power of Peace.

War and Religion, heavenly pair,
Twin constellation, fierce and fair,
Oh cover with your sheltering wings
The dangerous source where knowledge springs.

Reason's sociologist follows and betrays him. He argues that war is caused by hunger, and can be prevented by a plentiful food supply. But his enthusiasm for science leads him up through Danish eggs and Brazilian coffee to the wireless and the cinema and the radioactive bomb. This conclusion is greeted with applause by the assembled nations, and the cause of Reason seems lost. Now comes the crisis. Reason summons his last witness— Passion; the head invokes the heart. Violence exults, for Passion is always on the side of war, and he joins in the dithyrambic invocation, but when the discords resolve it is not into a military march but into the choral movement of Beethoven's Ninth Symphony. Passion has enthroned Peace. What one may call the spiritual construction of the drama is excellent. How it would act is another matter. The prologue was once performed by puppets in Roger Fry's Omega Workshops for the benefit of Belgian refugees, but I did not gain from that any idea of the work as a whole.

There is another mystery play among his manuscripts, *The End of Man*, which is of the same date as *War and Peace* and teaches the same lesson. There is also a pleasant unfinished dialogue of post-war date between some statues round a pool, which was suggested to him in the garden of his friends the Morrells, near Oxford. "It occurred to me at Garsington that spirit and matter are the two sides of the bellows of life," he writes to Lady Ottoline Morrell. "They blow out the wind but they never touch naturally and they are always moving in different directions." Was the dreamy fanciful aspect of his character re-emerging? Were his anxieties about civilization at an end?

5

The Magic Flute, unlike *War and Peace*, ends on a note of interrogation. Reason and Youth have proved their worth, but the victory remains undecided, and it is with a heavy heart that

Sarastro retires to his castle. He could give the Queen vision, but she cries: "I want no vision. I love the night." This pessimism is significant. For the happier mood of 1919 soon passed and the next few years were the saddest he ever knew—sadder than the war years because they did not provide him with such definite work. His friends were all resuming their old jobs or interesting themselves in new ones. Fry was painting, Schiller at business, McTaggart at philosophy, Wedd and Grant teaching, while as for the young men all they wanted was rest and amusement and they were not the least inclined to rise in their hundreds and demand a new world. He complains to Ashbee (14 January 1920):

> Cambridge has resumed precisely as before the war or more so. No change of outlook is visible in young or old. Just tradition reasserting itself, equally the good and the bad. Men are plainly incapable of experience, which, as Oscar Wilde remarked, is an instinct.

With a bad Peace and an unsatisfactory League on his mind, he could not understand such levity, nor always distinguish between levity and resilience. In another letter to Ashbee, dated the following year, he refuses an invitation to Palestine with some tartness; though the "bar" referred to was soon lifted:

> I find it rather difficult to write to you when every letter of yours treats me as a kind of imbecile needing "cure" (from Jerusalem of all places!). Perhaps if you were at home you wouldn't think it so foolish to be preoccupied with the parlous state of Europe. At any rate the difference in our interests is rather a bar to correspondence.

The same feeling of tension appears in this letter to Leonard Woolf:

> King's, Cambridge
> April 1923
>
> Dear Leonard,
>
> I should like to write for the *Nation*, if only to get a little money, but I don't know whether I shall be able to. Henderson sent me Papini's book, but really I can't handle such tripe; a sort of sentimental sliming over a quite unreal Jesus. How religious people spoil even their gods! And through the mist one seems to divine in Jesus a really remarkable man. I will do Forster's book however. Only there again is the difficulty of writing on a personal friend, a situation which leads us Cambridge people to underestimate virtues and gifts for fear of being too partial. Oh dear, I wish I could think of *anything* to write on, or any way of writing, but this damned state of Europe keeps my nose on a peculiarly unpleasant grindstone, and the only result is that one's nose wears out, and the grindstone doesn't. As I am here now,

I shall hardly get up to the Labour International Committee. I hope that will not disqualify me, for I particularly wish to continue a member.

I have been rereading *Jacob's Room*. It's full of good stuff, probably better stuff than I know, and beautifully written. But the disjointed effect still worries me, though I realize the point of it. Hope you both enjoyed Spain. I shall in fact be in town next week, for two days, and attending that conference about Europe on the 9th.

G. L. Dickinson.

To his concern for Europe, he added a more personal melancholy. He had for many years been offering affection where it was not needed, and the knowledge that he had made a mistake and was in a sense blameworthy sank into him and saddened him. He writes to me that he must be "almost the only man who has ever lived with whom no one has ever been in love": an extraordinary remark, and not the less depressing because it was untrue. Later in his life happier relationships awaited him, but he was now passing through a dubious autumn, when the leaves would not fall from the trees. At moments he felt that nothing except the movements of the heart have any value and that his own had oscillated uselessly between yearning and disappointment.

Worse was to come. While he was in this mood of mistrusting himself and the world, he suffered a terrible blow in the death of his sister Janet. Janet has not often been mentioned in this biography for the reason that few letters were exchanged with her, but she was constantly in his thoughts. She had led an active practical life. Like May, she shared his love of music and his political outlook; all three sisters were in heartfelt agreement with him throughout the war. She was taken seriously ill in the autumn of 1923. Most men are inadequate in the presence of illness and become hysterical and irritable when it continues; Dickinson, so sensitive, might have been expected to react in this way. But his sensitiveness was always at the service of his love. As soon as he realized that it would comfort Janet to see him constantly, he gave up his Cambridge life and came to London, and he visited her every day from November to the following March, when the end came. There is, of course, no external test by which affection can be measured, yet one cannot help comparing this steadiness with the conduct of the so-called "strong man", and wondering where strength lies. On this account his sister's death has to be mentioned, and also on account of its lasting influence upon him; he had never worried much about his own fate, and now he became still freer from personal fears. He wrote to me the following day:

> Up to the last, she was fully conscious, and one might almost say happy. She had no fear and some kind of unshakable faith that it was all right. . . . I think she was an almost perfect spirit. I say "almost" because those words are so insensitive, after all. She was full of humanity and therefore of the little frictions of humanity. But there was a sort of overshadowing beauty which took charge completely. These last weeks I got very close to her and that I know was a great joy to her, as it must always be happiness to me, so long as I am capable of thought and feeling.

In the *Recollections* he says:

> I used to read to her, sometimes some of my poems, which it appears, though I did not know it, she had always liked and read and reread. . . .
> Always thinking of other people, her friends. . . . She asked whether she would get better, for she did not want to go through it again. May said: "No that would be too cruel." She said: "Oh, nothing is cruel. But I know what you mean." She spoke of dear God and was sure she was going somewhere safe. No fear, no complaint. She said to me how good it had been to get so close to me. Surely a spirit made perfect. Yet I do not *believe* though I do not *disbelieve* that anything remains.

Can one speak of death without becoming affected? Goldie seems to me to have that rare gift. He can state his grief without exhibiting it, and without the understatement which is another form of self-consciousness. Janet's death convinced him not of immortality, but of her belief in it. He felt henceforward that if there is a key to the universe something surprising will be revealed. However, that wasn't the point. What she had really done for him during those four months was to reveal additional goodness on earth.

Mrs Lowes's husband had died the previous year. After Janet's death, she and May decided to live together. They finally took a flat in Beaufort Street, Chelsea, which was to be the last of the long series of his London homes.

6

Since he had helped to evoke the League of Nations, he naturally followed its movements intently—movements so cumbersome and so involved that they gradually reduced him to despair. The new machinery installed at Geneva bore little resemblance to the ardent desires and generous hopes for a better Europe which he had brought to birth among humble audiences at home. He did not object to its size, but had it any purpose? Was it benignant? Might it not be a "dangerous façade" concealing from ordinary people the indifference and the cynicism of their governments? Above all, would it work quick enough? "I should not mind the League moving slowly if events didn't move fast," he once remarked. As the end of his own life approached he felt more and more that civilization must hasten if it wants to be saved. He had the impatience and the irritability of the political theorist, and the impression he made on officials at Geneva during his frequent visits was not altogether favourable. They realized better than he did the dangers of hurrying. Their perspicuity has not helped us! He may not have been right, but they have proved wrong.

His feelings about the League varied. This letter to May records an early visit.

Geneva
10 September 1922

I am more hustled than I have ever been. Today, being Sunday, I have had the morning for an article to the *Manchester Guardian* (a little less hasty than one's wires) which I am sending by post. It's an awful business, as there is Assembly in the morning, the committees, and no end of people buzzing round, and no time to reflect or get anything right. Everything in Assembly is repeated both in French and English, which is a waste of time I am not sorry for. But as everything is printed very quickly, one might almost as well not be there! I find Reuter is also reporting to the M.G. which makes it difficult for us to know what to send and what not. I am really impressed by what the League does within its powers, but of course it is mostly complicated and continuous and does not lend itself to quick grasping or reporting. The great thing is that people of different nations have to sit together and give account of their actions or their governments'. When dinner engagements are added to all the work it becomes really desperate. However, I suppose I shall get through, and endeavour not to fuss. I have had to take veronal twice, which I don't approve of and must endeavour not to repeat. But if one doesn't sleep one is a rag next day. Moorsom is a great comfort, so helpful as well as so cheerful. He is off however for the week-end walking somewhere, and of course it has come on to rain.

At this date he is definitely hopeful, after 1923 he begins to get sceptical, partly owing to the League's failure over Corfu, and partly owing to an experience of his own. In 1927 he became again hopeful, thanks to the admission of Germany, but then came the aggressive policy of Japan in the Far East and the League's inability, from whatever cause, to protect his beloved China. He did not live to see the withdrawals of Japan and of Germany, but he had witnessed enough to write in his *Recollections*:

> Sooner or later a crisis with a Great Power is bound to arise, and then we shall know whether the League will face the music and win. I think the most likely thing is that there will be no declaration from the Council of who is the Aggressor (the British Government, by repudiating the Protocol, has rejected the only complete definition of an aggressor) and that the members of the League will range themselves on opposite sides.

Only in the case of a comparatively small problem (such as the threatened Greco-Bulgarian conflict) was the Council prepared to act effectively—in other words to act quickly. As soon as powerful interests were involved the machinery slowed up.

To his mind the most urgent question before the League was the treatment of Germany. He held the opinion—and it is an opinion which was once common among Englishmen —that when a war is over it is at all events over for the victors, and that no further punishment need be imposed. Moreover his cultural sympathies were German rather than French: how could he condemn as barbarous the country of Goethe, Hegel and Wagner? He paid a short visit to Berlin in 1920, largely under the auspices of the Quakers, and the misery he saw there among the educated and professional classes made a deep impression on him. So did the sinister atmosphere. "The most terrible city I ever saw," he writes to May: "all *planned* (not muddled into like London) and planned without a sign of heart or feeling. It's really typical of the capitalist militarist epoch." He hoped that the Germans were going to react against the brutality in their tradition, and he knew that they would only react if they were treated in a civilized way by the French and others. Their misery was the most pressing of the evils to be righted at Geneva.

He only once took an official part in League affairs. It was in July 1923, when he served on the Committee on Intellectual Cooperation, and a significant incident occurred. This committee had been appointed by the Council of the League. Its chief duties were to examine into the state of learning and culture, and propose measures of relief in distressed areas. Professor Gilbert Murray, the British member, was unable to attend its second session, and Dickinson acted as his deputy. He at once disconcerted his colleagues by raising the question of establishing contact with Germany and of helping the German universities. The name of Germany was mentioned as seldom as possible at Geneva. She had not yet joined the League, and many of the members had suffered from her during the war and were disposed to withhold relief from her, if possible on high philosophic grounds. And, as if he had not shocked them enough by mentioning her, he went on to suggest that an immediate appeal for funds should be made in America and elsewhere. He urged that the situation was critical, that it concerned not only Germany but civilization as a whole; clearly he felt that here was a test as to whether people were willing to meet a human need in a field which ought to be non-controversial.

The president of the committee (Henri Bergson) thereupon rose with his accustomed tact and said that there was no question yet of appealing for funds; the committee must continue to examine into the state of learning, and he particularly deprecated any appeal to America; it was without precedent, and might lead to criticism both of the League and of the committee. Dickinson replied that if the appeal was an innovation it was one which he would welcome. He was next told that it would be very difficult to help the German universities because they were state-owned, but this did not wipe out from his memory the starvation he had seen in Berlin. Unable to silence him, the committee then became every inch a committee and set to work to draft a set of alternative resolutions on the lines of his own, but less drastic and more open to interpretation. These he accepted, confident that at all events something would be done for Germany. He took little further part in the debates of the session.

The incident had a sequel. After his return to England he received in due course a list of the national committees which had been set up in the various countries under the auspices of the League for the purpose of intellectual cooperation. Nearly every country, distressed or not distressed, was on the list: Austria, Belgium, Brazil, Bulgaria, etc. But Germany was absent. He was furious and believed he had been tricked. Gilbert Murray shared his indignation and wrote a strongly worded letter to *The Times* pointing out that the omission of Germany was bound to bring discredit on the League. He himself wrote to the *Manchester Guardian* and also corresponded with M. de Halecki, the secretary of the committee on which he had served. M. de Halecki apparently rebuked him for writing to the press and asserted that though Germany was omitted from the list there was no intention of discriminating against her. Dickinson was always at the top of his form when rebuked, and he replied: "I do not of course question that you had no intention your circular should produce the effect it does produce, and if public correspondence should bring out clearly the fact that funds for Germany will be accepted by the Committee, nothing but good will have been done to your objects." The episode left him with the suspicion that ill-faith, as well as timidity, lay entrenched at Geneva.

In spite of his growing doubts he continued to support the League. He saw no other alternative to anarchy, and he felt that, if men like Lord Robert Cecil and Sir Arthur Salter believed in it, it must be good. Also he realized, during his frequent visits, that the permanent secretariat was almost unconsciously acquiring an international attitude, and this cheered him. He usually stopped with Elliott Felkin of King's, who was working in the secretariat with Salter. Occasionally Dickinson acted as correspondent to the *Nation* and to the *Manchester Guardian*. Between his visits he was constantly writing to Felkin on points connected with the League. One of these letters shall be quoted in full, to illustrate the closeness with which he followed events. The document on which it comments is "the Protocol for the pacific settlement of international disputes of 1924". This Protocol had attempted to close what is known as "the gap in the Covenant" by providing an automatic test for defining aggression. It was rendered useless by the refusal of the British to sign it—a refusal to which reference has already been made (page 154).

King's
5 November 1924

Dear Elliott,

Many thanks for your letter and enclosures. It's really extraordinary how difficult it is to ascertain what any official document means. You say, e.g., and it seems to be borne out by the resolutions of the Assembly 1921, that "it is the duty of each member of the League to decide for itself whether a breach of the Covenant has been committed". But on turning to the amendments supposed to carry out these resolutions of the Assembly one reads "it is for the *Council* to give an opinion whether or not a breach of the Covenant has taken place", which seems flatly to contradict the other. However, that is not the immediate point. So far as I can see, the Protocol is *formally* watertight in its provisions for preventing war: for apparently, even in the case of "domestic questions", if one Power seems inclined to attack, or does attack, the Council can instantly impose an armistice and then the party not acceding becomes the aggressor. The argument that the Protocol would not *work* therefore seems really to amount in fact to saying that some states would break their agreement. I am far from disputing this. But it strikes at the Covenant as much as at the Protocol. I see, now that we have a Tory Government, that this blessed country, after affirming its love of peace, etc., will be the one to wreck the Protocol, to which even the small states opposed to the treaty of mutual guarantee and the incorrigible France have come round. Truth is, the British really can't bear not to be able to make war when they want it—adding, of course, that they never could want it, and never have wanted it, except for the sake of "justice", "liberty", "right", et hoc genus omne. If Curzon is to be Foreign Minister, I should prophecy war with both Turkey and Russia in a very near future. If on the other hand—quod est impossibile—they were to make Cecil Foreign Minister? But no, they couldn't. . . .

I work continuously at my book on pre-war diplomacy, but without any idea that it is much use. No one will read it, and if they do no one will profit. However it keeps me occupied, and in an odd kind of way (rather morbid) interested. There are some nice young men here as usual, and I am contented enough, though rapidly approaching old age and losing my memory.

Yours,
G. L. D.

The book referred to is *The International Anarchy*, at which he was working during his Geneva period. Perhaps the sense that history was repeating itself helped to disillusion him with the League. But he remained at the service of the League of Nations Union. Here is a letter telling May about a lecture at Cambridge in 1926.

My lecture went off all right. There were about 150 people including an admiral and two generals. The admiral was charming, the breezy kind. I having remarked that no doubt most soldiers and sailors regarded the League as "tommy rot" (the nearest I dared approach to the probable language) he said, "The phrase 'tommy rot' does injustice to the British Navy. The real language is of a kind I can't repeat, but infinitely stronger." He dotted all my eyes [*sic*], and said afterwards he could not think how I had discovered so much of the truth! The general, or one of them (the "junior service" as he remarked bowing to the admiral) was less candid and made an effort to pretend soldiers were pacifists. Of course he could cite one or two. I asked him if he personally knew any who were, and the answer was silence. The other general didn't talk, but asked intelligent questions I didn't know the answer to.

This pleasant letter reminds me of the mess room at Peshawar fourteen years before, when the delighted officers made him swallow the prairie oyster. The date of it is significant; in this year *The International Anarchy* is published and the final period of his life begins.

chapter thirteen
The International Anarchy
1926

The war, for Dickinson, ended not with the Treaty of Versailles but with the publication of *The International Anarchy*. That was the date when he established a truce in his own heart. He could do no more against the powers of evil, he had no new weapon in his armoury, he knew that if he attacked again he would become mechanical, hysterical, non-human, an automaton repeating arguments without waiting for the replies, and shrieking peace peace through a megaphone. Some critics will say that he had worn himself out with worry. Others, more discriminating, will say that he had worked the poison of the war out of his system by producing a big book on it, and could now settle down to a cheerful old age. Both are wrong—the first because they ignore the vitality of his last years, the second because they ignore the melancholy mingled with the vitality. He had not come to the end of his powers, but he had with merciless honesty surveyed them. He had always been clear-sighted. In his youth he had settled down to be a don because it was the best career of which he felt himself capable. In his old age he forced tragedy into the background because he could not handle it fruitfully any more. He was not complacent, and it would be an error to round off his career complacently. Churchill, Mussolini, Hitler, Gandhi and other menaces to peace still exist and he never forgot them.

The International Anarchy is important both in itself and because it initiates this truce. At the time he began to write it he was in the deepest gloom, which he has recorded in a long manuscript note, dated 30 October 1921:

> Through all this chaotic horror I find one thread running which seems to me true and beautiful; that is, the activity of the Quakers. Wherever in Europe is trouble—and where is there not?—these few men and women are to be found, talking little, doing much, bringing relief to Germany, Austria, now to Russia, while the big guns talk and do nothing. That is one way of life which is clearly good. But it is not my way. I set myself at the beginning to discover all the truth I could

and to state it. The result is meagre enough: perhaps it is less than nothing. But I have no other path. I do not know whether this frame of mind will persist to the end, which may be yet several years, or whether it will lighten and clarify. Meantime, since I can do nothing else, I have settled down once more to the pre-war diplomacy, with the idea that perhaps I might yet write something that would be of use.

For the last few days I have spent most of my time reading dispatches. It is dreary work enough, but there is a kind of dramatic interest in it, to see this catastrophe approaching, to see everyone afraid of it, yet everyone hoping to profit by it, to see how inevitable it is while the European system prevails, and how necessary a complete change of system is, if mankind is not to move quickly to its final destruction. . . .

Everyone around me, all my best friends even, seem to have settled down to live as before, pleasantly, cynically, or whatever may be their attitude. I, almost alone, arise and go to bed with the constant obsession, is there to be a continuance of the old, to the new war, or a radical transformation? The pain becomes almost unendurable, and I can only stave it off by plunging into some kind of work, which yet must bear upon it.

The work of preparation was formidable. Some preliminaries had been done in *The European Anarchy*, but now he read all the diplomatic documents, including the new matter published by the Soviet Government. He tried out some of the material in lectures at King's and at the London School of Economics, and found it rather intractable. He writes from Cambridge to Elliott Felkin (10 February 1922):

I'm lecturing here on pre-war diplomacy, badly I fear, and with much labour to myself. The stuff of course is damned complicated and it's very difficult to arrange and make clear and interesting to the ignorant. Besides why does one? This little fly, shaking a remote corner of the spider web of the universe, must look absurd to an onlooking Spinoza-god, who likes to feed the spider. So long, and may what we call society last long enough for you to run a happy course.

This is an unusual mood in which to settle down to four or five years' research. The book produced at the end is remarkable from two points of view. Remarkable in the first place for its learning, logic and lucidity. It has mastered and digested all the available facts, has given an account of the pre-war diplomacy which will never be superseded, has shown how that diplomacy was bound to produce war, and will produce war. Remarkable in the second place because it contains no exhibition of emotion. The violent feelings which agitated the writer, the indignation and irritation, the sorrow and despair, are suppressed, lest they endanger his appeal. He refuses to show his readers how much he suffers, in case they are diverted from the facts and discount the argument. And so, paradoxically enough, *The International Anarchy* ranks high as a work of art. It is supported by an intense emotion which is never allowed to ruffle the surface. It has the quality which, working through another temperament and in another medium, has produced Bach's fugues.

This quality becomes plainer if we compare it with a book which seems more artistic at the first glance: *The Magic Flute*. *The Magic Flute* deserves the praise given to it in a previous chapter. It is serious, profound, inventive, fanciful, beautifully written. But it has one defect: as soon as it describes war the writer's emotions get out of control, and we have him lamenting or denouncing instead of creating. He wrote it too near the events he was trying to exorcise. The war had to sink deeper into him, its causes and its consequences had to penetrate more elaborately, before he could attain the agony which is serenity and write *The International Anarchy*.

The writing of the book is contemporaneous with his visits to Geneva and the League. At last it was accomplished, and on 2 June 1927 he concludes another remarkable work, the main version of his *Recollections*, with the following words:

I have published (last November) my big book on the origins of the war. . . . I know that this is a good book—I believe it to be possibly the best book on the subject; because it is the only one I know which stresses the only important fact, that it is not this or that nation nor its policy, but the anarchy, that causes wars. The book was considerably and favourably enough reviewed, but it has not sold as much as a thousand copies. Another testimony to the general truth that truth is the last thing people care about.

Meantime I have been occupying myself largely with the translation of *Faust* which Miss Stawell and myself have been working at, and which is now complete. It has been, and is, an infinite relief to me to deal with a mind so sane and so great as Goethe's. But we have not yet found a publisher for our book, and I anticipate the usual fate for it. I don't seem to care much now. I am getting very old and have little left to do but to keep myself innocently occupied so long as I can, or must. I still enjoy myself much and often. This term in particular Cambridge has been so lovely in the almost perpetual sunshine that it has been enough to be alive and look at it. And still the young men exercise their perennial fascination, the few I know, who are certainly also fit.

He has written a book which he knows to be good and which might save Europe if its lessons were heeded, and under a thousand copies of it have been sold. As in the business of the Boxer indemnity, two years previously, he has been brushed aside. Practical men don't want him. He retires without bitterness and without self-consciousness into his castle, and the Queen of the Night continues her genderings beyond mind.

chapter fourteen
The Truce
1926-1932

The rooms in Gibbs's Building, G staircase, which Dickinson occupied for the last twenty years of his life, had been decorated under the advice of Roger Fry, and I remember them as the most beautiful college set I knew as well as the best-beloved. They were above the arch of that Jumbo House which has previously been described. One room, crimson-papered, looked into the front court, through the great semicircular window. There were two of Fry's pictures here—an early portrait of Ferdinand Schiller, and a landscape of Taormina, ridge beyond ridge and Etna behind. The second main room looked over the Backs. Its walls had a grass-paper of gray-green, and on the floor was a Chinese carpet, featuring four thin pale-purple dragons on a biscuit-coloured ground. Besides the bedroom, there was also an attic, with a little circular window up in the middle of the pediment. Here Dickinson sometimes slept, and anyone who came into college late could see the small round eye of his light—the highest habitable point in King's.

Almost a century earlier another eminent Kingsman had occupied the set—Charles Simeon, the evangelical divine. Simeon's elderly friends had found the climb to the second floor tiring, so a handrail had been placed for their convenience on the staircase, and it is still called "The Saint's Rest". Painted chocolate, it leads upwards, through ghosts and draughts. The staircase looks built for eternity, so solidly it stands, but a few years back the death-watch beetle was discovered throughout Gibbs, and there was a fear that the upper dons might fall through onto the heads of the lower. This was averted, and during the repairs the colour of Dickinson's front wallpaper was changed. For me, however, it remains crimson.

Though he had occupied the set for so long, it seemed to become his own in this final period, when he had done what he could for peace and might retire to his castle and wait. In the vestibule, like weapons at rest, lay the documents he had used in *The International Anarchy*: "books more for gentlemen really" as a bedmaker rightly remarked. Books were everywhere, but he had a serviceable rather than a valuable library, and was never a bibliophile. The pictures, the Chinese objects, the honourable family furniture, made a stronger impression than the books. The atmosphere was hot: gas, electricity, cosy-stoves, valor-perfection lamps, sizzled and roared. He was determined to get comfortable, why not? and his plaintive appeals mingled with those of other dons bent on a similar ideal and poured into the ears of the Bursar. He succeeded. There was even a bath which had, in the end, no need to be filled with kettles off the ring; there was even that rarest of all academic birds, a W.C. The mixture of luxury and hardship so characteristic of Cambridge retains no charm for a man who is approaching seventy. It is the privilege of the young.

But was he approaching seventy? When his friends argued, as they sometimes did, whether he was very old or very young, they had no doubt about the superlative: he was certainly neither rather old nor rather young and he might be approaching seventeen. His appearance at a distance; his air of discouragement and fatigue; his bad memory; his occasional petulance; the garrulity which would pour out an account of the book last read, the play just seen—all these suggested a man at the term of life. Then, in a flash, he seemed younger than anyone, his mind more elastic, his gestures more natural. His sympathy, in particular, had the quickness of youth—that was what made it so precious. And his judgement—thank goodness!—was sometimes at fault. He never acquired that canniness about character which is so depressing in the mature. Although he was shrewd about historical evidence he could blunder over his acquaintances, because he accepted them at their own valuation. If you went up to him in his rooms and told him you were virtuous and able and poor, he would for a time believe you; your merits would be extolled, your qualifications advertised, your wants relieved. And even when he found you out you retained the right to be a bore. He was generous— in every sense of the word—and as the years passed his generosity got more instinctive. Heaven knows what he gave away in cash; and his other gifts which could be more easily discerned were so spontaneous, they fell onto the recipients before they knew where they were.

One hesitates to call him "a popular don", for the words suggest some cheery empty creature. He never tried to ingratiate himself with the young: he was too modest and also too proud. When they returned to Cambridge after the war, he felt out of sympathy with them, and when the change took place, and both young and old wanted his company, it would have annoyed him to be told he was a success. I remember watching a perky undergraduate ferreting about in his books and him saying to me gently: "I don't know his name—he calls me Goldie." This expressed a general relationship. The younger generation entered, scarcely knocking at the door, and called him Goldie because they forgot his age and their own.

Another undergraduate, whom he came to know well, has written an impressionistic sketch of a first visit. I will quote from it. Date about 1930. I compare it with my own early memories of Winchester cutlets, and find it in every way superior to them. "Liebling", as he calls himself, is pounding up G staircase with no thought of "The Saint's Rest". He bursts in and:

a musty smell as of a world silted up with unwanted books met him at the door and a hot air rushed past him down the staircase and out into the cold strenuous winter world where it perished quickly, and Liebling rubbed his feet cautiously according to directions then paused uncertain which of a variety of doors to choose. "Come in" cried a distant voice and through tobacco smoke past seated figures stiff and monumental past a large table eager with knives forks tumblers wine glasses he went up to an old mandarin or perhaps it was the holy Larmah seated on a large padded chair with a book rest and a great iron stove in front of him which was roasting everyone in the room except the mandarin who seemed accustomed to the most intense heat and heard a quiet kind voice that never flowed exactly in periods yet was never harsh or frightening say "So glad to meet your father's son, how do you like King's?"

I don't quite catch the words of greeting, but the heat, the big table, the doubts on arrival are all authentic, as is the banquet which develops:

Food was carried in in large silver plates the mandarin grew nervous and excited as to whether it had really all come could so little food possibly feed so many guests and with his gesture he indicated vast hungry hordes hanging on the outskirts of the table, more silver dishes were brought in, more sausages floating, no reposing on soft beds of mincemeat, like a cockney in his bath, were uncovered steaming, what are they drinking the Larmah asked, and obediently guests became unstuck, moveable, manly, corks popped cider frothed over even the Chinese student began giving advice sausages and mincemeat were conveyed to their final destination the Larmah seemed satisfied somehow the hungry were fed only a miracle could really explain it, the tension relaxed the conversation began.

Various topics occur, such as birth-control, do reformed sinners make the best schoolmasters, are there compulsory chapels in China. Finally:

They don't mind dying much in China, do they? shouted Liebling to the Chinaman, hoping to introduce a story he had heard about how one could buy a substitute to be accepted for one. "Always dying" said the Larmah "millions by starvation flood plague at this moment so thick on the ground." That explains why they believe in meta-morphosis don't you think said the clever student confidentially to the Larmah. "May be its true for all I know" said the Larmah shaking his hands towards the two remaining sausages reposing on their cold beds of mincemeat, and just for a moment Liebling was quite certain that in the whole world there was only this funny old man sitting in front of two cold sausages saying I don't know my dear boy, and feeding the starving.

Then the second course comes in—an enormous apple pie with cream—and Dickinson characteristically tries to change all the plates himself. Everyone jumps up to help him, and the vision closes.

Besides undergraduates, dons, and constant visitors male and female from London, my own vision of those rooms includes some college servants—more particularly his bed-makers Mrs Newman and Mrs Richardson, Mrs Asplin, and his gyps Rose and Fuller. It surprised him that people who went to and fro and had not even a permanency of masters should be so loyal to the college; among his Cambridges, the Cambridge of dependents was never forgotten, and he was always active on its behalf at college meet-ings. Not that he was always tactful with his entourage. His innocency bordered on social rashness. He would call out "Again no slop basin? Your memory's as bad as mine!" or he would use up all his tea, forget he had done so, and inquire "Wherever can it have gone to?" The entourage, on its side, had to do a good deal of clearing up and searching. He was not practical, and I can still hear him damning his sleeve-links in the morning because they wouldn't go in, or his hot-water bottle at night because it puffed in his face when he filled it. He swore constantly, and no wonder. For he was unhandy with "so-called inanimate objects". They were always splashing or scalding him, or beating a merry retreat at the moment he needed them most. "Here you are, yes of course," he would say, lifting a sheet of paper, and there beneath it, after the locksmith had been sent for, would be the bunch of keys. It surprised us after his death that all his papers should be in perfect order, until we remembered his unselfishness and independence; he had spent the last weeks sorting and docketing, so that if the end did come his executors should have the minimum of trouble with his affairs. His will was both thoughtful and affectionate, and the names mentioned earlier in this paragraph are recorded in it among his other friends.

As regards college administration, he was conscientious rather than active. He was diffident at meetings, and he put what he had to say clearly, but not forcibly. Besides being a member of the Congregation, the governing body to which all Fellows of King's belong, he was sometimes elected to the Council, and he was invariably chosen to be a Fellowship Elector, and a member of the Tribunal. He had strong opinions about the development of the college estates, and when it involved the destruction of natural beauty, as it sometimes did, he was not easily appeased. Nor did he favour throwing open the grounds of the college for military parades.

Outside King's he had various interests, as was natural in view of his long residence. He was a vigorous member of the Cambridge Preservation Society, and he was for a time President of the Council for the entertainment of foreign students at Cambridge. In London he was a Fellow of the Royal Society of Literature. The list of his little honours might be extended, but I am unwilling to make it sound important, for he was not interested in posts or in having letters after his name. What he cared for was love and truth. What he hoped for was a change in the human heart. He did not see how the civilization which he had tried to help could be saved unless the human heart changed, and he meant by "saved" not some vague apotheosis but salvation from aerial bombing and poison gas.

Let us follow him now from his rooms, down the sloping lawn, over the bridge, through the avenue, across the Backs, and let us leave him in his outdoor home.

In Fellows' Garden, 4 May 1928:

Yesterday and today sunshine and lovely May weather. A great thunderstorm Wednesday cleared away the clouds at last. I have been sitting in the garden this morning browsing partly on Goethe partly on Rylands's book, *Words and Poetry*, partly on the flowers—the cherries past their best but scattering white snow on the grass, tulips yellow red and white, irises, bushes of pyrus japonica, all dazzling in the sun. Beauty becomes more precious as it is more precarious for me. One takes the moment—"verweile doch du bist so schön". I saw clearly this morning that Goethe is a seer rather than a poet. Never I think has he the magic of words as Shakespeare had and so many English poets (any German?). But he sees everything and sticks it down . . . and what clearness of visual impression . . . and good songs and good ballads, where simplicity is everything and freshness and genuineness . . . and how profound and human, e.g. "Gott und die Bajadere", also read this morning. How brave and unmorbid, how Chrĭst-ian (not chrĭstian), how continually and persistently wise! And at times how great in lyrics—as in the close of the classical Walpurgisnacht.— The young men in The Orchard yesterday at tea apple blossom everywhere—and on the river, as lazy and lovely as ever—also, being English, as unconscious and unimaginative. This too happens in the world, and I take off my hat to it.

2

The books written during these years of respite all have roots in a pre-war world. The studies on Goethe and on Plato both go back to the innocent and unblockaded Germany of 1884 and to the Heidelberg pine woods. The life of McTaggart evokes the Cambridge of the 'eighties and 'nineties where he had found McTaggart, Fry, Wedd, Schiller. The dialogue *After Two Thousand Years* goes back to the same Cambridge, city of friendship and truth, Elysian Field where the old man who is eternally young converses with himself under the semblances of Plato and Philalethes, and it also goes back to Mistra, Greece visible, birthplace of Euphorion, where the inspiration of writing in the dialogue form first came. It was not until his political work had been concluded by *The International Anarchy* that he resumed his earlier allegiance to imagination and poetry. His last books do not by any means retreat into fairyland, but they do escape from the struggle with facts and from the enumeration of facts which had occupied him since 1914.

Goethe and Faust: An Interpretation (1928) was written in collaboration with Miss Melian Stawell. It is mainly Miss Stawell's work, and he would have had this stated on the titlepage but for her resistance. She had finished a rough draft with which she was

Kings Coll Ca mb Dec 8

Dear Julian

I ve been reading your poems I have always thought
that you were the oneman who might be a pote among theose of
the younger generati n I happen to have read   certainly
t nk so t he more now. There is one poe towards he end in
particular marsh birds pass ober L ndo which impressed and
moved me very much. But the are all interest ng and there I
ex ect one s hould stop. But wil ne ertheless add that I th
th n k you try to much to do in petyr what only painting
cando owever all t is close observatio and record is no
d ubt much mor hopeful and promising than the usua outpour
ing of i mature emoti s sympathetic thoug I am to this lat
ter. nd hakespeare certainly began like that. The other
sma   point s that I thin k y are to fond of the device o
adjecive at the end of one ine and noun at the beginning of
the next I su p se you do it for the sake of stress But som
how think it has become ra her a trick. Howver th point is
that I thin you may be a poet and wish you all good speed
Your departue t the country f r which o doubt y u have goo
reasons has rarher cut y u off from my ken t oug not from
m y affections

Letter to Julian Bell, 1930

Age 69. Wearing Chinese cap. *Photo by courtesy of N. Teulon-Porter*

dissatisfied and had asked for his help, since she knew that he had returned to *Faust* after the war. His function was mainly that of a critic and a condenser, though they discussed every point and attempted a common style. Miss Stawell has given me a list of about forty passages in the book which are entirely his: they include the description of the opening of the Second Part (pages 118–22), and the comparison between the final heavenly joy and the finale of the Fourth Act of Shelley's *Prometheus* (pages 256–7). The translations are hers—except for some of the Mephistopheles items. The book is a competent sensitive guide, and it should become popular if an interest in Goethe ever revives in this country. Miss Stawell and he also completed a translation of both parts of *Faust*, which remains in manuscript. Furthermore he broadcast on Goethe. His idea was that a renewed study of Goethe at this crisis of our history might lead to a new advance, and he was delighted when men of the younger generation— Robert Nichols for instance—encouraged him. On the whole he received little encouragement. The British public remains cold to the colossus, however tactfully and enthusiastically he is presented. Possibly now that Germany has raised the cry of "Deutschland ohne Goethe" we shall begin to read him, but not in the spirit which Dickinson enjoined.

After Two Thousand Years: A Dialogue between Plato and a Modern Young Man (1930) is one of his finest books. It pays its double tribute to Plato and to Cambridge, and the superb passage of prose with which it ends has an oratorical splendour which shuts out daily life. But it is coloured by recent experience, for it is the result of his friendship with the post-war generation. It reveals his ability to learn from the young. We can all like the young, envy them, and fear them, but to learn from them is more difficult. The conceit of experience, the pride of established position, get in our way, and if we do learn we hope they don't notice it in case it makes them uppish. Dickinson was above all such pettiness, because he was in a state where the years do not count: Plato enters into the young man's outlook in order to develop his own, and he himself is as much the young man as he is Plato. The book—which incorporates part of a manuscript dialogue—is more intimate and frank than most of his publications. He seems to be liberated from conventions which have hampered him, and can discuss easily and quietly such subjects as love between people of the same sex, or the artificial control of population. The first half of the dialogue is concerned with the means towards a good life, the second with the good life itself. "Yes, the book is my testament and I can now say 'Nunc Dimittis'," he writes to Robin Mayor. He hopes "to clear off the memoir of McTaggart and I should like if there were time to do something about my father for our own satisfaction", but the serious work of his life is over.

Next year the loyal and affectionate tribute to McTaggart duly appeared. He was not well satisfied with it. Various friends had contributed chapters or paragraphs at his request, and these, however excellent in themselves, blurred the main outline. Moreover, the complexity of his own emotions may have confused him. His intense admiration for McTaggart, their war differences (which McTaggart chose to regard as mystically non-existent) and their tacit reunion after the war did not make for literary detachment. McTaggart was a remarkable figure, possibly a great man, certainly a very strange one, and, biographically speaking, such a man needs rather ruthless handling if he is to come alive. Dickinson only brought sensitiveness and piety. It is a pity that he could not go on to the projected memoir of his father. The relationship there, though less intimate, was probably more amenable to his treatment.

The other two books, *Plato and his Dialogues* (1931) and *The Contribution of Ancient Greece to Modern Life* (1932) were offshoots from other activities. The *Plato* enlarges some excellent broadcast talks. He was a good broadcaster and his gentle husky voice came through well. Besides the talks on Plato and Goethe, he introduced and closed a series called "Points of View", and contributed to the series called "What I would do with the World". The interest he aroused showed that a larger public was awaiting him. One day I came across a man in a train who had been listening to "Points of View"—a series which included Wells, Shaw, etc. He was half clerk, half sailor, and wholly un-academic, and he said that the speaker he really did like was the one he had never heard of before—someone called Low Dickens. I was not surprised. I had always known that Low Dickens existed inside the lengthier designations of the don.

The pamphlet on ancient Greece in its relation to modern life was a reprint of a lecture delivered to a summer school. It was published a few days after his death. He was due to broadcast on the same subject in the autumn of the year, and one of his anxieties when he went into hospital was that he might be inconveniencing the B.B.C. officials who had engaged him.

3

I end with several letters. Letters have to pass two tests before they can be classed as good: they must express the personality both of the writer and of the recipient. Dickinson's letters pass the first test but not the second. When he writes, he is always himself —interesting, thoughtful, sympathetic, never failing in comfort or counsel. But there is not the final touch of magic in virtue of which the recipient, as it were, shines through the paper upon which the words are written. It is a magic commoner in talk than in writing, and even in talk many people fail to achieve it, and say their how d'ye do or yes in tones unvarying. And one would not even look for it in his letters, were he not so sensitive and selfless. He, if anyone, might be expected to reflect the unseen features of his correspondents and to echo their inaudible heartbeats. I do not think that he does; to be precise, the personalities of his two great women friends, Mrs Webb and Mrs Moor, have not come out clearly through what he writes to them. Except for the differences in the subject-matter, what is addressed to the one might have been addressed to the other. When he spoke to his friends or spoke of them all altered at once; he vibrated to wave after wave, and as he turned his head from guest to guest at one of his lunch parties one felt that a new universe was seated on every chair. That was his strength, that was his glory, and if that could be communicated in a biography he would appear for what he was: one of the rarest creatures of our generation. His letters are a misleading substitute; they tend to exhibit him as merely sympathetic and kind.

These later letters are much the best. They are fresher and more translucent, the meditative whirlpools are fewer, and they have a quickness of movement unusual in a writer of his age. Moreover, many of them are written to the young, so that they show what he signified when he was in his sixties to correspondents who were still in their twenties and thirties. Their manners are perfect. They don't condescend or chirrup or instruct, nor have they that uneasy ingratiating note which spoils the communications of many well-meaning old men.

They are typed; and the typing is even more remarkable than the handwriting which it superseded. He is said to be the only man who could make a Corona type upside down. He struck the keys rapidly and violently, thinking of what he thought and not of what he did, with the result that he doubled lines, halved them, threw capitals in the air, buried numerals in the earth, broke out into orgies of ?????? or %%%%%%, and hammered his ribbon to shreds. George becomes "Geroge", Gerald "Gerlad", perhaps "perhpas", and there are even happier transformations such as husband into "humsband", and soul into "soup". A semicolon in the middle of a word means "I". When the page was finished he had by no means done with it. He seized his pen and frantically coursed to and fro, correcting, connecting, obscuring, exclaiming "oh dear!" or "damn" in the margin. So charming was the result that his friends could scarcely believe it was unintentional. The whimsicality and gaiety in his nature seemed to have found a new outlet and machinery to be of some use after all.

I have arranged the letters in alphabetical order of recipients, and added notes in square brackets.

To Clifford Allen. [Lord Allen of Hurtwood; they discuss the manuscript of *After Two Thousand Years*.]

King's Coll. Camb.
4 August [1928]

Dear Clifford,

I have long thought you the most intelligent and helpful of critics and I think so now more than ever. What you say is exactly the kind of thing that helps, and it seems to me all perfectly true. Writing is the devil, especially as one has to write into a void, not knowing who will read. Over simplifications sometimes seem necessary, if one is to make any effect at all. But it is true that they exasperate. It is also curiously true that a single word may lead to exasperation. I occasionally feel inclined to say that it is better to exasperate, since people won't attend at all otherwise. But I know that really that isn't my game because I never want to do it in conversation. I shall lay your comments aside with my MS. and rewrite at leisure, if I am allowed either leisure or time at all. It's so queer how one suddenly drops out without warning, and one naturally considers that at my age. I do hope my dear Clifford that you will have continual opportunity for that face-to-face verbal persuasion of people actually in politics which seems to me both so important and so difficult, and for which you have such gifts. For aught I know to the contrary, you have gifts of writing too and will use them. But the other seems to me a remarkable speciality, yours, and I hope and expect that health and circumstances will always allow it. I am glad to think of you enjoying that place and I hope better in health. It is true, I think, anyhow, that you and me apart, that the whole order of society which made it possible is vanishing. So perhaps is all English country, inevitably. I hate the thought, but see no way of doing more than save a few bits.

Did you see in the *Nation* a really interesting article—as I thought—on youth and the war?

An upset has occurred in my plans not worth writing about, which may mean that I have to change them—plans for the summer, I mean. By the bye, I'm reading Shaw's book. He really *is* a writer! And as full of blind spots as men of genius usually are, and apparently must be.

Yours,
G. D.

To Julian Bell. [In a previous letter, which is reproduced at page 168, he discusses Bell's *Winter Movement*, and greets him as "the one man who might be a poet among those of the younger generation". "Arms and the Man", the satire here criticized, has appeared in a shortened form in the anthology *New Signatures*.]

King's College, Cambridge
17 July 1931

Dear Julian,

Dadie handed me the other day your poem. It was charming of you to dedicate it to me, and I am rejoiced to think that there is at least one young man who hates war. But—these buts! forgive me I am getting an old man and venture to take an old man's offensive liberties. I feel that your poem will be nothing but provocative and offensive to every kind of man that reads it. You will reply that you mean it to be. Yes, but I am thinking of the main thing, what will tend to change opinion about war. I have spent years over this business, not too successfully, and I get more and more convinced that one's only chance is to understand and believe that one is up against an extraordinary complex of atavistic feelings genuinely held by quite good people. (I grant you the others, but I think it is the mass opinions, fears, devotions, despairs, boredoms, poverty, which are the real obstacle.) I regret now every escape of irritation satire and rage which I have let escape, and, to be honest, I feel that, if I accept this dedication from you, I shall be supposed to endorse your methods. Will you understand and forgive my dear, and perhaps reconsider the whole poem? For I feel it in my bones that if you publish it you may regret it later, and that it may do you harm in a way which you yourself will regret. I would not say this latter if I did not feel that you have the chance to write good poetry (which I don't feel about many of the young, though that may be only the imperception of old age) and I would like you not to throw unnecessary obstacles in your own way. Write and forgive me anyhow.

Yours always,
G. Lowes Dickinson.

To Bernhard Berenson. [The opening reference is to the *Letters from Italy* of Mr Lowes Dickinson which had been privately printed. "Tomcat copulation" was then on his mind, for the same month he writes to another correspondent, Mrs E. B. C. Lucas: "The sexual goings on of the present young seem to me very disastrous and very sordid, and I don't think this is a matter of mere silly Victorianism. I think that some of our best intellectuals are simply throwing themselves into the mud till they can savour nothing else." These strictures are not characteristic; he spent but little time in being shocked by the young. The *T.L.S.* article on Goethe, was, he believed, by Middleton Murry.]

King's Coll. Camb.
27 March 1932

Dear B. B.,

I am very glad to get your letter and that you found my father's interesting. They have always been very interesting to me and I think he had a very good vivid Victorian style of letter writing. He was a most charming and delightful man, as I am discerning more and more as I read through a number of old family letters. His marriage with my mother was as near the perfect as anything can be in this world, deepening affection on both sides to the end. As I observe from the outside the ways of the modern young, it sometimes seems to me that they are losing everything in a kind of tomcat copulation of the most miscellaneous kind—but I know it is an old and perhaps inevitable vice of the old to grouse at the young.

I was very sorry to hear how ill Mary has been. Please give her my kindest remembrances and sympathy. I am glad to see that she is better, and I shall look forward to the possibility of seeing you both in the autumn. To you old age is only a threat, to me it begins to be a reality and of course an unpleasant one. Among other things I have almost lost what little memory I ever had. Still when one is well, and one's mind active, there is something soothing about old age. It's no use fussing any more. I wonder whether you read an article on Goethe in this week's Literary Supplement of *The Times*, I think it most remarkable and am anxious to know who could have written it. It seems to me just right. For years I have felt Goethe to be more important than any other man and now I see more clearly why.

As to the world about one, I have the chronic feeling of living in a lunatic asylum and I can hardly suppose that a débâcle of unimaginable dimensions is not imminent. If only I could depart before it comes!

Yours sincerely,
G. Lowes Dickinson.

To Mrs O. W. Campbell. [He much admired her *Shelley and the Unromantics*. The following passage about religion is suggested by her *Camilla's Banquet*.]

King's
11 March 1932

I find that my own view or feeling or whatever one should say changes in old age. I have always valued the peculiarly Cambridge attitude about truth and I do so still, and always shall, since it is our only safeguard (if it *be* one) against the wild superstitions always fermenting below, and always breaking out in times like these. There is something to be said for supporting the Roman Church as the only prophylactic against worse evils. But I see that when it comes to what one is to make of the world (and many people at any rate have to try to make something of it for practical rather than speculative reasons) our intellect can't do much for us. We are too ignorant by the very fact of our little natures and senses, etc. You put forward a position which was also Goethe's, that all experience must contribute to any-thing one may be able to believe. Of course if one is a little person incapable of much experience one's thought will be little too, and may easily be (often are) merely imbecile. But if one is a great person like Goethe then one gets into touch with great things.

To Herbert Corner. [When Dickinson summed up the "Points of View" series of talks in 1930 he appealed for the views of the young and received a manuscript which greatly interested him and which he tried to get broadcast. The writer was a junior technical engineer in a municipal electricity works in the north. A long correspondence ensued, from which I have taken the following letter. It shows him in contact with someone whose upbringing and experiences had differed from his own, and it shows how little such differences matter when there is intelligence and sympathy on both sides, as there is here. It is also of the nature of an apologia. Corner's visits to Cambridge were a great success.]

King's College, Cambridge
17 March 1932

My dear Corner,

I have several letters of yours which I must make some attempt to reply to. First as regards Whitsun, I will keep that week-end for you, so make what arrangements you can and for as long as you can. But if you find some other time more convenient let me know as soon as you can, as I am apt to get filled up. Easter is no use as I shall be away. I expect to leave on Saturday, and shall not be free again before the 16th April.

No, I doubt whether I shall attempt to "set down in book form a simple account of my philosophy of life". What is it? It grows and changes, and the more so as I get older, and one can't get such things across to anyone else. For people can only understand and receive what they have lived into. About abattoirs, I was once at Chicago and saw cattle killed by hundreds, an infinite line of them, one blow on the head of each with a hammer and they fall to the ground and are skinned almost before they have ceased to quiver. It's enough to make one hate meat. But there it is—nature's fundamental law, or one of them, that creatures live by preying on one another. Man distinguishes himself only by also murdering his own kind. There are times when I think him the vilest of all creatures and then remember that he is also the finest—as witness the saints and the martyrs of every kind. How could one state diagrammatically or otherwise all the puzzledom of that? No I don't understand relativity and I expect one can't without mathematics; so at least my mathematical friends always tell me. But then of course I don't think mathematics really teaches one much important truth, though it's a useful tool for some purposes, and the relativists themselves seem to be all at sixes and sevens.

I could lend you some day McTaggart's book on *Some Dogmas of Religion* if you would care about it. But I should say you would not get much out of philosophy. My own view is that what is important in it is the same thing, in a way, as in poetry. Spinoza is a wonderful spirit like Plato, like any philosopher who is a man of genius and not a mere logician. I believe that poetry lets in light; but perhaps only parabolically.

Do you mean that you want to study Greek and Latin in the original tongues? I wonder whether it would be worth your while. I doubt it at your age. I expect it would be more worth your while ("worth whileness") to read the best English writers. But we can discuss that. Anyhow what you need at present is concentration and coherence, the structure of writing before you attempt the ornaments. Or so I think, and McT.'s style is a model of those qualities.

Now your letter of the 7th March, though I don't know that there is much more for me to say about it. I expect you don't know how provocative and irritating your treatment is certain to be to those who fundamentally disagree. The question is, whether you do good or harm by stirring them up even to anger and indignation. And that is a question hard to answer. I can only say now that I regret all the provocative things I have said in my books about the war. It seems as if they only please those who agree with one, put off the others. And I should think that is more the case, not less, with the uneducated than the educated.

As to your question about forgiveness, the literal translation of the passage is "remit our debts as we have remitted those we owe to our debtors". As far as I can see, this does not mean in *proportion* as etc., but *sheer* remission. Of course Jesus is using a metaphor. However, I daresay there is no end of discussion about that, and I am no scholar in the New Testament. My difficulty about Christianity is and always has been that Christians make the centre of their faith the historical existence of a man at a certain age. I daresay he *did* exist, though that has been doubted. But if he *did*, what was he really like? I cannot think religion can depend upon such uncertainties, and of course you agree. Then there is no doubt at all that Christian theology has been enormously influenced by Platonism and by many other influences. Dean Inge is certainly right about that. Only I don't understand how he connects the Platonism with the historical Jesus. My main point, however, about all this is that so deeply are people's religious beliefs entangled in their traditional church teaching, that one can't tear down the one without the other. Hence a certain reticence, which I feel more and more as I get older. When one is actually talking to a given person one can feel one's way. But when one writes a book one hardly knows what one is doing. See the quotation from the Platonic Socrates on page 55 of my Plato book. For the rest, I am not a sufficient student of the history of Christianity to discuss fruitfully your other points.

Yes, that "running round after your own tail" is really the gist of my criticism. It seems worth while criticizing you, because you see the point yourself, and therefore can probably amend it. As to your repetitions I think there is a great difference between lecturing and writing a book. In lecturing, it is true that one ought to repeat, and not to crowd too much into the hour. But the art is to repeat without people realizing you are doing it. But when you are writing and print-ing, you assume that the reader has your book in his hands, he can pause and think over what you are saying, and that is what he ought to do. If he is intelligent, he will merely be irritated by constant repeti-tion, especially in the same form of words. That is the essence of your fault as a writer.

But perhaps something too much of all this. On the larger question, I don't expect to find a final philosophy. That, like life itself, is a growth, and in living minds the growth itself never stops. That is why some of the wisest men have held that death is not an extinction but a release to some higher life. Whether it is, I don't know, and don't expect to till it is too late for me to come back and tell any one! You will see, in our book, what Goethe thought. I have been endeavour-ing the last week to say something about his beliefs for a broadcast talk. He is one of the men I would rather follow than anyone else. But of course I don't know whether he really *knew*. He certainly did not return to tell us! and I doubt if we do much good battering our heads against that wall, though we may try to insinuate ourselves.

I have been much struck lately by reading a book of Lady Welby's correspondence. I met her in the past, and she was a woman of genius, and I keep finding in her echoes of Goethe. Unconscious I think, for there is no evidence that she ever read him. If your librarian is amenable, ask him to get *Echoes of Larger Life*, edited by Mrs Henry Cust. It might interest you. By the way, Goethe is often treated as an egotist, but it is a very inadequate account of him. Besides, it is true what he said, that the value of egotism depends on the value of the egotist!

Let me know about your coming here as soon as you know yourself.

Yours sincerely,
G. Lowes Dickinson.

To Bonamy Dobrée. [About *After Two Thousand Years.*]

King's College, Cambridge
3 July 1930

Dear Dobrée,

Many thanks for your very friendly and perceptive review of my dialogue. It is the only one I have had which goes into the heart of the matter, as is perhaps to be expected. I think what you say on the most fundamental issue is true. We are all confined and cribbed by our own natures; and it would be chimerical to expect to escape that. I hate conflict and love friendship. However in old age one begins to emerge from one's burrow and realize that other people are in theirs, and that theirs are different; and hence these struggles and horrors. What it's all up to I don't know; but I have always felt that the view that it is up to nothing is absurdly inadequate. The creeds, all alike, seem to me not only guesses but bad ones. There is more to be got out of the shooting at the stars which is great poetry and music. I don't think men need to "create" their tragedy. It would always be there, even if all I think possible were achieved. But I don't believe it need be this hideous tragedy of destruction and war. There I am unrepentant—that is I am myself. Many thanks again.

Yours sincerely,
G. Lowes Dickinson.

Pardon my typing.

To Elliott Felkin. [Selected from a long correspondence.]

Hôtel de l'Abbaye, Talloires
27 September 1927

Dear Elliott,

. . . I don't quite know how to deal with your many kindnesses and Joyce's. "Thank you"? Why, yes, of course. But that's a word, and one would like to arrive at things. Anyhow my dear I do thank you and both of you, for all. I had many thoughts, lying in bed this morning after breakfast—always the best time of day. But they evaporate. You will not yet realize, nor for many years, how odd it is to be quite fit and happy yet well aware that at any moment one may be precipitated—into what? It's idle to speculate, and Spinoza was right when he said that a wise man never thought about death. If the human race would have so done, what might we not have been spared. I have also been reflecting on Goethe's use of the word "daemonic". It seems to mean the unintelligible irrational element, which is the world we are caught in. I should translate it "energy". Daemonic men have that, but not at all necessarily intellect or goodness, e.g. Birkenhead and Churchill are daemonic, so is Mussolini. Perhaps Caesar was, but one knows so little about him. However he must have been. And Bismarck. Goethe himself, having also intellect and love, may count as one of the few men not only daemonic but great. Byron of course was daemonic. What a screed about nothing! But every now and then one seems to get aperçus about the commonplace. It looks lovely out today, blue sky behind shifting clouds, which are oddly creeping down the hill opposite. I am glad to get a feeling of rest. I suppose old age is mostly felt in getting exhausted more quickly. Otherwise, when one is well, it's rather pleasant. One takes stock. I don't seem to myself very different to any other man whom I contemplate—just one more bubble popping up on the stream. The stream is the thing that matters. But *how* does it matter? It is the Sphinx. In Goethe I came across yet another definition of genius—"that power of man which by its deeds and actions gives laws and rules". That's an unusual one! Well, till Sunday. Would you and Joyce care to come back to dine with us at the Beau Séjour?

To E. M. Forster. [The first letter, referring to *A Passage to India*, is printed for the reason that it well expresses his feelings about life as seen through an Indian medium; cf. his letter to Mrs Moor, page 116.]

The Shiffolds
2 June 1924

Dear Morgan,

I have now finished your book. I think it so good that I haven't much to say about it. For it is always easier to pick holes. The theme —the incompatibility of Indians and English—is done as perhaps only you could do it—with the power of understanding both sides. But then there are all sorts of behind suggestions; and I have a feeling —rare for me at my age—that you have lifted a new corner of the veil. What you see behind it is indeed disquieting enough; but we cannot shirk it for that reason; at least I don't want to. But it is one of the puzzling things about life how "cheerfulness will break in". So that in the midst of my intellect's most hopeless despair or rage

I know that, in fact, I think there may be some point in the terrible business, which, *if* one knew, one might approve. Aziz I think a triumph —so alive and so consistently inconsistent. . . . You will know well by now, and no doubt knew before, the crux of doubt—what did happen in the caves? Why mayn't we know? Why mightn't we know all the time? I expect however that you had good reason for your handling of this and I don't much mind myself. More important is that, whereas in your other books your kind of double vision squints—this world, and a world or worlds beyond and behind—here it all comes together. One doesn't know the fate of books. But one would think this should be a classic on the strange and tragic fact of history and life called India. Anyhow you will feel that you have pulled it off, a satisfaction that will abide underneath the never to cease dissatisfaction which belongs to life, and is life, if one lives at all.

. . . I can't be made very unhappy now, anyway, because I sort of see all the time the illusion and unimportance of these things. But then "important—unimportant", as the White King meditated. Carpenter is coming over here for the night. I feel a little anxious, wondering . . . how it will go. . . .

Yours,
G. L. D.

[The next letter begins with a display of independence on the part of the typewriter and the marginal lament "Oh dear!" The stories referred to are in *The Eternal Moment*.]

London
19 April [1928]

Dear Morgan,

I propose to go to Cambridge on Saturday. But this weather rather knocks me. More particularly, looking through my papers, I found a letter of yours of last August which I was glad to reread. You will have forgotten it; but you cite Blake and also Vicary re mystic experiences. Which brings me to your stories. I am not well satisfied with them. Your constant pre-occupation to bring realistic life into contact with the background of values (or whatever it is) is very difficult to bring off, and I am apt to feel the cleft. This I say only because we *do* say how we feel about things. I daresay I am wrong, in the sense that you succeed with other people, e.g. Melian Stawell, whom I told to write to you. Not altogether, I gather, with my sister, who was delighted that you sent her the book. It was just one of those perceptive things you do. I like best the first and last stories. It is good that someone should take the Wells–Shaw prophecies and turn them inside out. I have just returned from addressing theological students on science. I liked the young men, but I'm not sure it's much good trying these stunts. To begin with, the old can hardly meet the young—really meet I mean—and then theology and "Jesus". It all seems to me so "off", the way they hold it. Why is it "Jesus" that inspires them—or rather, as they say, is *there, alive, directing* them? In some way that no one else is. Surely these coils will shuffle off one day, for some of them. But meantime that is the way they formulate experience that, sometimes at least, is genuine, if commonly merely traditional and not experience at all. Du reste, most of them seemed fairly open-minded, except the high Anglicans. Romans majestically abstained, but otherwise the gamut ran down (or up) from Anglicans to Quakers. Somebody said you intended to come up this term, and if you do I hope we may meet. In that case perhaps Joe would also come. He called here the day I left for an Easter visit to my brother, so I missed him. I was at Bessie's last week-end in the sleet, but there was no telephoning to you and anyhow you could not have come over, nor I to you. . . . Well, so long. I must get on with duller things. Furness (J. M.) writes that he much admires and enjoyed your book on the novel. My best remembrances to your mother. I hope she keeps well and warm and enjoys her little tinkle of wireless. What would happen to her if she were obliged to hear a real orchestra in a real concert hall?

Yours,
G. D.

K. C. C.
17 January 1932

Dear Morgan,

I have been reading Forrest Reid's *Uncle Stephen*, which I picked up at the club and then took out of *The Times*. It's extraordinary rather, what a curious effect it produces in me. Years ago when I was a boy, I read a book called *The Boy in Grey*, I think, and I think it was by Henry Kingsley. The point was that a prince who wore a ruby met in the courtyard of a palace a boy in grey, with a token, and had to follow him. I have never forgotten the impression of this book, though I have never looked at it since and should hardly care to, for it may be rot. Well, *Uncle Stephen*, at the age of seventy, produces something of the same effect. Not the Uncle Stephen part proper, but the part when he becomes the young Stephen and fascinates Tom. Both the boys are so well done I think. But of course the kind of interest it wakes in me is what they call a wish fulfilment, and I get a whiff of that old feeling "nothing else would be worth while except that". I don't know why I should tell you this except that it strikes me as curious and rather ironic. I have no further news. Things here are as usual and I'm rather glad to have got back to my own rooms and to have solitary breakfasts with a book. How odd it is that, with catastrophe waiting round the corner, one can still enjoy Bridge and idle talk. I wonder how long I shall be able, or want, to hold on to life? If only there were no one dependent on one!

G. L. D.

[The next letter was written shortly before he went into hospital. The Goethe poem enclosed in the postscript is "Sagt es niemand, nur den Weisen" from *Der West-Östliche Divan*; it is translated on page 56 of *Goethe and Faust*. The postscript also quotes "Vielfach wirken die Pfeile des Amor . . ." from the third of the "Römische Elegien", and recommends *Goethes Lebensweisheit* by Emil Ludwig "if you want to know about Goethe—I daresay you don't".]

King's Coll. Camb.

12 July 1932

Dear Morgan,

Thanks for your letter. . . . It seems as if one is making a lot of fuss about nothing, but I prefer to make preparations for every alternative. I am quite enjoying myself here, and there is something pleasant in the arrest of time; like I remember feeling years ago between one's tripos exam and the result.

I don't know whether you know the enclosed poem of Goethe's. It always seems to me to be profound, and your remarks about sex remind me of it. I think that all forms of love, including the physical, point to something beyond, and I trust Goethe's account of experience, because he had so much and so varied and wrote so much down, and never bothered about being consistent, which indeed it is absurd to be, for one is an oscillating and growing (or declining) creature, and experience too oscillates or grows (or declines). It looks to me now as though I might have to wait the full ten days before the room is vacant, and the longer the better so far as I am concerned, because I want to enjoy the warm weather.

G. L. D.

[In connection with the foregoing here is an extract from an earlier letter; I had sent him some remarks on personal immortality which Edward Carpenter had left behind for his friends.]

Many thanks for sending me those words of Edward's. They give all the most beautiful side of his character. I don't know whether what he says is true, except in feeling, and if one begins to think and argue about it there is no end. But it seems to me that love, so understood, is more attainable and better worth having than most things. . . . It is I suppose old age that makes me think now that the sex element is rather a disturbance than a consummation. Yet without it, I suppose, love would not attain the height it sometimes does. But I must not chatter.

To Gerald Heard. [Commenting on an early draft chapter of

The Ascent of Humanity. When the book was published three years later, he wrote a short Introduction to it.]

The Shiffolds, Holmbury St Mary, Dorking
15 September 1926

Dear Gerald,

This method of address must be reciprocal, though I observe that some people are naturally called by Christian names and I appear to be one of them. Others, though one becomes very intimate, never are. I suppose there is some psychological ground, but I don't know what it is. My oldest friend, a woman whom I have known for fifty years nearly, I have never called by anything but her surname, nor have any of my sisters. "But to resume" or rather to commence. Your MS. is a most puzzling proposition. I think, as I did with the former fragment I saw, that you have got an idea which ought to work out very interestingly, but must be worked out on a large scale, with a lot of detail and references, etc. This chapter, like the former, seems to be a kind of either summary or introduction. I suppose it to be intended so. Your full view seems to include history (from the anthropologized beginnings), psychology and mysticism. Your strength should be in the fact that your mysticism is not shot out of the blue, but emerges from your science. In fact, it should thereby cease to be what is properly called mysticism and be rather psychical research. And that subject also you will have to include. This large scale, as I understand, is really the point of your projected book. I feel as if it might really reorient our thought, if you get the leisure, and command (as no doubt you will) the patience, to work it out to the necessary detail. This is for the matter, and is about all I can say about it.

For the manner, I can say more. Your style is at present a remarkable combination of epigram (often good epigram) and pedantry and obscurity. You will have a rather laborious task, I think, in clarifying it, and no one but yourself of course can do that. I notice however a few points [details given].

I see that you have a very difficult problem of style to write what is scientifically clear and accurate, and yet to get a literary quality. You will perhaps solve this because, as I see it, the faults are not those of a man who will never have a notion of writing, but of one who is struggling with the medium and will probably emerge into some new mastery. I *think* you may have to check your epigrams.

The sum of all which is, that I wish you, as soon as may be, leisure for doing this book which is germinating in you, which will take I think a long and laborious process to do, and which might be very important when done.

G. L. D.

To Kingsley Martin. [Addressed to the present editor of the

New Statesman and Nation, and extracted from their graver correspondence.]

K. C. C.
24 September 1925

Dear Kingsley,

On examining my box I find in it the shirt and some collars. There is also a pair of socks, which may be yours, but they are grey and I think you said yours were khaki. I have worn the pair in question, and I rather thought they belonged to Savary. However I send them along, in case. There are no others. I found a pleasant little party here, and had a game of bridge, in which I lost 2*s.* 6*d.* and won 2*s.* 6*d.*, and ended up as you were, a most satisfactory arrangement. Since when I have been strolling in the Backs, under a cloudy sky, which just lets through a dim light, showing all the reflections in the river; an owl hooting, otherwise silence and darkness, very beautiful and peaceful. I do hope you will be feeling better for Scarborough, and will endeavour "nichts bereuen". I am still vague as to how long I shall stay here, but at latest I leave Saturday for a little round of visits.

Yours,
G. L. D.

To Robert Nichols. [A subsequent letter discusses Goethe and the daemonic (cf. page 179). The reference here is to R.N.'s *Fantastica.*]

King's Coll. Cambridge
17 November 1928

Dear Mr Nichols,

Many thanks for your letter and for your book which I have been reading with interest and sympathy. It is always good to find another mind touching one's own even if only in passing, and especially, at my age, a young mind. What you say about myth is very much what I also have felt. Many years ago I tried to say that, in a little book on religion. But the trouble about myths is, that they cannot now become generally credible. I believe men ought to find what they want in poetry and music. But then so many aren't sensitive to those things. My notion is, a little round of light illuminated by science, increasing, one hopes, in illumination and range; and outside, twilight and night, to be filled by art—I mean serious art. Perhaps I should say imagination. What has been the trouble with religion is that it has turned myth into dogma, and out of dogma bred persecution and priestcraft. When you return I hope perhaps we may meet and have a talk, for letters are unsatisfactory, unless one knows the other fellow so well that one can be sure to be rightly understood.

184

I thought it very nice of you to write, for I have been feeling very isolated.

Yours very truly,
G. Lowes Dickinson.

To Dennis Proctor. [Selections from a long correspondence. The reference in the first letter is to my friend Frank Vicary (page 180), who had stayed with Dickinson at Cambridge.]

K.C.
14 June 1930

Dear Dennis,

I meant to show you the enclosed for I know you are interested in Life, and this seems to me to have a singular beauty. The writer (I forget whether I spoke to you about him) has been a miner, fisherman, ship's steward, torpedoed, miner again, pig breeder. I came across him through Morgan Forster, who is a great friend of his and I too feel a great friend now. How people are spread about through all classes, who have the sense of life, and how tiresomely class limits most of us. That is really the principal reason for trying to improve society. Give me this back or send it as I value it. I leave here tomorrow and shall be at Beaufort Mansions till I leave on Saturday. Bless you my dear.

G. D.

Hotel Europäischer Hof (they so call themselves), München
7 August 1930

Dear Dennis,

This in haste, in case I catch you in town. We are staying here until the 15th, and that day expect to move on to Salzburg. There will therefore as I gather be only the 15th that we shall be in Salzburg together. You might communicate with us on the 15th evening. We are staying at Salzburg until the 30th and after that go to France. Glad to get your letter and news, and know that you are well and happy. I have been for a fortnight odd in the Engadine before joining my sister here. Weather there was better than in most places and I'm the better for it. Here the climate is bad and very unsettled. We were interrupted by a storm of rain at an open-air concert yesterday evening which was broken up just as we were beginning to hear Schubert's quartet of Der Tod und das Mädchen. It was all very schwärmerisch and romantic. A song to the harp was sung from the top of a high tower, illuminated for the purpose! Being romantic myself I loved it, but I think your generation could hardly endure it. I find the Germans very pleasant. The young men might be attractive, as they all go about in shorts and open shirts, without ties, but alas they are seldom physically beautiful. I generalize, as I have often done before, that the

Germans are the ugliest and least distinguished people God has thought fit to produce. But they are civilized to a degree inconceivable to our English philisterei and insensitive good nature. However I must not run on now. We start the Ring tonight. Wonder if I shall still be an enthusiast. I think I shall. The enchanter always corners me, though I rebel next day. I have now got proofs of my long dialogue through, and suppose it will emerge in the autumn. Nobody of any kind will like it, but I am used to that and imagine myself not to care. . . . I wonder what your mysterious "triumph" was?

Yours,
G. D.

Montrésor, Indre et Loire
21 September 1930

Dear Dennis,

Owing to the usual muddles and delays of forwarding letters yours of the 27th August reached me only yesterday, hence my delay in replying. I was very glad to hear from you and at such length, the more so as I was not expecting you to write. After you left Salzburg we had a week of wonderful weather. This was during the heat wave, but at Salzburg though it was hot in the day it was fresh and cool at night. We had delightful music of which however I think I wrote; then returned via Innsbruck, my sister to London and I to Paris and thence to Tours, where I met Roger Fry and his delightful sister Margery, who is as able as he and more all round. She is at present head of Somerville, but will not be for long. I have enjoyed my stay with them at this little town, though weather has been very dicky and the hotel uncomfortable to my ageing body. It's nice country, rather like Suffolk, and full of ruins of great Abbeys, now turned into farms. There is a castle inhabited by a Polish countess. Pippa and Pernel Strachey, sisters of Lytton, have also been here. I have never been with a trio of such able women. One felt ashamed of one's sex! Delightful women too, which is not always the case. What will be my next move, I don't quite know. At the moment Roger and Margery have determined to fly to the south of France, but it hardly seems worth while to go there for a week or so on the chance of sunshine. I may go to England. At any rate, when I do get there, I will call you up and hope to visit you in the new house. I'm all in favour of people writing their autobiography, if they can do it, and beginning early, but it's a task most people abandon. My friend at Geneva has kept his most elaborately for years, with documents, photos, and all the rest of it. It will be a most interesting document if ever it sees the light, which I daresay it won't. I have written nothing and hardly read anything. I play a good deal of chess with Roger, who usually beats me and I get very sulky about it, having very bad chess manners. It's really very ridiculous. Then I walk a bit about the rather charming country. The others have the resource of painting which is inexhaustible to them. For Margery, who has always been an executive woman, really likes nothing so much as painting and playing the flute. She is also an expert on birds. I was interested to hear of your induced mysticism. There are very queer things to be learnt and done about oneself. Your admiration for Proust strikes me as excessive, though it is shared by so many of your contemporaries. He certainly describes well the little slip of life he deals with. But what a little slip it is. Parisian society of a rather snobbish and frivolous character. How much does that really tell about "Life"? which extends so infinitely through time and space, is so incredibly various, even if one confines oneself to humans. And when one takes in also the animals and insects! Not to mention the stuff the physicists deal with. I can't do much except gape at it now, and stretch my little imagination as far as it will go before it bursts like a bubble. However that is a matter of age and not for you to bother about. . . . I append a translation of a queer little poem by Goethe, which rather intrigues me. My love my dear,

G. D.

[The poem which follows occurs in Goethe's posthumous works. It is sometimes printed as two poems, the second, with the title "Dreifaltigkeit", beginning at the third stanza.]

> "The history of the christian church,
> What it amounts to I can't conceive.
> There's such a lot of stuff to read—
> Tell me what you yourself believe."

> "Two champions standing up to box,
> The Aryan and the orthodox.
> For centuries they kept up the fray,
> And will do till the judgement day.

> "Embodied in creation's riot
> The Father is eternal Quiet.

> "A mighty task the Son assumed
> It was to save the world he came;
> Much good he taught and much endured,
> In our own time it's still the same.

> "Descended then the Holy Ghost
> At Whitsun operative most,
> But whence he came and whither goes
> For all our efforts no one knows.
> Brief was his moment, then it passed,
> Although he be the first and last.

"And thus repeating faithfully
The ancient creeds we all agree,
Worshipping with unfeigned zeal
The Three in One and One in Three."

1 Beaufort Mansions, S.W. 3
Saturday, 4 October 1930

I wonder Dennis dear how you got on with the Choral Symphony. I listened to it on the wireless at Miss Stawell's. Listened to it? No rather to a husky and malicious ghost parodying it with occasional interpolations of a zany or a lunatic, perpetual atmospherics, and in all the softer passages the sound of some fool broadcasting on some irrelevant topic. Moreover it was obvious even so that Wood was conducting disgracefully, and that the chorus could not sing the music, but that is invariable and partly Beethoven's fault for writing the music so high. Nevertheless I listened all through since even this parody served to recall the greatest music in existence, unless it be the Mass of Bach. And you I hope would not realize the defects. . . . I imagined you puzzled by the first movement, overwhelmed as I hoped by the amazing scherzo, deeply moved by the adagio, and especially by the second theme that comes in on the cellos. Then comes that queer almost childish-sublime introduction to the last movement, when all the previous themes are repeated and rejected by the basses. And then that amazing theme which is like a bud that opens and opens into a great rose like the rose at the end of Dante. I wonder what you did make of it my dear. I lay awake a long time thinking about you and I am starting the day telling you what I am thinking, merely to help me to endure the spectacle of the world with which one has to occupy most of one's time. Grim and grimmer it is and will be, but as it becomes more terrible becoming also more mysterious and perhaps up to something greater than we can conceive. But such thoughts are not for you, or for any young man. I am intending to turn up on Friday (is not it?). I shall be rather like the symphony as heard on the wireless, and I shall see you only through a mist of cocktails. So long my dear. By the bye I went yesterday to have my hair cut at a place in the King's Road. The barber informed me that he had taken his holiday in London, investigating the churches and other sights. Of course he had seen much that I have never seen, or forgotten, among other things the church where Pepys is buried with a long eulogistic inscription to the wife he was always deceiving and always quarrelling with. He's (the barber) a Devonshire man and lives with a Devonshire family in Fulham where he gets Devonshire dishes such as soused mackerel. He instructed me firmly and kindly in history and other things, where certainly I need instruction. He was inclined to think that the Pepys Library is at Oxford not Cambridge but there I had to be firm. How nice the English working people often are with that curious sweetness and kindness. I wonder how long it will last out against the present and future conditions.

Well my dear I must go out from this haven and resume such labour as I have and such thoughts as I cannot escape from. . . . Sursum corda my dear.

G. D.

[The sonnet referred to in the next letter is in the 1896 *Poems* and begins:

> Thou knowest, love, of love's immortal tree
> Strength is the root and tenderness the flower.]

K. C. C.
21 January 1932

I ought not to be writing to you my dear but to be preparing an address I have to give tonight. Still I want to write because last night I heard the 3rd Act of Siegfried, and so, I think you said, did you. We have a wireless which to my astonishment can give Wagner's orchestration almost as if you were in the Hall. I listened subconscious of the long windedness and superficiality of Wagner, but nevertheless in a kind of ecstasy. What a miracle he was! He does not tell you about it, he just *gives* it. And that heroic love, which includes all the other and transcends it, is I expect really the point of life (see my sonnet No. 25). The long years since, and especially the last fifteen, have pretty well killed me. But I see that the "thing", whatever it is, persists underneath. However, as usual, I begin writing to myself and not to you; so indestructible is egotism (or would you say egoism). I think we ought to make a distinction. One is suffering from the ego, and the other is loving it. You won't and should not feel now what I do about love, but everything must proceed by stages. But there's always something on before, so follow the gleam!

Dein,
G. D.

To D. H. Robertson. [The economist. References to IT are frequent in later letters and talks. The implication is usually sinister.]

King's Coll.
29 July [1930?]

Dear Denys? Dennis?

I have now read a good part of your book, all the latter part, I think. It seems to have all the best qualities of the Cambridge mind so rare, so exasperating to so many people, and as I think so precious and indispensable. I have enough of it to sympathize. But I have also another devil in me who becomes more insistent as my time draws to an end. He says "nothing important can be proved" and adds "what I want to know is what *you* stand for in this chaos of different standpoints." You no doubt have that devil too, but you never let him speak in this book so I don't know what he would say. Mine says "I hate fighting and all the fine coverings under which it defends itself. I hate empire. I hate nationalism. I hate war. I would rather see the whole of mankind finally destroyed than see it proceed as it is now proceeding." I reply—that is the other devil replies—"well what's the good of that? You won't stop any of that by hating it." And the second devil says "well then, you ought at least to have the guts to be a martyr." All this is not very relevant to your book, but perhaps it's all I can say. For in the subjects you deal with you are the expert and I the mere amateur. And I find you an admirable exponent, with humour, candour and common sense. The last word lies with what I am in the habit to myself of calling *IT*. IT is probably up to something though perhaps to nothing that interests us ephemerals. It can only be confronted by ? plus Poetry.

Yours,
G. L. D.

To D. K. Roy. [This important reply to an Indian inquirer may be compared with his letter to Corner. He again explains himself to someone whose experience of life differs, but he is here more aware of the difference.]

King's College, Cambridge
18 January 1931

Dear Mr Roy,

I shall find it very hard to say in a brief space, or indeed to say at all, what I feel about the mystical question you ask. This is not merely reserve; it is my sense of the gulf which lies between an Englishman and an Indian, in all these matters, even when on both sides there is good will. When I was a young man I became much absorbed first in Plato, and then Plotinus. I am one of the few Englishmen who have studied Plotinus from cover to cover, though that was years ago. I thought then that there must be some way of reaching ultimate truth (or perhaps I should say ultimate experience) by some short cut. I suppose the principal thing that happened to me, in the course of my life, was the disappearance of this idea. *I feel now that we are all very ignorant and quite incredibly and unimaginably inadequate to deal with the kind of questions we ask about ultimate things.* I know however that there do exist what are called mystic states and I am interested when I come across any one genuine who claims to have had them. But what they signify really, when had, I cannot of course pretend to judge. I am now pretty near to death and naturally my mind moves in that direction. What death really means no one can tell, perhaps it means different things to different people. I am content and indeed obliged to "wait and see". You say that you have read the book on Goethe which I wrote. The attitude he had towards all these things is very much my own. I "wait" hoping and expecting to "see" if there is any thing to see. Meantime "Alles Vergängliche ist nur ein Gleichnis" etc. may be a guess at truth. I expect that yoga comes in in this connection and I am quite ready to believe that in your country men have discovered much in the way of the control of the body by the mind, and the engendering of conditions which most Europeans know nothing about. But how important that may be I cannot judge; I have never, since I was a young man, been interested in those things, and have always had the fear that there may be much danger and delusion there, even if there be possible achievement.

To turn from those things to more "practical" ones, as Englishmen are apt to say (I am not defending our national attitude), my own instinct or judgement, or whatever it is, is all against attempting to deal with political questions as if they were religious or mystical, etc. When one enters into politics one enters the region of passion, interest, prejudice, and at last, fighting, which, however it begins, always ends in the destruction of all that was best and most generous in those who perhaps inaugurated it. I have heard, of course, from every side the kind of criticism you bring against the League of Nations: it *is* a most imperfect document. But its imperfection represents that of the nations and peoples who framed it, or, by their mere presence in the background, caused it to be framed as it is, and not otherwise. To say it is *bad* is to say what is true: that political mankind is bad. But political mankind will not be made better by scrapping all the poor stuff it tries to do, and crying for the moon—that is for a different humanity. If one is working for that latter, it must be by other than political means, or, if one adopts political methods, one must cut them according to the cloth of the *now* existing mankind. I have written you all this that you may know where I stand, since it is these things you ask me about.

Yours sincerely,
G. Lowes Dickinson.

To Virginia Woolf. [For *Jacob's Room*, see page 151. These two letters are about *The Waves*. The first of them is a sort of critical rhapsody of which I know no other example from his pen. I have inserted some punctuation but not standardized it otherwise. Bernard etc. are all characters in the novel.]

King's College, Cambridge
23 October 1931

Dear Virginia,

I have been living the last week almost entirely in your company whether I have been actually reading you or not and I have kept up such a conversation with you that I am urged to try to put some of it down. But there is such a lot of it, and what one puts down is dead as it touches the paper.

Your book is a poem, and as I think a great poem. Nothing that I know of has ever been written like it. It could I suppose only be written in this moment of time. And now I understand or think I do to what you have been leading up all these years. The beauty of it is almost incredible. Such prose has never been written and it also belongs to here and now though it is dealing also with a theme that is perpetual and universal.

Oh dear what words, and even so only touching the least essential. For there is throbbing under it the mystery which all the poets and philosophers worth mentioning have felt and had their little shot at. I have only read it once and I see and know that it ought to be read often though I don't know whether I shall do that since I brood more and more and read less and less except to get information which is not reading but mugging up. I am an old man now and find age curious. My mind is all right though I suppose it may go tomorrow as my memory is going fast. But oddly enough the imagination functions as never before and about things one can't write down. The world is incomprehensible and must remain so to us animalcules, though the best thing about it is our shots to comprehend it. You make no shots because you will not make the shallow and the stale ones. Possibly though you agree with me (though very likely you don't) in this. The universe (or universes) is not without significance. It is apparently indifferent to our values it is certainly indifferent to our happiness our well being our goodness or badness our morals our loves. "Our." But what are we? Waves, yes? but waves in the sea part of the sea inseparable from the sea bound too each of us to be this wave and not that (whence much if not all of our trouble) but able and increasingly able as we get older to perceive that the other waves have their life too and that while we are clashing with them we are somehow they. Those sort of things, which I find in your book (I don't think I merely put them in, though that is the most common thing we do with other people's thoughts and makes us recalcitrant to new truth).... Anyhow I feel it like that. Also life seems like a dream as one comes to the end of it. One's separate individual skin ceases to hold one, it cracks all over, nightmares come in and visions and terrors and ecstasies till finally one rides at death, like your Bernard at the end. Oh dear, words words words as you also so vividly feel.

To change the tone, I walked down the river the other day. The eights were thick over the water and the fours a kind of inextricable tangle, and to every eight and every four a young man (what children they look now) shouting to them from bicycles and horses in every kind of tone, hortatory abusive encouraging desperately earnest. Among them of course Percival. Firmly but kindly he was saying "It isn't one of you, it's all of you that are wrong." How profoundly and everlastingly true! Then once more firmly and kindly—"Now I'll tell you the best way." But alas his words fade on the wind and before he knows or we hear the only way the youth who was piloting an aeroplane will have dropped bombs neatly on him and on all the Percivals before he is brought down himself by a machine gun, falling with the proud sense that he is "doing his bit" for the dear old country. Courses were being done, the coxes yelled, the October sun shone out in the garden by the river, where some don's wife entertains bored boys, and folks gossip about the matrimonial affairs of the fellows of King's, the dahlias and chrysanthemums burned; someone was upset in a whiff (as we used to call them) and came swimming in laughing (he too was Percival), a very old and disreputable man held open a gate and cursed under his breath when he was not tipped. Louis walked along the tow path ashamed because he could not row, and Nevill, looking for new prey, and I, thinking of you and your book, was aware in the back of my mind that I was coming home to a cup of tea, that there was a fraudulent election on and how should I vote; that I ought to call on so and so and so and so, that I might be dead tomorrow and that nothing mattered except to break through this mesh as decently as one could into—what? At which point, as George Meredith says somewhere, my imagination "tottered in dots". Oh dear, too much of this. But, my dear Virginia, you will pardon me for it is the best and only tribute I can pay in return for what seems to me a great book. Leonard's book still lies on the table and before I can get to it I have others to at least look into. Why will people send me their books? What do *you* do when they send them to you? Of course the simplest plan is to write at once saying one hopes to read it, and then not read it, but there are a few cases where this is impossible.

I don't think I shall correct this typing. I'm told it only makes it worse.

Yours always,
G. Lowes Dickinson.

King's Coll. Camb.
13 November

Dear Virginia,

I have just finished your book for the second time and I feel like beginning it again at once. I cannot and will not try to tell you how much it tells me in my old age—how beautiful and how profound

I feel it. But I shall give you a motto which I came across in the paralipomena to Goethe's Faust, which expresses one side of it (one only):

> Des Menschen Leben ist ein ähnliches Gedicht,
> Es hat wohl einen Anfang, hat ein Ende,
> Allein ein Ganzes ist es nicht.

Don't answer this. It's only a second exclamation. And incidentally this book makes clearer to me what literature really is. It's not (as it is so often in fact) a kind of antithesis to science. It's science made alive. There's a passage about the Old Man on page 317 which says everything about that bit of anthropological psychology (this is the language of science!) and turns it all from a pale ghost, a thing of words, into a living reality. What makes science so awful is its insensitiveness and consequent pedantry. But what heroes some men of science are. I'm beginning to chatter. Forgive me. I ought to be like Bernard in your wonderful passage, page 310.

Yours,
G. D.

It is a happy chance that these letters about *The Waves* should close the series and emphasize his interest in contemporary writing and its experiments.

chapter fifteen

The Last Months
June–August 1932

> thou dost wait
> At the sad city's open gate.
> But though the mark is on thy brow
> No bondman of the flesh art thou,
> And though thou enter, thou dost bear
> This in thy heart for comfort there:
> Only the morning reads aright
> The sombre secret of the night;
> Only the free divine the laws,
> The causeless only know the cause.
>   G. L. D. (written in 1893)

Body. Wait till the last, the fiercest struggle, wait
Till I invade in force your every gate,
Flow over every passage, every cell
Of the proud fort you engineered so well,
Till you become a passive registry
Of the triumphant agony that is I. . . .

Soul. All that you can and may, I don't deny it,
You have the power and if you will can try it,
But this I know, up to the bitter end,
I to my purpose all my force will bend,
Believing that the passion of the soul
Is rooted in the nature of the whole.

Body. So, last as first, you miss the best of life,
Waging with me this vain and desperate strife.

Soul. That was imposed upon us by our fate.
But listen! Though I fight, I do not hate.
For you, my enemy, have been my friend,
Driving me desperate to my proper end.
We enter now the last most tragic scene
That sums in symbolism all that's been.
Do you your worst, as I shall do my best.
What lies behind us both must do the rest.
                G. L. D. (written in 1929)

In the summer of 1932 a group of Cambridge friends dined
together in London. There were informal speeches and Goldie
had been asked to reply to the toast of "Eternal Youth". Well
qualified for such a task, he performed it with the expected insight and wit, but introduced a note of farewell which deeply

impressed his audience. Two of them wrote down afterwards what they remembered of the speech, and their letters shall be quoted, because they are in a sense a reply to the letters in the last chapter. Something has been said about the Cambridge whom he loved; here is the Cambridge who loved him.

The writer of the first account is a man of about my own age. He writes to May:

When he, Goldie, got up he told us that he wasn't going to talk about "Youth" at all but proposed to tell us what it was like to grow old. He said that he found he got, as he grew older, not exactly less and less interested in the world about him but more and more detached from it, he found himself more and more in the role of spectator rather than participant—he described how he would lie awake in the early morning "watching himself thinking"—detached from himself, not responsible for himself or his thoughts, an amused spectator of himself from the outside, less inclined to praise or blame, just watching himself and others. . . . The proposer had rallied him in his speech, giving it rather as a sign of Goldie's youthful interest in everything, that Goldie found the society of such very dull people entertaining. . . . Goldie met this challenge by saying that he felt more and more that all human creatures were somehow equally important or unimportant in the scheme of things as we know it now—and it was then in his speech (if I remember the connection aright) that he said he didn't know whether he would be with us next year, very possibly he wouldn't (I had the feeling at the time that he felt he probably wouldn't) and he went on to suggest (I can't quote) that the interest of growing old lay in the getting nearer to the time when this queer universe would be seen to be less and less queer, when the irrational and seeming immortal power whom he called "It" which seems to control events would be seen in its proper perspective, and he half suggested that some sort of vision of the truth might be given to old age even this side of death.

I have put this very badly in summarizing my recollections and I have perhaps made rather more definite what he was putting rather tentatively. He did it of course with much humour and charm—you know his way when he was trying to find words for an elusive thought, lifting his eyebrows, interlocking his fingers, the muscles rather taut, with a steadfast refusal to dogmatize and then laughing at himself for some paradoxical expression of his point.

The writer of the second account is a young man.

I wish to goodness I could remember more of what he said. But I remember very vividly the impression it made on me at the time.

I think I was more moved than at any other time in our relationship. I was sitting almost opposite him, and after he had been speaking for some time, I practically did not take in the words at all, but fixed my eyes on his face and felt such a tenderness for him as I had never had before. It was almost as though he was having then and there as he spoke a "mystical experience", which he had always said he had never had in his life. He had a rapt smile on his face, as though he were in a state of blissful happiness such as he had never known, and obviously his surroundings were completely lost to him. He had been asked to speak to the text of "Youth", but on the pretext that old age was second childhood he talked about old age and death instead. Ostensibly he was summing up the condition at which he had arrived, but as he talked on, more and more abstractedly, going over the advantages and happinesses of old age, I felt that really he was penetrating at that moment further than he had ever done before in his constant enquiry, and that he was actually experiencing a happiness that transcended the state of resignation and composure which he was describing.

He seemed to assume without any question that it was the last time he would be there, and somehow he made us feel the same thing. Although there was no reason why he should not live for any number of years more, it was somehow quite evident that this was his farewell speech. I think he probably said as much, but I can't remember for certain: the impression was so strong, that everyone must have felt it, whether he said it or not. For me it was the saddest moment of all my time with him, and it came back to me with a shock of recognition when I first learned that he was dead.

He died two months later (3 August), as the result of a severe operation from which, however, he appeared to be recovering. He wrote to me just before that he felt no fear of death, only a sort of excitement, but dreaded pain. Everything seemed to be going well, he had no excessive discomfort, and he was planning to spend his convalescence with the Trevelyans and Elliott Felkin. Whatever he may have felt in June he had no misgivings now, no more had his family and friends. I was with him on the Tuesday; the following evening I had the news through Ferdinand Schiller and could not at first believe it. There is something unreal about it still, probably for the reason that he never staged himself as an invalid. He was chiefly occupied in saving us trouble and in sparing our feelings. Oddly enough he succeeded. A character of his strength manages to sustain those who cling to it and I have "minded" more the deaths of people I have loved much less. Perhaps he conveyed to us the impression which he himself had received at the death of his sister Janet. There was no self-consciousness or cynicism in his departure, no sentimentality, and no "message"; it called for no special tone of voice because he had never used one. Yet it was not pagan, unless the music of the priests in *The Magic Flute* can be given that name. It did not suggest either that he had become one with the universe or that he had gone for ever.

Much could be added. The memorial services in the college chapel and in London expressed in different ways what had been lost. In London, the words of Spinoza, read by Roger Fry, and his own words, read by Dennis Proctor, reminded us that the free man thinks not of death, *nihil minus quam de morte cogitat*, and that man stands upon only one step of an infinite ascent. Eulogies, tributes of affection and esteem, sympathetic obituary notices, the extraordinary impression he made upon the doctor and nurses who attended him in their hospital routine—they could be recorded but they throw no more light. The truest words about him were said by his former bed-maker at Cambridge, Mrs Newman: "He was the best man who ever lived." That is what I feel about him myself, and it is what those who knew Socrates say of Socrates at the close of the *Phaedo*.

Epilogue

Mephistopheles, who should inhabit a cranny in every biography, puts his head out at this point, and asks me to set all personal feelings aside and state objectively why a memoir of Goldsworthy Lowes Dickinson need be written. If I say "Because I want to" the answer is "Who are you?" If I say "My friend was beloved, affectionate, unselfish, intelligent, witty, charming, inspiring" the Devil will reply: "Yes, but that is neither here nor there, or rather it was there but it is no longer here. I have your word and the word of others that this once was so, and I do not query it, but is there nothing which will survive when all of you also have vanished?"

I ponder as this bleak question is pressed, and I have to admit that one important item of interest for a reader—external adventure—is absent from Dickinson's life. It is difficult to think of a life where so little happened outwardly. He was never shipwrecked or in peril, he was seldom in great bodily pain, never starved or penniless, he never confronted an angry mob nor went to prison for his opinions, nor sat on the bench as a magistrate, nor held any important administrative post, he was never married, never faced with the problems of parenthood, had no trouble with housekeeping or servants. From the material point of view Fate gave him a very easy time, which he frankly appreciated, and if his biographer tried to romanticize and imply the contrary it would only move the Devil to laughter.

"Was he a great writer?" Mephistopheles continues. "Do you claim immortality for him on literary grounds?" And here I am constrained to quote from a letter of a friend of Goldie's and of my own, who belongs to a younger generation, and who embodies, like so many of that generation, the spirit of kindly diabolism. Acute, irreverent, light-hearted, he has been appreciating the educational value of *Plato and his Dialogues*, and then, fearful of praising indiscriminately, he adds:

BUT . . . you know I always find a "but" about Goldie's writing. He would be so inclined to clarity in conversation (with me anyway) but so beautifully unclear with his pen. I get mesmerized when I read anything he writes (except *John Chinaman*) and then have to read it all over again. It's so like travelling in a first-class compartment. It rolls gently on and I am never certain what has been said—what station I have been carried through. Do you find this? No, I bet you don't. As a literary gent you are beyond hypnosis.

I find it a little. Not in *John Chinaman*, nor *A Modern Symposium*, nor *The International Anarchy*, nor in the best of *The Magic Flute* and others of his books. But there frequently is this hypnotic effect, although the argument is taut and the language apposite. Something is wrong—or perhaps too right—with the style. Many readers will differ and think Mephistopheles could easily be routed here, but in the keen air which I am trying to breathe it seems to me that the words "great writer" won't do for Lowes Dickinson except in the low laudatory sense in which all writers of distinction and integrity get called great.

From Parnassus to Pisgah. Heartened by his two victories, Mephistopheles now points towards the Promised Land and says: "Has he brought *that* any nearer? What has this dreamer effected from the humanitarian point of view?"

The answer to this question lies in the future, but the terms in which the answer must be expressed are obvious. The one big practical thing for which Dickinson worked was a League of Nations. Before the war he worked for it unconsciously, his lecturing and writing imply it, though it has not crystallized in his mind. The war instantly brings it to the surface, and he does as much as any one man in England to promote it. After the war, he watches it with misgiving—and he did not live to see the worst. If the League pulls through it will vindicate him as a publicist, and show that his work for civilization took a practical direction. If it fails he will join Shelley and the other ghosts who have protested vainly against the course of doom and fate—for that is all that an idealist amounts to in the terms of Mephistopheles's brutal question: a ghost.

The fourth question, "Is he important as a thinker?", must be answered by his fellow thinkers. Some say that he is, but the majority endorse his own verdict, and according to that he ranks as a Cambridge philosopher below either McTaggart, Moore or Betrand Russell, and takes no place in the philosophic hierarchy of the past.

The case of Mephistopheles would appear to be watertight, and a biography of my friend and master uncalled for.

But two things must have been noticed about the Devil from the days of Job to those of Faust. In the first place he is always defeated on ground which he already occupies, in the second place he assumes that two and two must make four. Blinded by arithmetic, deaf to the warnings of poetry, he assumes that a man is only the sum of his qualities, and it is to the qualities named at the beginning of this epilogue, the "beloved, affectionate, unselfish, intelligent, witty, charming" which were so easily brushed aside, that I return for his overthrow. These qualities in Goldie were fused into such an unusual creature that no one whom one has met with in the flesh or in history the least resembles it, and no words exist in which to define it. He was an indescribably rare being, he was rare without being enigmatic, he was rare in the only direction which seems to be infinite: the direction of the Chorus Mysticus. He did not merely increase our experience: he left us more alert for what has not yet been experienced and more hopeful about other men because he had lived. And a biography of him, if it succeeded, would resemble him; it would achieve the unattainable, express the inexpressible, turn the passing into the everlasting. Have I done that? *Das Unbeschreibliche hier ist's getan?* No. And perhaps it only could be done through music. But that is what has lured me on.

G. L. Dickinson: A Tribute

Forster's first published account of Dickinson, apart from a brief supplementary tribute in The Times (Spectator, *13 August 1932*)

Tributes are empty things, yet when one has known a man for over thirty years and thought him great something has to be offered. Great? This is clearly the wrong word for Lowes Dickinson, it suggests inaccessibility and the power of making others feel small, whereas he had the power of bringing people out. While they were with him they were happy and amused. When they left him they found he had extended their sympathies and exercised their intelligence, so that the earth and the universe became larger places—this earth for which he has little hope, despite its beauty and fascination, that universe in whose light the earth will perhaps be reinterpreted. He has, indeed, the maieutic power which Plato ascribes to Socrates, and he has been called Socratic; the epithet is kindly meant and is no doubt thought suitable for a don. But whereas Socrates proceeded by snubbings and traps, and with a pertinacity which would drive any modern youth to drink or the gramophone, Dickinson, as far as his method was concerned, belonged to a different tradition, indeed, he hadn't a method, he just lived his ordinary life and because it was so precious it leavened the lumpishness of his hearers and made them his friends.

So, whether at Cambridge, where he is best known, or at the London School of Economics, where he lectured for over twenty years, or at Geneva, where he focused his hopes for our earthly salvation, or in America, India and China, or in that unexplored country which has just been discovered by the microphone, or in that other country, nonexistent he sometimes thought it, which psychical research has indicated—wherever he went he brought his liberating power and a modesty that never degenerated into humility, and a courage untouched by aggressiveness, and respect for the opinions of others. He also brought charm. Charm, in most men and nearly all women, is a decoration. It generally belongs to them, as a good complexion may, but it lies on the surface and can vanish. Charm in Dickinson was structural. It penetrated and upheld everything he said and must have remained through suffering and old age. It was nourished by his affection with us, and how deep that affection was one can see from his books. Does anyone suppose that he wanted to bother on and on about the War when that glorious affair was over? He had no love for international politics, he thought them loathsome, but until they were diagnosed and purified he knew they would lead to another war in which millions more young people will be choked, maimed and killed. All his work hangs together. If he had not had the impulse to write *The International Anarchy* he could not have written *The Magic Flute* or even *The Greek View of Life*. Both history and poetry, in his opinion, are the servants of the present, they exist to help us here and now, and to steady us through the greatest crisis humanity has yet encountered.

The moment for a survey of his work and influence has not yet come, and these remarks are not offered as a critique. They are only a tribute, which may perhaps send a few readers back to his books. Those who have never read him should begin with the *Letters from John Chinaman*; then they should try *The Magic Flute*, which, though a fantasy, combines many aspects of his genius. Of his dialogues, *A Modern Symposium* contains the best characterization, but the last published dialogue, *After Two Thousand Years*, is in some ways the most remarkable of all his works: it takes place between Plato and a modern young man, who explains to the Greek what developments the world has evolved since his day—if developments they can be termed. Economically and politically and socially we are heading for disaster. Nevertheless, the end is not yet, the reinterpretation may come.

"No! The world is full of gods, ascending the golden stairs, although your feeble vision cannot see them. Rising out of the deep abyss, the long ascent of life reaches up into the heaven of heavens; and of that chain you, on your little step, are but one small link. For the whole universe groans and travails together to accomplish a purpose more august than you can divine; and of that your guesses at Good and Evil are but wavering symbols. Yet dark though your night be and stumbling your steps, your hand is upon the clue. Nourish then your imagination, strengthen your will and purify your love. For what imagination anticipates shall be achieved, what will pursues shall be done, and what love seeks shall be revealed."

Dickinson was an old man when he wrote these words. They were read aloud at his funeral. Who, among those who were present, will retain such splendour of diction and warmth of emotion at the age of seventy? Who will have gained such wisdom?

A Great Humanist:
E. M. Forster on Goldsworthy
Lowes Dickinson

Broadcast talk, published in The Listener, *11 October 1956*

Goldsworthy Lowes Dickinson was born on 6 August 1862. (For I want to preface this talk with a brief account of his life. It was not a dramatic life. So let us get it out of the way.) He was born, then, of cultivated middle-class stock. His father was a portrait-painter of note. His mother had a connection with a well-known firm of publishers. The marriage of his parents was a happy one, and with one brother and three sisters he passed a very happy childhood. "Goldie" they called him. He went on to a preparatory school and to Charterhouse, at both of which institutions he was uniformly miserable. Not until Cambridge did the clouds begin to break. King's, the college to which he went, just suited him, mainly because there is a tradition there which he did all he could to promote: that of easy intercourse between old and young. Dons at King's do not live in one box and students in another. Anyhow, they need not unless they want to.

He read Classics, left the university, and turned to political studies. He also tried to work with his hands on a cooperative farm, also tried to be a doctor. These attempts were abortive but are symptomatic. He was trying to give away what he was beginning to receive, and to help his fellow creatures. A more appropriate avenue was opened in 1887 when King's made him a Fellow; he went into residence there and began a career of teaching in Cambridge and London. Subjects: political history, analysis of constitutions, that sort of thing. He also wrote books. He also travelled: to Europe constantly, twice to America, and once to India and the Far East. I went with him to India.

And then came the 1914 war. It is impossible to convey to a younger generation what 1914 felt like. It was such a surprise. That word is a feeble one, yet I can think of none more appropriate. It certainly gave Dickinson a surprise that lasted him for the rest of his life. He knew the war was coming or might be coming, he was prepared for it intellectually, but he could not foretell his emotions. His feelings are best conveyed by an analogy: they resembled the feelings which arise when a promise has been broken by a person whom one loves. One knows all the time that the promise will not be kept, perhaps cannot be kept, yet the shock is none the less mortal. In 1914 civilization broke its promise to him, and he never felt sure of it again.

Not that he collapsed or despaired. His old values held firm. In the very first fortnight of the war he jotted down on a half-sheet of notepaper a scheme for a League of Nations which should prevent future wars. The phrase "League of Nations" did not exist then, but he had, earlier than anyone, the idea. For the next fifteen years he was concerned with the inception and the organization of the League, did propaganda for it in America and elsewhere, and constantly attended at Geneva when it took up its quarters in that city. His great work, *The International Anarchy*, where the war's origins are analysed, dates from now. Its importance must be emphasized—especially to those who still assume that a don does not trouble himself with outside affairs.

During the last years of his life he had a respite from anxiety. He had done what he could and he sat back. He was in Cambridge again and found it as congenial and charming as ever and a place where the old could still learn from the young. And the young seemed to be learning from him. Then he fell ill. An operation was advised and apparently succeeded, and when I saw him in the hospital he was cheerfully planning for the future. But on the following day he died—3 August 1932. He was three days under the age of seventy.

So much for the life of Goldsworthy Lowes Dickinson. What of his work? He was a prolific writer. His complete bibliography totals nearly 400 items. Most of these are newspaper articles or letters or translations, but there are over twenty books, from which I must now choose. I need only mention in passing *A Modern Symposium*. *The International Anarchy* stands at the head of a group of war books. *A Modern Symposium* stands at the head of a little group of dialogues. At the head of a little Greek group stands *The Greek View of Life*, to which I must now refer.

I must be brief, because I am saving up my time for two other books— the *Letters from John Chinaman* and *The Magic Flute*. *The Greek View of Life* was published in 1896, and it exploded the fallacy that only those who know Greek can know Greece. It has run into about twenty editions, and must have introduced thousands of young men and women to an inheritance they were in danger of neglecting. The ancients are modern. That was Dickinson's contention. They are modern, first, because many of their political and social problems have been ours, and have been expressed, particularly in Athens, with a lucidity beyond our power. Our passions colour our judgements—and are bound to, or we should not be alive. Ancient Greece has the advantage of being remote from us in time. It can be studied dispassionately. And it has a further advantage. It is not just a convenient laboratory for the social scientist. The joy of living and the greatness of existence are also to be found there. It is the greatest literature the western world has produced. It has one disadvantage. It can only be read by people who have sweated at the language for years, and they often cannot read it as well as they pretend. Translations are therefore imperative. *The Greek View of Life* might be called an introduction to translations. It is an attempt to show the non-expert the character and environment of hidden treasures, and to leave him amongst them. If Dickinson were alive today—which for many reasons he would not wish to be—he would anyhow be cheered by the excellence of popular translations from the Greek: T. E. Lawrence's *Odyssey* and Mr Rex Warner's Thucydides are two that come to my mind.

From Greece let us hasten to China. *Letters from John Chinaman* came out, quietly enough, in 1901. It purports to be addressed by a Chinese official to an English friend, and it describes the charm and the sanity of Chinese civilization, and the approaching threat to it from the economic imperialism of the West, and its possible vengeance on the West. It appeared anonymously but was rightly assumed by English readers to be by an Englishman. In America it had a more dramatic reception, which shall be described in Dickinson's own words:

> It then penetrated to America, and there everybody seems to have accepted naively its Chinese origin. It was attributed to the then Chinese ambassador; and Mr Bryan, the famous politician, thought it worth while to write a special reply to it, in which he observed, among other things, that clearly the author had never seen the inside of a Christian home. Before publishing his book, he ascertained that the author was really an Englishman, and he said as much in his preface. But he thought his book none the less worth publication, and it is not for me to dispute that it may have been.

If only a politician will speak strongly for or against a book that book will certainly sell, and good Mr Bryan sold *John Chinaman* like hot cakes. We today—reading the book after the excitement is over, and after the prophecies contained in it have been but confusedly fulfilled—read it for the sureness of its touch, the exquisiteness of its style, and the truth of its feeling. It is the loveliest of his works—too smooth maybe for some tastes and bearing little relation to the China of today. To the China of his day it was germane. Eleven years after writing it, he visited the country, and was not disappointed. "China is much as I imagined it," he wrote to me from Peking in 1913. "I thought I was idealizing, but I now doubt it." He may have been idealizing. He certainly experienced the emotion of love. There was some deep affinity. When he got old and felt the draught he used to wear a little Chinese cap—or rather a series of caps, for he kept losing them—made out of black silk with a tiny red button on the top. Foreign trimmings do not as a rule suit the Britisher but his were appropriate. They suited him.

Since I have mentioned this cap, I will allude to the physiognomy beneath it. Here is what he looked like in his later days. Clean-shaven; features strongly marked; spectacles; the complexion not good; the head bowed a little forward from the shoulders when he walked, though the shoulders themselves, like the body generally, were shapely and strong. The hands—to proceed with this inventory—were large. The clothes erred on the dowdy side—dark blue serges, shirts of indistinction, podgy ties. Thus caparisoned, he did not present a commanding figure, but there was about him a most commanding charm. Charm, in most men and nearly all women, is a decoration. It genuinely belongs to them, as a good complexion may, but it lies on the surface and can vanish. Charm in Lowes Dickinson was structural. It penetrated and upheld everything he did, it remained into old age. It conferred on him a beauty which cannot be given that rather patronizing label of "spiritual", a beauty which, though it had nothing to do with handsomeness, did belong to the physical, so that his presence was appropriate amidst gorgeous scenery or exquisite flowers.

And now for *The Magic Flute*. This remarkable little fantasy came out in 1920, shortly after the First World War had ended. It recalls the opera of Mozart, and it adapts for its own purposes the libretto that Mozart set to music. The Queen of the Night stands for instinct: she dwells on the other side of Mind, in the dark, creating while she sleeps. She is Queen of the Night, but not of the heavenly bodies, whom she hates because of their brightness and their order. Sarastro stands for reason—and for something else: what else Sarastro stands for we shall one day see. Pamina, their daughter, is the world's desire. Tamino, in quest of Pamina, is Every Youth; his ardour and his nobility are matured by experience until he reaches the goal and understands the nature of the goal. For it is not what Tamino first supposed it would be. He passes through the fires of agony and the waters of doubt to no ordinary consummation. The mystic side of Dickinson has taken charge. It also inspires two profound and profoundly moving episodes that he has introduced into the Mozartian story: the episode of the Hermitage of Jesus and the episode of the Lotus Lake of Buddha.

The story opens with the Queen of the Night persuading Tamino to rescue her daughter, who, she declares, is imprisoned by Sarastro in his castle; untrue: Pamina remains with Sarastro of her own will. The foolish enterprise turns into a war—not with Sarastro, who will not use force and cannot be touched by force, but between the deluded peoples of the earth. It is the war through which Dickinson had himself just passed. Tamino fights, kills his enemy, and then it is revealed to him, through the power of Sarastro, that he has killed his friend. He leaves the battlefield and preaches peace—to find that the civilization he trusted has betrayed him. He is thrown into prison and into fire, and through the fire the spirit of Pamina leads him—she and the music of his own flute, which, unknown to him, had once played in the castle of Sarastro.

The allegory then gathers strength. The war section is the weakest in the book: Dickinson stood too near to the horrors he was trying to exorcise. It is when Tamino has passed the test of the fire, and is approaching the test of the waters of doubt, that the author's genius finds scope. Tamino has been purged of selfishness. He desires Pamina no longer for himself but for the whole world. He seeks her and knows that he cannot find her unless he finds truth. With truth as his aim he sets out for the desert.

At the very edge of the desert is a house surrounded by a garden, and over the garden gate a man is leaning—an elderly man with an ironical mouth and kindly eyes. It is Candide—Voltaire's Candide. They take to each other and Tamino stays with him for a time and helps him cultivate his garden. Candide—ever since his mistress Cunégonde left him to run a brothel on the Bosphorus—has known few inconveniences. He is intelligent, humane, considerate, gay, he has no pains, no pleasures, no desires, no philosophy, no interest in truth. He is a congenial companion except in one respect: Tamino cannot mention Pamina to him, for he would only take her for another Cunégonde. So he has to continue his journey into the desert.

Candide accompanies him a little way into it—partly through friendliness, partly because the road passes a ruined building, called the Hermitage of Jesus, which he is curious to visit. Not that he is interested in antiquities, but there is an odd rumour that Jesus has returned there and he would like to verify this. They are overtaken by another traveller, a handsome and agreeable man. He also has heard the rumour and is bound for the Hermitage. He adds: "I have a special interest in this matter, for I met Jesus there once before. . . . My name is Satan." Candide is delighted to meet Satan, and cries: "So you are revisiting the scene of your discomfiture." Satan answers: "Say rather of my triumph. For such it was, though it has been misrepresented in the popular story. . . . I offered Jesus the three things which alone could have made his mission a success—imposture, science, and empire. He rejected them all, and so doomed himself to failure, as I intended he should." This leads to an interesting talk, and Candide shrewdly asks why he took the trouble to tempt. Satan's answer brings us up against one of Dickinson's profound beliefs: his belief in some unity that exists beneath Good and Evil. "I acted under orders," he answers. "I do not profess to understand why these orders were given. . . . But . . . apparently the result has been satisfactory to my employer, for he is sending me again on the same errand."

By this time they have reached the Hermitage and find quite a company there. A Spanish Jesuit, a French *abbé* of the modernist type, a Scottish Presbyterian and a Russian priest have all heard the rumour and have come to meet Jesus. They have been waiting for several days and their relations have become strained. Satan and Candide establish a pleasanter atmosphere, they all sit round the fire, with the darkness and the sounds of the wilderness at their backs, and each of them explains in turn the bearing of this new event (if indeed it has occurred) on his particular creed. The Jesuit begins. In a thoughtful and brilliant speech he expounds the importance of the Church, which "took up the truth revealed by Jesus, interpreted it to the intelligence of mankind, and applied it to their institutions". And he warns his hearers not to confuse the Jesus of Eternity, whose revelation was absolute and final, with the Jesus of Time, who visited the world nearly 2,000 years ago, and who—if indeed he is returning to it—will find much to bewilder him and will need the expert guidance of his own Church.

Tamino is impressed, but becomes aware of the sounds of the desert and of something—or is it someone?—who stands outside the circle of their fire. The same sensation recurs during the address of the second speaker, the French *abbé*, who explains the doctrine of Progressive Revelation and informs the irritated Jesuit that the heresies of one generation are the orthodoxies of the next. Brilliant eyes fix Tamino—set in the night and brighter than the stars—and a possibility enters his mind. Then the Russian priest speaks—most touchingly, for the Jesus he waits for will not belong to the clever or the influential, or the advanced, but to the poor. And again the gaze beckoning out of the night, the possibility becoming a certainty. Finally the Scottish Presbyterian speaks. He has some sharp words for Candide, whom he understandably mistrusts, and the Jesus he expects is or should be hard, for hardness is what this backsliding generation needs. They are not fit for the Sermon on the Mount. Tamino he characterizes as "a nice laddie", who must go back to his work, accept the teaching of his own Church, and expect to find it true when he is old enough to understand.

Tamino does not hear this sound advice. For the possibility has become a certainty and without speech he speaks to Jesus.

"Lord, was your gospel true or false?"

"True and false."

"What was true in it?"

"Love one another. Forgive your enemies."

"What was false?"

"The scourge of small cords, and the coming on clouds to judge the world."

"Are any of the Churches your Church?"

"None of them are mine."

"Do I belong to your Church?"

"You may."

"How?"

"By following me."

"How shall I follow you?"

"By following Truth in Love."

"How shall I find Truth?"

This last remark he makes aloud and the Presbyterian answers tartly: "I have already told you that Truth is found." None of the Churches have been aware of Jesus, and Satan says: "It must have been some hallucination." But Satan has seen him and has to admit it, adding: "He is more impracticable than ever. . . . I shall not even trouble to tempt him. . . . Fortunately, [these gentlemen] have me to direct them, and between us, I daresay, we shall build a tolerable church, strong enough to stem the anarchy." Tamino then realizes that Satan is Fraud, that the Church he hopes to build is for the worship of the Golden Calf; and he hates him.

The next stage of his quest for Truth is the Lotus Lake of Buddha. This is a solemn and exquisite place, inspired by what Dickinson had seen in China, and Tamino at first mistakes it for the Castle of Sarastro. But it is a monastery, whose inmates follow the quest of Eternity, and he himself, since he follows Pamina, is a child of Time. He undergoes the discipline of the monastery. He sat in a wood lost in meditation, and preparing to pass into the final, the eighth stage, from which there is no return—and then a traveller came through the wood, thieves set on him and left him for dead. He called for help but Tamino could not give it, he was too far away, and by the time he returned to the body the man was dead, and he saw in his eyes that look of the man on the battlefield, who had been both his enemy and his friend. He went back to the monastery. In the setting sun, one of the statues of Buddha glowed, and Tamino held with it a voiceless colloquy, such as he had in the Hermitage of Jesus.

"Lord Buddha, was your gospel true?"

"True and false."

"What was true in it?"

"Selflessness and Love."

"What false?"

"Flight from Life."

The light fades from the statue, to illumine the lotus buds on the lake, and they flower into the face of Pamina. He must go back to life. And having passed the Waters of Doubt with the help of her spirit, and the music of his flute, he enters the Castle of Sarastro.

This, the climax of the book, is rather unsatisfactory: too much has to be worked in. The *décor* is again Mozartian: Tamino has passed the tests, and is initiated into the Order of Truth. Who else has been admitted into the Order? Not Plato. Why not? Because Plato fell back in the end under the dominion of the Queen of Night; he came to prefer religion to reason, authority to liberty, and the State to the individual. And these are the three great heresies which no one holding can remain a member of the Order. Is Candide here? The answer is no; Candide almost qualifies but he lacks the one thing needful: the sacred fire.

With this reference to the sacred fire my attempt to recall Lowes Dickinson draws to its close. You see the importance of the reference: Dickinson believes in reason but is not a rationalist. He believes also in the sacred fire, and the fusion of these two beliefs is attempted in his conception of Sarastro. How can they be fused? How can water and fire combine? Certainly not in the material world. But when we consider the complexities of the human spirit fusion becomes, if not possible, at all events comprehensible.

I have used the phrase "to recall Lowes Dickinson" and I fear it is an apt one, for I do not think he is much read or much talked about today—not even in King's College, Cambridge, the tiny corner of the world which once contained him. I am sorry about this, not for his sake, but because he has so much to offer. He challenges the materialism of our age. He also challenges the religiosity, the revivalism, the insistence on sin that are so often offered as correctives to materialism. In place of those false goods and gods he offers the human spirit which tries to follow reason, knows that reason sometimes fails, yet when it does fail does not scuttle to take refuge in authority. Add to this his belief that it is through poetry and through music that man comes closest to the sacred fire, and his claim to be remembered is confirmed.

He has also a tangible memorial. When you are in London, and if you are in the neighbourhood of Kensington, go and look at Edwardes Square. It is a charming square to the south of Kensington High Street. No. 11, Edwardes Square is the house where Dickinson's sisters lived, and where he lived when he was in town. A plaque has been put up to him on the house. It describes him as a writer and a humanist, and the word humanist also describes Sarastro.

Forster's Preface to
The Greek View of Life

Written in 1956 for a new edition, and reprinted here by courtesy of Methuen & Co. Ltd

In his unpublished *Recollections* Lowes Dickinson describes the genesis of this little work: "It came to me in our dining-room at All Souls Place, in the old armchair, now long vanished from my life—who bought it, I wonder? Does it still exist?"

When he sat in that chair he was a Cambridge don in his early thirties, whose main job was the teaching of Political Science, and whose previous books had been about modern France or parliamentary institutions. He had been brought up on Latin and Greek, it is true, but in a stupid and wasteful way, the classics had meant little to him, and had sometimes bored him, and it was only when he got away from them and studied contemporary affairs that he began to discover what they meant. The ancients are modern. That, in brief, was his discovery. They are modern because many of their problems are ours, and have been expressed, particularly in Athens, with a lucidity beyond our power. We cannot be lucid, we are too much involved. Our passions colour our judgements—and are bound to, otherwise we shouldn't be alive. Ancient Greece has the advantage of being remote from us in time; we can therefore study it with detachment, and we can bring back from it help for our problems today. Greece hadn't science, it is true, and she had no global commitments, but she encompassed within the tiny circuit of her city states much that affects and afflicts the modern man in his relationship to society. And, because her writers were intelligent and because they were sensitive, she has been able to send us news on these urgent matters which is still fresh, although it is over two thousand years old.

That was one of the considerations that occurred to Lowes Dickinson when he sat down to write *The Greek View of Life*: the political consideration. He was a student of politics right up to his old age (when he produced *The International Anarchy*) and he naturally gives space to them in this work of his youth. But it was not his only consideration. Greece was not just a convenient laboratory for the social scientist. The joy of living and the greatness of existence were also to be found there. Greek literature combined beauty and depth, wisdom and wit, gaiety and insight,

speculation and ecstasy, carnality and spirit; it had variety; it had con-
structional power; it was the greatest literature the world had yet produced. There was one disadvantage attached to it. It could only be read
by people who had sweated at the language for years, and they generally
could not read it as well as they pretended. Translations were therefore
imperative. And whilst admitting that most translations impair the
colouring, and even distort the proportions, he preferred them to
nothing at all. His book might be called an introduction to translations.
It is an attempt to show the non-expert the character and environment
of hidden treasures and to leave him among them. In his own judgement
he succeeded: "I still feel that I have got hold of . . . the central thing,
the thing that makes Greek of permanent value to civilization."

The four sections of the book deal with the Greek attitude towards
Religion; towards the State; towards the Individual; towards Art.
Religion is a puzzler: all-pervading yet having little connection with
what the Christian regards as faith or as conscience; mainly concerned
with making Man feel at home in this world, and offering him only the
vaguest intimations of immortality. The State is a puzzler of another
sort: unthinkably small, so small that the people in it know each other
personally, and the same citizen could be farmer, judge, legislator,
soldier, etc. The Individual is easier to grasp, but remains definitely
B.C.: if fortunate, he is well-to-do and healthy and so can enjoy the
operations of his body and his mind and can contact other fortunate
individuals; his life is not a preparation for a better one, and the end of
it is regrettable unless he has become unfortunate. And Art: art is aesthetic, but it is also ethical; it is individual but it is also social, for the
reason that the individual is closely integrated in his city-state.

The above is a most crude summary. Still it may help the reader to
start off on the four sections. He will notice that Dickinson says nothing
of the origins of Greek civilization; it was not his purpose to do so, nor
did he know as much about them as is known today. He will also notice
that his outlook is mainly Athenian, and that the keystone of his work is
Plato. Plato was indeed one of his three guides—the other two being
Shelley and Goethe—and he found in the Platonic dialogue, and even in
the Platonic myth, a congenial road to truth. It is significant that the
longest of the quotations (pp. 189–200) is from the *Symposium*. There
Plato expounds, in a famous passage, his theory of love and his belief
that the highest love is homosexual. To Dickinson, as to many critics,
such a theory seemed characteristically Greek, though other critics
have denied this: Dr Charles Seltman, for instance, in his alluring
Women in Antiquity. And after Plato the emphasis falls on Aeschylus and
on Thucydides.

The book was published in 1896—exactly sixty years ago. It had an
immediate success both here and in the States, was used extensively in
education and must have introduced thousands of young men and
women to an inheritance they were in danger of neglecting. It may be

trusted to do the same today. The fallacy that only those who know Greek can know Greece has been exploded, and, though translations can never function as originals, they lead the reader much nearer to the shrine than was once supposed. So may good fortune attend this, the twenty-third edition! It appears at an appropriate moment, for a plaque has recently been installed to Dickinson's memory; not on that house at All Souls Place which contained the armchair and has itself disappeared, but at 11 Edwardes Square, Kensington, his home in later days.

In 1899 he paid his first visit to Greece. His impressions are worth quoting:

> I had been depressed and worried. But from the moment of landing at the Piraeus life renewed itself in perpetual interest and delight. The Acropolis at Athens revealed to me the meaning of the architectural mouldings I had seen parodied all over Europe. It was like hearing music at last played in tune, after a long perversion by slight discords.

It was an experience I had myself this very spring. Like him I saw the Acropolis, the columns at Sunium and the charioteer at Delphi, and I also experienced something he does not record: the fundamental good-will of the Greeks who inhabit Greece today. His own visit had other consequences. One magical evening in the deserted ruins of Mistra above Sparta "there occurred to me the idea of writing a Dialogue on Good, which I carried out in the following year or so". The dialogue form was particularly suited to his genius. *A Modern Symposium* followed, and at the very end of his life, closing as he began, he wrote *After Two Thousand Years*, when Plato and a young man of the present century converse in the Elysian Fields and discuss their contrasted yet comparable civilizations.

Forster's Introduction to *Letters from John Chinaman and Other Essays*

Written, together with brief Notes on the Essays, for this selection (1946) of Dickinson's work, and reprinted here by courtesy of George Allen & Unwin Ltd

Goldsworthy Lowes Dickinson (1862–1932) was a Cambridge don whose life was outwardly calm and academic. Appearances can deceive, and he was really in close and constant touch with the problems of his day and a prophet of much that has happened since his death. He was, it is true, a scholar, a philosopher, and something of a mystic, he was, in his private life, a charming and considerate companion, who understood friendship and valued and respected the young. But he was also a vigorous student of public affairs, he went about the world and learned, he was horrified by the coming of the 1914 war and by the threat of worse war to follow, and he worked with all his might for the League of Nations and can claim to be one of its originators. Diversely gifted, he was an individual who managed to live both for himself and for humanity, and perhaps that is the only sort of life worth living.

Dickinson's hopes failed, and he will always be dismissed as a failure by the type of person who used to hail Mussolini as a success; the type is still prevalent. But when mankind has digested its recent achievements, when it has gone everywhere and done everything, and has encountered at the end of every vista its own bloodstained face, it may perhaps pause and try to think. Should it do so, it will certainly listen to the message, and—more important still—will hear the accents, of Lowes Dickinson, who believed in reason, integrity, tolerance, compassion, love, and art (yes: in art), and who had the mental strength to fight and suffer with his eyes open.

The following essays, which have been selected by his publishers, well illustrate his interest in the East and in religion, and also indicate his debt to ancient Greece. But he was many-sided, and some of his aspects have necessarily been missed out. There is, for instance, the mass of political work which culminated in *The International Anarchy*. There are the dialogues, amongst which the exquisite *Modern Symposium*, though not technically a dialogue, must be classed. There is the fantasy of *The Magic Flute*. Perhaps the present selection may lead readers to his longer books, and if they should wish to know more about his life there is a detailed biography of him, written by myself.

appendix e
Pilgrim's Progress

Forster's review (Daily News, *8 February 1921*) *of* The Magic Flute

Since Christian escaped from the City of Destruction there have been so many changes in the spiritual landscape that it is impossible he should now find his way to Mount Zion. The Slough of Despond, the River of Life, the Hill Difficulty, the Delectable Mountains, still exist, because they are parts of the soul of man, but they are no longer in their original positions, nor independent, as they used to be, of one another. Fusion and complexity have increased during these three hundred and fifty years. There are precious jewels now even in the armour of Apollyon, and the joys of Mount Zion itself will not be absolute. They were absolute for Christian, who "shall not see again such things" as he saw when he was "in the lower region upon the earth, to wit, sorrow, sickness, affliction and death". But when Tamino, the Pilgrim of Mr Lowes Dickinson's Fantasy, has passed through the Fire of Action and the Water of Doubt, and has won to the Castle of Sarastro, he finds that it is not a haven of attainment, but a record of those who have attained, and that when his name has been entered he must go back to the world. Nor is Sarastro himself omnipotent. He would rescue the Queen of the Night from the misery she causes herself and mankind, but he cannot, she will have none of him, preferring the darkness. He says, "Lord, how long?" but no voice answers him, and with this interrogation the Fantasy concludes.

And, if the starting-point and the goal have both been altered since Bunyan's time, still greater changes have occurred in the road that connects them. To Christian the road was straight. To Tamino it is essentially not straight, it is crooked, winding, sometimes narrow, sometimes broad. If he went straight ahead he would never arrive anywhere. If he listened to the Scotch Presbyterian in the Hermitage of Jesus, who says to him: "Get back to your own work, accept the teaching of your own Church, and expect to find it true when you are old enough to understand it," he would never deflect his eyes from the argument, and see, glowing through the darkness, the eyes of Jesus, and talk with Jesus beyond speech, and, finding not in Jesus the goal, alter his direction, and pass on to the Lotus Lake of Gautama, nor would he pass on again thence. . . . Honesty and singleness of purpose are as precious in the twentieth century as in the seventeenth. But they must be combined with sensitiveness, to moral there must be added aesthetic apprehension; Salvation will never again be found by following the mathematically straight line. It would be amusing to confront our two pilgrims with one another. What would Christian call Tamino? Mr Facing Both Ways perhaps. While Tamino would see in Christian and his mere strength of will a traveller not less pernicious than Monostatos, and in his Sacred Scrip a barren and ungenerous guide through the living landscape.

The Magic Flute is Tamino's own guide—for Mr Lowes Dickinson has found in the famous opera of Mozart a fresh and most beautiful mythology. Whether Mozart would also find it, I doubt. I have never (difficult confession!) been able to hear the greatness in Mozart's music, nor to see more in his *Magic Flute* than a masonic pantomime containing one or two serious numbers. But this is beside the point. The mythology is to Mr Dickinson's purpose philosophically, and he also builds it into a touching and lovely story. Sarastro stands for Reason, for regulated emotion, while the Queen of the Night is undisciplined Instinct, who dwells on the further side of Mind, creating while she sleeps. She does not understand, she does not wish to understand. And Pamina is their child. It is the Queen who first incites Tamino to seek Pamina, pretending to him that Sarastro forcibly detains her. Tamino tries force (Monostatos), but force is useless, because Pamina remains with her father by her own wish. Thousands are slain in a war, until Tamino's eyes are opened, he understands the nature of Sarastro, and he sees that he has been slaying his own friends. He would withdraw, but his own side turn against him now, and he is cast into prison. There Pamina appears in a vision, the test of Fire is consummated, and he passes out after her through flaming walls that say:

> I crackle and blaze!
> Bear me who can!
> Who cannot I craze—

and the Magic Flute, the spirit of Sarastro, is with him, and answers the flames:

> But I am a man—

and he wins through. It is the test of the Water (speculation) that he must approach next. And wandering about, as our modern pilgrim must, he visits in turn the Garden of Candide, which is scepticism, the Hermitage of Jesus, where the religious sophists are in assembly, and the Lotus Tank of Mysticism, where Reality is attained, it is true; but at the price of renouncing Humanity. Reality thus won is useless to a follower of Sarastro. Tamino continues. And at last, in a mountain gorge, amid roaring waters, the vision of Pamina reappears, as once in the prison, and he follows her through the spray and the cold this time, while the Flute answers:

> But I am a man.

And, a man, he enters the Castle of Sarastro.

Such, in brief, is Mr Lowes Dickinson's argument. But the graciousness and persuasion of his writing, the humour, the poetry, the sane yet emotional outlook—these cannot be conveyed. A sense of security is with us as we read, and though the closing scene in the Hall provides no ultimate vision we have a belief that something has been achieved, or at least recorded, which can never be erased. This hall is no vulgar repository of All the Talents. Poets come here not because they are great poets, but because they are followers of Sarastro. Wordsworth and Dante are excluded. Plato came, but in his old age he seceded to the Queen of the Night: "he came to prefer religion to reason, authority to liberty, and the State to the individual. And those are the three great heresies which no one holding can remain a member of our Order." Candide did not come because he did not think it worth while; he had every qualification but one—the sacred fire.

In one respect, however, Mr Lowes Dickinson does belong to the past. He does believe in a Pilgrim's Progress, whereas most of our contemporaries believe not in Pilgrimage, but in Adventure. They have not the sense of a goal, and in consequence their writings and conversation lack ethical flavour. Mr Dickinson's main catogory is, indeed, not Good and Evil, but Light and Darkness, and *The Magic Flute*, like all his books, inflicts no moral lesson. All the same, it contains the moral sense, because its climax is not an escapade, but a goal.

The first and third sections of the book are the best. The second, which deals with war, inevitably deals with the War, and even if one agrees with Mr Lowes Dickinson's opinions (I do) one feels that he has not freed them enough from the sorrow and indignation of the moment. The conscientious objector, the journalist, the embittered mother, the bloodthirsty old man, are universals, no doubt, and therefore apt to his allegory, but he has not always succeeded in universalizing them, or in "reindividualizing" them, to coin a clumsy phrase. Character-drawing is, indeed, not his strong point. Bunyan beats him here. Christian is a rare walker—one can see his legs at it the whole blessed way, and he walks in his own fashion and talks to correspond. But Tamino gives no sense of personal functioning, and though his face and thoughts are fair and appropriate he seems but an abstract figure of youth, such as occurs in the pictures of the Italian Renaissance. However, these are small defects in the general scheme. The writer's aim has been to present "The Choice before Us", and he has never presented it more subtly, more beautifully, or with greater persuasion.

A Broadcast Debate

Forster's review (Nation and Athenaeum, *10 May 1930*) *of*
Points of View (*no. 313 in the Bibliography*)

Points of View prints a series of broadcasts from Mr Lowes Dickinson, Dean Inge, Mr H. G. Wells, Mr J. B. S. Haldane and Sir Oliver Lodge. Mr Bernard Shaw also broadcast, but characteristically refused to toe the line and be printed with his colleagues, and his place has been filled by Sir Walford Davies. The B.B.C. is to be congratulated both on the series and on the prominence it gives to Mr Dickinson, who opens and closes the debate, and writes a general introductory note. Mr Dickinson has, of course, won an audience through his books, and he is particularly well known to readers of the *Nation*, but he is not a familiar name to the general public, and something has here been done to repair the public loss. Last year, just after the series had been delivered, the present reviewer took a railway journey with an excited and intelligent young man, half clerk and half sailor, who waved copies of the *Listener* about and cried: "I've heard of all the others, but who's Low Dickens? He's far the best of the lot, he sets you thinking for yourself." That has, of course, always been Mr Dickinson's aim, from *The Meaning of Good* onwards, and it is the aim of the series generally, and those of us who believe in thought must thank the B.B.C. and wish it many years of freedom from commercialism. It has its faults. Its demure gentlemanliness is often trying, and it is menaced by that subtle evil, public-school good form, which always end by throttling originality. But at all events it is not tricking us into buying something. The speakers are not suddenly switched off so that somebody's patent poison may be dinned into our ears. This happens in other countries, and it would happen in Great Britain if proper control were removed.

Why do we believe in thought? All the speakers, except Sir Walford Davies, stress their belief in it. They desire to find out what the universe is like and to make deductions from the discovery. Not even Sir Oliver Lodge exalts intuition, not even the Dean of St Paul's takes refuge in authority. We believe in thought, surely, for two distinct and perhaps incompatible reasons. In the first place it seems "up to us" to think; it is a noble and human activity, something that men ought to do. In the second place, we hope that by thinking we shall avert certain evils from ourselves and society, particularly the evil of war. "Men always want to fight when they ought to be trying to understand," is the way Mr Dickinson puts it, and he weaves the two reasons for thinking into a single thread more closely, perhaps, than do his colleagues. He would weave in everything, love as well as thought; he feels that until human nature has expanded fully we cannot either be saved or safe, and views civilization as a pilgrimage towards a harmony which may never be realized, but it is our only proper goal.

Democracy, psychology and biology are among the subjects touched upon in the debate; it is not possible to give a complete list of them in this brief notice, and still less possible to indicate the points of difference between the speakers. The addresses are not of equal value. Sir Walford Davies's is the least satisfactory; there is a sort of coy mysticism about him which does not wear well, and when he says that "the galactic universe is perhaps one stupendous Rondo of the Almighty" neither astronomy nor music seems to advance. Dean Inge makes, as always, some fine and acceptable remarks, but he seems dispirited, although he professes to be in better spirits, and he snubs his colleagues without enthusiasm. Mr Haldane is interesting, and severely statistical as long as it is a question of comparative mortality in occupations; when he comes to marriage he gives, rather charmingly, no statistics, but, because his own marriage has been happy, recommends the adventure to all and sundry. His talk suffers from desultoriness, and the same criticism might be passed on Sir Oliver Lodge's. Indeed, how should these talks be otherwise? one feels inclined to say. "Points of View" are lived, not narrated; one can broadcast views, but not a point of view. So one would suppose; and then Mr Wells comes and proves one wrong: his talk, the best in the book, somehow manages to distil the knowledge and emotion of a lifetime into half an hour. He writes very simply, very sincerely, and all about himself, yet there is not a touch of egoism in his argument; he is a "fragment of a man" trying, through the microphone, to reach other fragments of men. It is clear that the medium was suited to Mr Wells, and that he would not have been as happy on a lecture-platform, and as one reads him one visualizes him sitting in the soundproof studio, anxious and excited, with that queer skull-like membraneous object hanging a foot from his mouth, and confiding to it his view of the human make-up. He is the most vivid and stimulating of the contributors. But one's abiding memory will be of Mr Dickinson. With Mr Dickinson sympathy and tolerance are not catchwords or even pious aspirations. He possesses them naturally, and yet they do not enfeeble his own outlook or make him compromising or hazy. He really can enter into the views of others and interpret them without abandoning his own, and that is why he is so perfectly suited to preside over such a symposium as this.

Beatrice Webb on
Goldsworthy Lowes Dickinson

Typed letter to E. M. Forster, now in the Forster archive at King's College, Cambridge; published with the permission of the British Library of Political and Economic Science

Passfield Corner, Liphook, Hants
24 April 1934

Dear Mr Forster,

It was ever so kind of you to send us a copy of your delightful study of Lowes Dickinson which, as I said to my husband, is "the description of one rare spirit by another". I have read it with very great interest as I have always wanted to understand exactly what Lowes Dickinson meant by his vision of an ideal culture. Your account of his life and analysis of his writings has revealed to me why I was never able to appreciate him as a thinker, though I admired one or two of his books—*John Chinaman* and the *Modern Symposium* for instance. The truth is that our scales of value were mutually exclusive—perhaps they ought to have been complementary! This is brought out vividly by his impressions of India and China.

It so happens that we were in those parts in 1911 and 12: for instance I note his liking for the Maharajah of Chhattarpur. We also stayed with that "tiny and fantastic figure": we thought him the last word of Hindu decadence and especially repulsive when he asked my husband to help him to save his soul. I may add that we sent him the *Art of Creation* by Carpenter, whereupon he implored us to send Carpenter to stay with him at his expense as he was sure that he was exactly the person to solve his difficulties. It is needless to say that we did not hand on the invitation—as we doubted the fulfilment of the condition even if that eminent prophet had been willing to leave England. Then again about China and the Chinese: we were in Peking, Tsitsin and Shanghai during the revolution in the autumn of 1911 and we saw many officials and revolutionaries who had been my husband's students at the London School of Economics and who introduced us to their friends: every one of them was betraying either the republic or the emperor and usually both alternately. We saw very little beauty in modern China and its furniture or in the modern temples; and when I cross-examined the German expert at his Embassy, who had lived there twenty years buying museum pieces, he told me that there had been no art in China for many hundreds of years, the last sign of it being some pottery about 250 years ago. One thousand years ago they seem to have had 100 musical instruments but all of them had been dropped except two which emitted horrid noises. We went to one or two Chinese theatres and the Chinese plays seemed to us the last work [*sic*] of vulgarity and senseless noise. Perhaps we were prejudiced but I gather from Pearl Buck's wonderful novel, *Good Earth*, that the home life is very ugly in its relationships, whether between husband and wife or parents and children. What puzzles me is the cause of this fundamental difference of judgement between us and Lowes Dickinson, because I readily admit that he had an exquisite sense of beauty and that we have very little artistic faculty. Moreover his conception of the good is so completely different from ours, which I am afraid is always based on the social value of an institution or law—that is, the way in which it will raise or lower the culture and development of what are called the common people. I imagine that Lowes Dickinson would loathe Soviet Communism which we think has discovered the root of the matter in its aims and methods. Then again Lowes Dickinson seems to have ignored science and its application to social organisations.

Why don't you write another great novel (analogous to the *Passage to India*) giving the essence of the current conflict all over the world between those who aim at exquisite relationships within the closed circle of the "elect" and those who aim at hygienic and scientific improvement of the whole of the race? I think the exact antithesis of Lowes Dickinson and his immediate followers may be found in Professor Hogben and his wife; and I am afraid I am instinctively on their side.

But forgive the lengthiness and cumbertiveness [*sic*] of this letter of thanks. If you are ever in this neighbourhood it will be so pleasant to see you.

Sincerely yours,
[signed] Beat Webb
Mrs Sidney Webb.

A Note on the Text

Goldsworthy Lowes Dickinson raises a number of textual problems. The least serious are the differences between, on the one hand, the first British and American editions (the latter being printed by photo-litho offset from the former), and, on the other hand, the various subsequent reprints, all of them British. The nature of these differences is clear: they all represent, unmistakably, corrections rather than the introduction of errors. The name of Kingsley Martin has, in the reprints, been added to the list of people thanked at the end of the Preface. Since this has necessitated resetting the whole of the original page vi,[1] the alteration, lower down on this page, of "W. A. R. Munro" to "J. A. R. Munro" might have been a compositor's error but for the fact that the same change occurs on pages 22 and 275. Another change in the corrected line on page 22—"T. H. Bowlby" to "H. T. Bowlby"—is in turn confirmed as a correction by its recurrence on page 271. On page 35 "schwärmerisch" has been given its w. On page 40 one quotation from Shelley has been given its quotation marks, another corrected by the substitution of "morrow" for "moon". On page 69, in a quoted letter, an interpolated comment has been enclosed in square brackets instead of parentheses. On page 73, in another quoted letter, a necessary "it" has been inserted after "comprehend". On page 76, middle, "reason" has been corrected to "reasons"; on the same page "Cima di Forno" has been changed to Bernina" (also "Pisoe" to the correct "Pisoc"), and an otiose "some" inserted, patently for the sole purpose of filling out the line; I have here omitted this word. On the last line of page 86 "explains" has been corrected to "exclaims". On page 135 the claim that Dickinson was "the holder, and the first holder", of an Albert Kahn Travelling Fellowship has been modified to "among the earliest holders". On page 156 another Shelley quotation has been corrected by the substitution of "this" for "the". On page 174, line 12 from the bottom, "mind" has been corrected to "mine". On page 206 a letter originally dated "Aug. 4th (1929?)" has been re-dated "Aug. 4th (1928)". Finally, on page 208, line 3 from the bottom, "fathers' " has been corrected to "father's".

The first edition was published by Edward Arnold on 19 April 1934, and the first reprint (May 1934, sheets of this forming also the cheap

[1] All page numbers in this paragraph refer, of course, to the original editions.

225

edition of 1938) was printed from the same type, with the corrections listed above. When, in October 1944, a further reprint became necessary, the basis was not the 1934 reprint—of which 500 copies had been destroyed in the war—but the first edition, corrected from the original list of errors, a copy of which must have survived. This is clear from the fact that some of the corrections have been effected in a slightly different way. In the earlier reprint, for example, where the substitution of "morrow" for "moon" caused a block quotation to over-run by a line, this was compensated by reducing from one line to three-quarters each of the four spaces above and below the two block quotations on this page. To achieve this result for a photographic reprint, a certain amount of paste-up work, or the resetting of the entire page, was required. Whether through oversight or laziness, a third alternative was adopted: the reprint dated 1945 (likewise those of 1947 and 1962, both of them photographic) has no space between the second block quotation and the following text.

The basis for the present text, then, is the 1962 pocket edition, as collated with the other editions or printings mentioned above. (No manuscript or typescript survives.)

In the Abinger Edition of *Two Cheers for Democracy*, pages 360–61, I described my practice over punctuation, spelling and the like (briefly, to regularize wherever it is possible to do so "without encroaching on the author's prerogatives of meaning, emphasis and tone") and over Forster's frequent misquotation of other writers (with rare exceptions, to correct). What I wrote there applies here and elsewhere. In the present volume, quotations from Dickinson's *Recollections* have been brought into line, in substance and in most of the minutiae, with the version now published in *The Autobiography of Goldsworthy Lowes Dickinson, and Other Unpublished Writings*. (An exception is noted in the next paragraph.) To the editor of this volume, Sir Dennis Proctor, I am deeply indebted, not only for lending me proofs, but for checking against Dickinson's original typescript the 250 or so points at which these proofs differed from Forster's quotation. In almost every instance the discrepancy was due to an inaccuracy on the part either of Forster or of the typist who produced from Dickinson's original typescript (heavily corrected in his barely legible hand) the fair copy on which Forster relied. In a tiny handful of cases Sir Dennis concluded that Forster's reading was the true one, and corrected his proofs accordingly.[2]

More problematic than quotations from the *Recollections* are those from Dickinson's unpublished letters. It is safe to assume that these too are riddled with inaccuracies; and in the case of several letters to Forster himself, to the Ashbees and to A. J. Grant the assumption is confirmed by comparison with the originals at King's College, Cambridge. Quotations

[2] One quotation, stated by Forster (page 152 in this edition) to be from the *Recollections*, is actually, Sir Dennis Proctor informs me, from a separate sheaf of papers on which Dickinson jotted down his reflections during his sister Janet's last illness and immediately after her death.

from these letters have here been corrected. In one instance this has necessitated a tiny correction to Forster's own text. At page 43, line 7, his actual words are: "Here is the letter to Ashbee, who was then in Germany"—followed by what purports to be a single letter, dated "May 5, 1885". What Forster has done, however, is to quote from the *Recollections*, inaccurately, an inaccurate transcript by Dickinson of linked extracts from *two* letters (2 and 12 May), and to add further to the confusion by interpolating from the original a passage which Dickinson had omitted—interpolating it, moreover, between two passages from the second letter, although it belongs to the first. With some hesitation, I have altered "Here is the letter to Ashbee" to "The following is to Ashbee", and unscrambled the two letters to the extent of giving the extracts in the right order and inserting correct dates at appropriate points.

In the second of the two letters just mentioned, and at one other point (page 136), the principle of fidelity to quoted sources has led me to restore, following the *Recollections*, a name given in full by Dickinson, which in 1934 Forster thought it prudent to reduce to an initial letter or replace by three dots. These restorations are indicated by square brackets; elsewhere in this volume, square brackets (in two cases replacing Forster's round ones) denote an interpolation by Forster, not by his editor.

It remains for me to list other editorial emendations, which in this volume are, with one exception, trivial enough to warrant summary treatment. With this one exception, they fall into two categories. The first represents a mere extension of the principle of quoting other writings correctly: to naming them and their works correctly, dating books (and in one instance a parliamentary debate) correctly,[3] naming other individuals correctly, together with institutions and places. Into this category fall the following (in each case the reading given here is followed by the reading given in all earlier printings; figures denote page and line):

3: 9–10 Smith, Elder / Smith Elder
35: 18 and 100: 41 Society for Psychical Research / Society of Psychical Research
45: 5 *Savages* / the Savages
51: 9 Building / Buildings
51: 31 Scholars' / Scholar's
52: 1 Garden / Gardens
68: 41 May / April
69: 2 The Convergence / Convergence
82: 37 *Living* / Life
95: 5 1908 / 1907
100: 19 Lecture / Lectures
107: 14 and 111: 2 Pittsburgh / Pittsburg
108: 17 Gardner / Gardiner

[3] See, however, the index entry under Moore, G. E.

109: 37–8 University of Wisconsin at Madison / Madison University
at Wisconsin
110: 42 Ida M. / I.M.
112: 31 *Civilisations* / Civilisation
122: 12–13 University of Wisconsin / University at Wisconsin
127: 16 17 December / December 18th
132: 22 Ferenc / Ferencz
167: 38 Fellows' Garden / Fellows Gardens
168: 1 Rylands's / Ryland's
178: 3 *Larger* / a Larger

Emendations in the other category represent what I believe, with varying
degrees of confidence, Forster (or in some cases Dickinson) to have
actually written—or, at the very least, *intended* to write:

7: 29 turning / turn
33: 33 even / ever
66: 7 demonstrably / demonstrately
70: 15 assumption / assumptions
71: 4 always / already
85: 11 1900 / 1904[4]
85: 21 serious-minded / seriously-minded
91: 3 methods / method
94: 24 had cared / cared
100: 39 planchettes / planchette
101: 33 there / then
105: 20 sang / sung
116: 31 night / nights
124: 20 moon rise / moonrise
157: 19 impossibile / impossible
169: 8 finale / Final
184: 35 notion / motion
185: 37 und / and
191: 19 national / natural
191: 31 made / much
208: 40 Pamina / Pamina's
220: 37 defects in / defects on
221: 15 (of text) sets you thinking / sets you start thinking

A number of other suspect readings seem, on balance, more likely to
represent an idiosyncrasy—whether on the part of Forster, Dickinson or,

---

[4] Forster cannot have intended 1904—three years after his departure from
the Cambridge scene. The only possible years for which 1904 is a likely misprint
are 1900 and 1901, and 1900 fits better with the date (1899–1900) of McTaggart's first course of "popular lectures on philosophy" (see Dickinson's *J. McT. E.
McTaggart*, pp. 60–61) and with the facts mentioned by Sir Roy Harrod in
The Life of John Maynard Keynes, p. 63.

for example, the man (page 147) who shouted "More likely to chuck in you" rather than the more natural "chuck *you* in". One sentence from which at first sight a verb has been omitted is probably a conscious echo of Luther; see "I can . . ." in the index.

The remaining emendation concerns the list, on pages 80–81, of Dickinson's lectures at the London School of Economics and Political Science. Earlier editions included, presumably through some form of dittography, a course on "The Bases of Political Obligation" which is merely a garbled version of the course correctly included as "Some Theories of the Basis of Political Obligation". On the other hand, this "complete list" omitted Dickinson's first course, and "began" with what was actually his second course. The list given here has been corrected in these two respects; some anomalies remain, but they are less serious. ("The Structure of the Modern State" was given not twice but three times; two other courses were given twice.)

Bibliography

by R. E. Balfour, revised by the Editor

Note

Though every endeavour has been made to make this bibliography complete, it is probable that some of Dickinson's writings have escaped notice. In particular it has proved impossible to discover more than a very few unsigned articles; some certainly exist, e.g. in the *Saturday Review* and in *The Nation*, though it is not likely that there were many such. Apart from those indicated as anonymous or pseudonymous, all the items in the following list were published under his own name or initials.

Descriptions have been made as concise as possible, but occasionally where the subject of an entry is not clear from its title a few words of explanation have been added in square brackets. It has not seemed necessary to specify when only minor changes were made in reprinting articles, and "reprinted" must therefore often be interpreted as equivalent to "reprinted with verbal alterations". Indication of the various publishers, English and American, are given in the case of each book, but it has not been practicable to give a complete list of editions. The size and pagination quoted normally refer to the earliest English edition.

The bibliography also includes such of Dickinson's letters to the newspapers as have been traced. Many of these are of considerable length—in some cases an entire column or more of the *Manchester Guardian*—and are valuable expressions of his views on current affairs. Only a very few letters of purely ephemeral scope have been omitted, but less important ones have wherever possible been mentioned only as references in connection with articles or other letters dealing with the same subject.

To the numerous persons who have helped me in my search for Dickinson's writings I owe a deep debt of gratitude. Without their help this bibliography would have been far more incomplete—could indeed hardly have been begun. A list of their names would occupy much space and they will know that my thanks are not less sincere for being collectively expressed. I would, however, especially thank the following: Mr E. M. Forster, Mr Roger Fry and Mr N. Wedd, my professed intention of questioning whom on every possible occasion must have made the prospect of meeting me a recurrent nightmare; the editors of the *New*

Statesman and Nation, the *Manchester Guardian*, the *News Chronicle* and the *Cambridge Review*, who allowed me access to their files; the editors of the *Atlantic Monthly* and the *New Republic*, the Librarian of Congress, and Messrs Doubleday, Doran & Co., who supplied me with invaluable information about American editions; and the officials and staff of the British Museum and the University Library.

R. E. B.

Ronald Edmond Balfour, historian and Fellow of King's College, Cambridge, was killed in action in March 1945, at the age of forty-two. After examining the great majority of the 345 items which he listed in his excellent bibliography, and discovering virtually no errors of fact, I concluded that the effort of trying to track down the remaining items would hardly be justified. Instead, I have attempted to bring the bibliography up to date—though I would be astonished if there were no fresh gaps—by adding new editions and translations, either (as Balfour's practice appeared to dictate) at the end or under existing entries. Mere reprints are excluded, as they were by Balfour. I have also transferred to the main sequence (and, as far as possible, to correct chronological positions within their respective years) the nine items, originally numbered 337–45, which Balfour inserted as "addenda"; to avoid renumbering hundreds of entries, I have had recourse to "decimal" numbers, e.g. 150·1. Otherwise the original entries and the original system are for the most part unchanged—although in adding new items I have not attempted to supply even the conventional bibliographical tags ("Cr. 8vo" and the like) provided by Balfour.

O. S.

1883

1 Doubt. [Poem.] *The Carthusian*, Feb., p. 214.
2 Ormusd. [Poem.] *Ibid.* April, p. 235.
3 Cyrene. [Poem.] *Ibid.* June, p. 246.
4 "Comes there a voice to me". [Poem.] *Cambridge Review*, Nov. 14, p. 77.

1884

5 A Remonstrance. [Poem.] *Cambridge Review*, April 30, p. 301.
6 Pindar. [Sonnet.] *Ibid.* May 7, p. 317.
7 Diana. [Sonnet.] *Ibid.* May 21, p. 348.
8 To the Student of Bohn. [Epigram.] *Ibid.* June 4, p. 381.
9 Hesperus. [Sonnet.] *Ibid.* June 11, p. 399.
10 Savonarola. A Poem which obtained the Chancellor's Medal at the Cambridge Commencement MDCCCLXXXIV. Occupies pp. 7–16 of *Prolusiones Academicae . . . A.D. mdccclxxxiv*. Cantabrigiae: Typis Academicis. Reprinted in no. 36.
11 Cologne Cathedral. [Sonnet.] *Cambridge Review*, Oct. 29, p. 46.

1885

12 Shelley. [Sonnet.] *Cambridge Review*, March 4, p. 253.

13 Vox Desperantibus. [Poem.] *Ibid.* March 11, p. 272.

14 SYLLABUS OF A COURSE OF LECTURES ON CARLYLE, EMERSON, BROWNING, and TENNYSON. [University Extension Lectures delivered at Chesterfield, Mansfield and Stamford in the Michaelmas Term 1885, and at Chester in the Lent Term 1886.] Derby: Bemrose & Sons. Demy 8vo. pp. 30.

15 Emerson. [Unsigned article.] *Church Reformer*, Nov. 16, pp. 248–50.

1886

16 SYLLABUS OF A COURSE OF LECTURES . . . POETRY, MODERN AND ANCIENT. [University Extension Lectures delivered in conjunction with R. G. Moulton at Preston and Southport in the Lent Term 1886.] Sheffield: Leader & Sons. Demy 8vo. pp. 20. Dickinson delivered the first six lectures on Browning and Tennyson, Moulton the remainder on classical drama.

1887

17 JACOB'S LADDER. [Poem.] Privately printed by the Monotype Printing Company, Clement's Inn. Pott 4to. pp. 22.

18 Carmen Mysticum. [Poem signed D.] *The Spectator*, Dec. 3, p. 1653.

1888

19 "My love I saw the roses glow". [Poem signed D.] *Cambridge Fortnightly*, Feb. 7, p. 8. Reprinted in no. 38.

20 Tynemouth. [Sonnet signed D.] *Ibid.* Feb. 21, p. 56.

21 Sunrise. [Poem signed D.] *Ibid.* March 6, pp. 74–5. Reprinted with the omission of two stanzas in no. 38.

22 The Burning of the Books. [A dream signed D.] *Ibid.* March 6, pp. 76–8.

23 The Professor. [Unsigned short story.] *Ibid.* March 13, pp. 92–7.

24 "Across the waves I saw their purple die". [Poem signed D.] *Ibid.* March 13, p. 99.

25 Hymn from the Prologue to *Faust*. [Poem signed D.] *The Spectator*, Oct. 13, p. 1392.

26 THE SEEKERS. [Manifesto for an informal society of his friends.] Privately printed. Demy 16mo. pp. 8.

1889

27 SYLLABUS OF A COURSE OF LECTURES ON "MILTON AND HIS TIMES". [University Extension Lectures delivered at Newcastle and Sunderland in the Lent Term 1889, Blackburn and Leicester in the Michaelmas Term 1889, and Ipswich in the Lent Term 1890.] Cambridge: Fabb & Tyler. Demy 8vo. pp. 18.

28 The Later Plays of Björnson. [Unsigned article.] *Macmillan's Magazine*, Dec., pp. 130–35.

1891

29 FROM KING TO KING. The Tragedy of the Puritan Revolution. [Dialogues in prose and verse.] London: George Allen. Cr. 8vo. pp. vii, 127. For revised American edition see no. 78.

30 SYLLABUS OF A COURSE OF LECTURES ON MODERN FRANCE. [University Local Lectures delivered at Norwich in the Michaelmas Term 1891.] Cambridge University Press. Demy 8vo. pp. 19.

1892

31 Plato's Later Theory of Ideas. A criticism on Dr Jackson's articles [in preceding issues]. *Journal of Philology*, xx, pp. 121–33.

32 Peer Gynt. *Cambridge Observer*, Nov. 1, pp. 2–3.

33 REVOLUTION AND REACTION IN MODERN FRANCE. [1789–1875.] London: George Allen. Cr. 8vo. pp. xii, 300. For revised edition see no. 289.

1893

34 "The Empty Purse" by George Meredith. *Cambridge Observer*, Feb. 14, pp. 3–4.

1894

35 Progress. *Free Review*, April, pp. 47–63.

36 Savonarola. Reprint of no. 10 on pp. 177–84 of *A Complete Collection of the English Poems which have obtained the Chancellor's Gold Medal in the University of Cambridge*, vol. 2. London: Gibbings & Co.

1895

37 THE DEVELOPMENT OF PARLIAMENT DURING THE NINETEENTH CENTURY. London: Longmans, Green & Co. Demy 8vo. pp. viii, 183. For French translation see no. 70.

1896

38 POEMS. London: privately printed at the Chiswick Press. Imp. 16mo. pp. 67. Cf. nos. 19 and 21.

39 THE GREEK VIEW OF LIFE. [A volume in the University Extension Series edited by J. E. Symes.] London: Methuen & Co. Sm. Cr. 8vo. pp. xii, 236. (New York: Scribners; republished by the Chautauqua Press, 1903; McClure, Phillips & Co., 1905; Doubleday, Page & Co., 1908.) For revised editions see nos. 90 and 342.

1897

40 Edition of Carlyle's *French Revolution* in the Temple Classics. 3 vols. London: J. M. Dent & Co.

1898

41 Edition of Shelley's *Prometheus Unbound* in the Temple Dramatists. London: J. M. Dent & Co.

42 Edition of Carlyle's *Sartor Resartus* in the Temple Classics. London: J. M. Dent & Co.

1899
43 Edition of Browning's *Paracelsus* in the Temple Classics. London: J. M. Dent & Co.

1900
44 Edition of Carlyle's *On Heroes, Hero-Worship and the Heroic in History* in the Temple Classics. London: J. M. Dent & Co.

45 Recent Political Theory and Practice. [Unsigned article.] *Quarterly Review*, Oct., pp. 359–80.

1901
46 THE MEANING OF GOOD. A Dialogue. Glasgow: James Maclehose & Sons. Fcap. 8vo. pp. xvi, 231. [2nd ed. London: R. Brimley Johnson, 1902; 4th ed. J. M. Dent & Co., 1907; sheets of 6th ed. transferred to Allen & Unwin, 1930.] (New York: The Macmillan Co.; reissued by McClure, Phillips & Co., 1906; transferred to Doubleday, Page & Co., 1908; reissued by Dutton, 1921.)

47 From the Chinese Point of View. Four letters, signed John Chinaman, to the *Saturday Review*, Jan. 12, 19, 26, and Feb. 2, pp. 47–8, 78–9, 109–10 and 140. Reprinted as the first half of no. 48.

48 LETTERS FROM JOHN CHINAMAN. [Anonymous till 1911.] London: R. Brimley Johnson. Fcap. 8vo. pp. 63. [7th impr. J. M. Dent & Co., 1907; 13th impr. Allen & Unwin, 1932.] An enlarged reprint of no. 47. For American edition see no. 50; for German, Japanese, Gujarati and Dutch translations nos. 268, 343, 272·1, 281·1 and 339; for edition with an introduction by E. M. Forster no. 340.

1902
49 "As Others See Us". [Letter signed Haji Mirza Ali Asghar Kirmanshahi.] *Cambridge Review*, April 24, pp. 265–7.

1903
50 LETTERS FROM A CHINESE OFFICIAL. Being an eastern view of western civilization. [Anonymous.] New York: McClure, Phillips & Co. Fcap. 8vo. pp. xiv, 75. [Transferred to Doubleday, Page & Co., 1908.] The American edition of no. 48, with a new Introduction, pp. vii–xiv. Reissued by W. Faro as "Hands off China!" 1932.

51 Optimism and Immortality. *Hibbert Journal*, April, pp. 425–40. Reprinted as ch. 2 of no. 102.

52 Ecclesiasticism. *Independent Review*, Oct., pp. 115–31. Reprinted as ch. 1 of no. 60.

1904
53 Motoring. *Independent Review*, Jan., pp. 578–89.

54 Tammany. [Review of Alfred Hodder: *A Fight for the City*.] *Ibid.* March, pp. 333–6.

55 Religion and Revelation. *Ibid.* May, pp. 530–41, and June, pp. 26–39. Reprinted as chs. 2 and 3 of no. 60.

56 Noise that you pay for. [Music.] *Ibid.* Aug., pp. 377–90. Reprinted in *The Living Age,* Oct. 1, pp. 45–53.

57 Faith and Knowledge. *Independent Review,* Nov., pp. 274–81. Reprinted as ch. 4 of no. 60.

1905

58 The Art of Creation. [Review of Edward Carpenter's book.] *Independent Review,* Jan., pp. 634–40.

59 "How Long Halt Ye?" [Christianity and Paganism.] *Ibid.* Feb., pp. 27–36.

60 RELIGION. A CRITICISM AND A FORECAST. London: Brimley Johnson & Ince, Ltd. Fcap. 8vo. pp. xi, 93. [3rd impr. J. M. Dent & Co., 1911; sheets of 5th impr. transferred to Allen & Unwin, 1930.] (New York: McClure, Phillips & Co.; transferred to Doubleday, Page & Co., 1908.) A reprint of nos. 52, 55 and 57. Reprinted in no. 340.

61 De Profundis. [Review of Oscar Wilde's book.] *Independent Review,* April, pp. 375–7.

62 Frenzied Finance. [Review of T. W. Lawson: *The Chapters That Have Gone Before of "Frenzied Finance".*] *Ibid.* July, pp. 115–20.

63 The Newest Philosophy. [Santayana's *Life of Reason,* vols. 1 and 2.] *Ibid.* Aug., pp. 177–90.

64 Some Wagner Letters. [Review of *Richard Wagner an Mathilde Wesendonck: Tagebuchblätter und Briefe, 1853–1871.*] *Ibid.* Nov., pp. 352–6.

65 A MODERN SYMPOSIUM. London: Brimley Johnson & Ince, Ltd. Large Fcap. 8vo. pp. 160. [Reissued J. M. Dent & Co., 1907; Allen & Unwin, 1930.] (New York: McClure, Phillips & Co.; transferred to Doubleday, Page & Co., 1908. Lahore: W. C. Kapur, 1935.) For German, Danish, Swedish, Chinese, Spanish and Japanese translations see nos. 87, 94, 122, 301·1, 341 and 343; for editions with introductory matter by Louis Filler, E. M. Forster and Harold Taylor see nos. 344–6.

66 Euthanasia: From the Note-Book of an Alpinist. *Independent Review,* Dec., pp. 476–80. Reprinted in *The Living Age,* Feb. 17, 1906, pp. 445–7, and as ch. 4 of no. 102.

1906

67 Dickinson was General Editor with H. O. Meredith of the Temple Greek and Latin Classics. 6 vols., 1906–7. London: J. M. Dent & Co.

68 Quo Vadis? [The relation of ideals to practice, and of liberty to property.] *Independent Review,* Feb., pp. 148–57.

69 Ibsen's Letters. [Review of *The Correspondence of Henrik Ibsen,* edited by Mary Morison.] *Ibid.* March, pp. 345–8.

70 LE DÉVELOPPEMENT DU PARLEMENT PENDANT LE DIX-NEUVIÈME SIÈCLE. Paris: V. Giard & E. Brière. Translation of no. 37 by M.

Deslandres, with a new preface by Dickinson, pp. lxiii–lxxiii.

71 Shakespeare, Ibsen, and Mr Bernard Shaw. *Independent Review*, July, pp. 83–8. Reprinted in *The Living Age*, Aug. 18, pp. 437–40.

72 War and Peace. [Review of *The Arbiter in Council*.] *Ibid.* July, pp. 113–20.

73 The Motor Tyranny. *Ibid.* Oct., pp. 15–22.

74 Free-Thought and Religion. [Review of J. M. Robertson: *A Short History of Free-Thought*.] *Ibid.* Oct., pp. 111–17.

75 Eastern and Western Ideals: being a rejoinder to William Jennings Bryan. *Century Magazine*, Dec., pp. 313–16.

76 The American Sphinx. [Review of H. G. Wells: *The Future in America*.] *The Speaker*, Dec. 1, pp. 261–2.

77 Leslie Stephen. [In connection with F. W. Maitland's *Life and Letters of Sir Leslie Stephen*.] *Cambridge Review*, Dec. 6, pp. 139–41.

1907

78 FROM KING TO KING. The Tragedy of the Puritan Revolution. New York: McClure, Phillips & Co. Large Fcap. 8vo. pp. vii, 129. [Stock taken over by Doubleday, Page & Co., 1908.] A revised edition of no. 29.

79 A Wild Rose. [Poem.] *Albany Review*, June, p. 250. Reprinted in *The Living Age*, Aug. 17, p. 386, and in no. 99.

80 Christianity and Civilisation. [In connection with J. McCabe: *The Bible in Europe*.] *The Nation*, Aug. 24, p. 934.

81 Peace or War? *Albany Review*, Nov., pp. 130–39. Reprinted in *The Living Age*, Oct. 14, pp. 668–74.

1908

82 A New Poet. [Review of Lascelles Abercrombie: *Interludes and Poems*.] *Albany Review*, March, pp. 642–8.

83 Sociology and Ethics. [In connection with a new edition of Leslie Stephen's *Science of Ethics*.] *Sociological Review*, April, pp. 175–7.

84 Knowledge and Faith. *Hibbert Journal*, April, pp. 515–29. Reprinted as ch. 1 of no. 102.

85 The Social Ideal. [Lecture delivered March 21.] *Working Men's College Journal*, May, pp. 334–9.

86 Machiavellianism. [In connection with the fourth series of Lord Morley's *Miscellanies*.] *Albany Review*, Aug., pp. 552–8.

87 Ein modernes Symposion. *Oesterreichische Rundschau*, Aug. 15, pp. 245–59; Sept. 1, pp. 285–99; Sept. 15, pp. 380–92; Oct. 1, pp. 47–55. Translation of no. 65 by Mrs J. E. Jacob. The last three speeches of the original were omitted in this translation from lack of space, and the projected issue of the whole in volume form was never carried out.

88 JUSTICE AND LIBERTY. A Political Dialogue. London: J. M. Dent & Co. Cr. 8vo., pp. vii, 229. [Sheets of 2nd impr. transferred to

Allen & Unwin, 1930.] (New York: The McClure Company; transferred to Doubleday, Page & Co.; reissued by the Greenwood Press, 1968.) For Japanese and Chinese translations see nos. 166·1 and 289·1.

1909

89 Cross-Correspondences [between automatic scripts. Paper read Dec. 14, 1908.] *Journal of the Society for Psychical Research*, Jan., pp. 10–15.

90 THE GREEK VIEW OF LIFE. London: Methuen & Co. 7th ed. Cr. 8vo. pp. xii, 250. (New York: Doubleday, Page & Co.; reissued, Boston: the Beacon Press, 1951; re-issued, Gloucester, Mass.: Peter Smith, and in paperback, New York: Collier Books, 1962.) Revised edition of no. 39, with a new preface, pp. v–vi. [17th ed., in the Gateway Library, 1932. Fcap. 8vo. pp. xiii, 261.] For edition with a preface by E. M. Forster see no. 342.

91 Is Immortality Desirable? *Atlantic Monthly*, May, pp. 586–95. Reprinted as no. 93, and as ch. 3 of no. 102.

92 The Socialised Millionaire. [Review of G. S. Lee: *Inspired Millionaires*.] *The Nation*, May 8, pp. 204–6. Reprinted in *The Living Age*, June 12, pp. 686–8.

93 IS IMMORTALITY DESIRABLE? The Ingersoll Lecture, 1908 [or rather, 1909]. Boston and New York: Houghton Mifflin Co. Large Fcap. 8vo. pp. 63. Cf. nos. 91 and 102.

94 ET MODERNE SYMPOSIUM. Copenhagen: Gyldendalske Boghandel. Translation of no. 65 by D. Grünbaum.

95 Culture. *Cambridge Review*, Nov. 18, pp. 110–11. Reprinted as ch. 10 of part 4 of no. 130.

96 Letters from America. *English Review*, Nov., pp. 574–86; Dec., pp. 33–46; Jan., pp. 198–207. Reprinted in *The Living Age*, Feb. 12, pp. 387–95; Feb. 26, pp. 526–35; March 12, pp. 651–8; and in part 4 of no. 130.

1910

97 The Issue with the Lords. Four letters to *The Nation*, May 7, pp. 205–6; May 21, pp. 277–8; May 28, p. 312; June 4, pp. 348–9. Cf. an earlier letter on "The Lords and a Referendum", March 5, p. 881.

98 The Stream. [Poem.] *Basileon*, June, p. 14. Reprinted in no. 99.

99 A WILD ROSE AND OTHER POEMS. Privately printed at the L.C.C. Central School of Arts and Crafts. Sm. Demy 4to. pp. 8. Also an edition in Demy 16mo. pp. 8. Cf. nos. 79 and 98.

100 The Social Ideal of Democracy. [Lecture delivered Nov. 12.] *Working Men's College Journal*, Dec., pp. 430–33, and Jan. 1911, pp. 18–19.

1911

101 Ideals and Facts. *Hibbert Journal*, Jan., pp. 263–74. Reprinted in *The Living Age*, March 4, pp. 526–32.

102 RELIGION AND IMMORTALITY. London: J. M. Dent & Co. Fcap.
8vo. pp. 88. [Sheets transferred to Allen & Unwin, 1930.]
(Boston and New York: Houghton Mifflin Co.) A reprint of nos.
84, 51, 91 and 66. Reprinted in no. 340.

103 A Case of Emergence of a Latent Memory under Hypnosis.
Proceedings of the Society for Psychical Research, Aug., pp. 455–67.

1912

104 Demoralising Literature. [The dangers of police censorship.]
Letter to *The Nation*, Feb. 3, pp. 743–4.

105 Five articles, signed Don, in the *Manchester Guardian*. April 12,
p. 17, Aetas Parentum; May 2, p. 14, "Women and Children
First"; May 7, p. 16, Travelling, Old Style; May 14, p. 16,
Intellectualism; May 29, p. 12, Greek and the Spring.

106 πάντα κόνις. [Unsigned poem on the wreck of the *Titanic*.] *Cambridge Magazine*, May 25, p. 361.

107 "The Crime of being Inefficient". [Criticism of a leading article
on mental deficiency.] Letters to *The Nation*, June 1, p. 326,
and June 22, p. 438.

108 The Man versus The Thing. [Culture the aim of education.] *The
Highway*, Aug., pp. 162–3.

109 The Illusion of War. [Review of J. W. Graham: *Evolution and
Empire*.] *The Nation*, Aug. 10, p. 702.

110 Travellers' Tales. A series of articles, signed Don, in the *Manchester
Guardian*. 1, Dec. 20, p. 16, Cairo. The series continued in nos.
111, 112, 115 and 116.

1913

111 Travellers' Tales. [See no. 110.] 2, Jan. 8, p. 14, In the Red Sea;
3, Jan. 14, p. 18, A Junta; 4, Jan. 17, p. 16, Ulster in India;
5, Jan. 21, p. 16, Anglo-India; 6, Jan. 29, p. 16, A Mystery Play;
7, Feb. 10, p. 14, An Indian Saint; 8, Feb. 18, p. 18, "Civis
Britannicus Sum"; 9, March 10, p. 16, A Village in Bengal;
10, March 14, p. 16, Sri Ramakrishna; 11, March 24, p. 11, "The
Monstrous Regimen of Women"; 12, March 28, p. 16, Indian
Art: a Question; 13, April 21, p. 14, Buddha at Burupudur; 14,
May 5, p. 16, A Malay Theatre. Reprinted, except nos. 8 and 12,
as part 1 of no. 130.

112 Travellers' Tales. [See no. 110.] 15, May 8, p. 16, Nanking; 16,
May 27, p. 16, Impressions of China. Reprinted in part 2 of no.
130.

113 The Englishman. [Article signed Don.] *Manchester Guardian*, June 3,
p. 18. Reprinted as ch. 5 of part 2 of no. 130.

114 The Chances of the Chinese Republic. [Letter written from China.]
The Nation, June 28, pp. 491–2.

115 Travellers' Tales. [See no. 110.] 17, June 17, p. 16, In the Yangtse
Gorge; [18, unsigned], June 30, p. 16, China Today; 19, Aug. 7,

p. 16, Pekin; 20, Aug. 21, p. 14, The Most Sacred Mountain. Reprinted in part 2 of no. 130.

116 Travellers' Tales. [See no. 110.] 21, Sept. 4, p. 14, First Impressions of Japan; 22, Sept. 8, p. 14, A "No" Dance; 23, Sept. 12, p. 14, Nikko; 24, Oct. 2, p. 14, Divine Right in Japan; 25, Oct. 7, p. 18, Fuji; 26, Oct. 14, p. 16, Japan and America. Oct. 22, p. 14, Epilogue. Reprinted as part 3 of no. 130.

117 ALBERT KAHN TRAVELLING FELLOWSHIPS. REPORT TO THE TRUS-TEES. London University Press. Demy 8vo. pp. 58. Reprinted as no. 132 and in no. 340.

118 Japan and the West. [Unsigned review of E. B. Mitford: *Japan's Inheritance.*] *Manchester Guardian,* Nov. 13, p. 4.

1914

119 Japan and the West. [Review of Yoshio Markino: *My Recollections and Reflections;* and Okakura-Yoshisaburo: *The Life and Thought of Japan.*] *Manchester Guardian,* Jan. 5, p. 4.

120 Greek Again. [Letter in favour of the abolition of compulsory Greek.] *Cambridge Review,* Feb. 11, pp. 273–4.

121 History as Progress. [Review of F. S. Marvin: *The Living Past.*] *Ibid.* April 29, p. 395.

122 POLITIK OCH SANNING. ETT MODERNT SYMPOSIUM. Stockholm: P. A. Norstedt & Söner. Translation of no. 65 by K. I. Anderberg.

123 Crime and Punishment. [Review of G. Ives: *A History of Penal Methods.*] *Cambridge Review,* May 6, pp. 409–10.

124 Is War Inevitable? *War and Peace,* May, pp. 221–3, and June, pp. 252–3.

125 A Soul in Trouble. [A conversation in India.] *Basileon,* June, pp. 2–3.

126 The Holy War. *The Nation,* Aug. 8, pp. 699–700. For Italian and German translations see nos. 133 and 147.

127 The Way Out. *War and Peace,* Sept., pp. 345–6.

128 The War and the Way Out. Preparing the Path to Peace. *Labour Leader,* Sept. 17, p. 3. For German translation see no. 147.

129 A Peace That Will End War. The False Moral and the True One. Letter to the *Daily News,* Sept. 17, p. 4. For German translation see no. 147.

130 APPEARANCES. Being Notes of Travel. London: J. M. Dent & Sons Ltd. Cr. 8vo. pp. x, 234. [Sheets transferred to Allen & Unwin, 1930.] (New York: Doubleday, Page & Co.) A reprint of nos. 111, 112, 113, 115, 116, together with 95 and 96.

131 "The Enemy in our Midst". Letter to the *Daily News,* Nov. 3, p. 4.

132 AN ESSAY ON THE CIVILISATIONS OF INDIA, CHINA & JAPAN. London: J. M. Dent & Sons Ltd. Fcap. 8vo. pp. 86. [Sheets transferred to Allen & Unwin, 1930.] (New York: Doubleday, Page & Co.) A

slightly revised reprint of no. 117. Reprinted in no. 340. For German translation see no. 269.

133 Il patriotismo di Caino. Translation of no. 126, published as a broadsheet by the Comitato Pro Umanità.

134 The War and the Way Out. *Atlantic Monthly*, Dec., pp. 820–37. Reprinted in the *New York Times*, Dec. 20; also as nos. 135 and 144. For German, Swedish, Japanese and Italian translations see nos. 139, 140, 150·1 and 175.

135 THE WAR AND THE WAY OUT. London: The Chancery Lane Press. Sm. Cr. 8vo. pp. 47. (The Hague: Belinfante Brothers.) A reprint of no. 134.

136 Introduction, pp. 3–4, to Romain Rolland's *Above the Battlefield*. Cambridge: Published for "The Heretics" by Bowes and Bowes.

1915

137 After the War. *Atlantic Monthly*, Jan., pp. 111–16. Reprinted under the title "How to End Militarism" in the *New York Times*, Jan. 10, p. 2.

138 The War and the Way Out. [Letter in reply to criticisms made in a leading article.] *New Republic*, Feb. 13, pp. 49–50. Cf. a letter to the *Cambridge Review*, Feb. 24, p. 223.

139 Ein Ausweg für den Krieg. *Milwaukee-Sonntagspost*, Feb. 14, 21, 28 and March 7. A slightly abbreviated translation of no. 134 by H. Hayssen.

140 KRIGET OCH VÄGEN TILL FRED. Malmö: A–B Framtidens Bokförlag. Translation of no. 134 by A. Jacobsson-Undén.

141 The War and the Way Out. A Further Consideration. *Atlantic Monthly*, April, pp. 516–24. Reprinted in nos. 143 and 144.

142 The War and the Way Out. A Positive Plan. *Ibid.*, May, pp. 691–700. Reprinted in nos. 143, 144 and 145.

143 AFTER THE WAR. London: A. C. Fifield. Demy 8vo. pp. 44. A reprint of nos. 141 and 142.

144 THE WAR AND THE WAY OUT. Boston: Atlantic Monthly Co. Sm. Roy. 8vo. pp. 39. An offprint of nos. 134, 141 and 142, published as a pamphlet.

145 THE FOUNDATIONS OF A LEAGUE OF PEACE. Boston: The World Peace Foundation. [Pamphlet Series, vol. 5, no. 2.] Large Cr. 8vo. pp. 20. A reprint of no. 142.

146 On "Punishing Germany". *War and Peace*, May, pp. 121–2.

147 Der Heilige Krieg. Ein Friede, der den Krieg beenden wird. Der Krieg und der Weg aus dem Krieg. Translations of nos. 126, 129 and 128, on pp. 1–3, 16–22 of *Kriegsgegner in England*. Munich: G. Birk & Co.

148 The German Socialists and the War. *War and Peace*, Aug., pp. 168–9.

149 Die einzige Lösung. Letter to the *Blätter fur zwischenstaatliche Organisation*, pp. 202–4.

150 How Can America Best Contribute to the Maintenance of the World's Peace? *Annals of the American Academy of Political and Social Science*, Sept., pp. 235–8.

150 SENSÔ ZEHI. Tokyo: Keiô Daigaku Shuppanbu. Translation of
·1 no. 134 by S. Koizumi and K. Sannabe.

151 A German on the War. [Dr. F. W. Förster's *Deutschlands Jugend und der Weltkrieg.*] *Hibbert Journal*, Oct., pp. 30–36.

152 Approaches to Peace. Two letters to *The Nation*, Nov. 27, p. 326, and Dec. 11, p. 388.

153 The Basis of Permanent Peace. An essay, pp. 11–36, in *Towards a Lasting Settlement*, edited by C. R. Buxton. London: Allen & Unwin. (New York: The Macmillan Co.)

1916
154 The Freedom of the Seas. *War and Peace*, Jan., pp. 56–9.

155 THE EUROPEAN ANARCHY. London: Allen & Unwin. Cr. 8vo. pp. 153. (New York: The Macmillan Co.)

156 The American "League to Enforce Peace". *War and Peace*, June, pp. 134–5.

157 De Profundis. [Anonymous poem.] *Cambridge Magazine*, June 10, p. 560. Reprinted as no. 167.

158 The Paris Conference and the Future of Europe. Letter to the *Manchester Guardian*, June 26, p. 7.

159 Democratic Control of Foreign Policy. *Atlantic Monthly*, Aug., pp. 145–52.

160 Economic Policy after the War. *War and Peace*, Aug., pp. 167–9.

161 After the War. A series of letters to the *Manchester Guardian*. Aug. 1, p. 10, The Choice before Us; Aug. 3, p. 10, Nationalism and Internationalism; Aug. 5, p. 4, A Proposed League of Nations; Aug. 7, p. 8, The Problem of Nationalities; Aug. 9, p. 10, The Problem of International Trade. Cf. a further letter in reply to criticism, Aug. 16, p. 10.

162 ECONOMIC WAR AFTER THE WAR. [A criticism of the resolutions of the Allied Economic Conference held in Paris during June.] London: Union of Democratic Control. Demy 8vo. pp. 20.

163 The Law and the Conscientious Objector. Letter to *The Nation*, Aug. 26, p. 664. Cf. a further letter on "The Treatment of Conscientious Objectors", Sept. 9, p. 729.

164 Views of Settlement. Letters to *The Nation*, Sept. 16, pp. 757–8, and Sept. 30, p. 824.

165 Freedom of Speech. [In relation to Bertrand Russell's dismissal from Trinity College, Cambridge.] *War and Peace*, Oct., p. 8. Cf. a letter to *The Nation*, July 29.

166 The Conditions of a Durable Peace. Four articles in the *Cambridge*

Magazine, Nov. 11, pp. 103-4; Nov. 18, p. 130; Nov. 25, pp. 158-9; Dec. 2, p. 201.

166 GENDAI EIKOKU NO SANGYÔ KAKUMEI. Tokyo: Seikyôsha. Transla-
·I tion of no. 88 by Etsujirô Uehara.

167 DE PROFUNDIS. [Anonymous reprint of no. 157 as no. 4 of a series of "Reprints from the *Cambridge Magazine*".] London: The Morland Press, and Cambridge: Galloway & Porter. Large Demy 8vo. pp. 4.

1917

168 The League to Enforce Peace. *War and Peace*, Jan., pp. 64-7.

169 Articles in the *Cambridge Magazine* continuing no. 166 but under separate titles. Jan. 20, pp. 213-14, The Significance of the American Note; Jan. 27, p. 244, The Allies' Note; Feb. 3, p. 271, President Wilson's Speech to the Senate; Feb. 10, p. 300, Nationality and the Settlement; Feb. 17, pp. 326-7, Rival Imperialisms; Feb. 24, pp. 357-8, The Choice before Us.

170 The "Fight for Right". [An article in reply to an attack upon himself by the "Fight for Right" Society in a letter to the *Morning Post*.] *Cambridge Magazine*, March 3, pp. 382-3.

171 Introduction, pp. 5-7, to *The American League to Enforce Peace. An English Interpretation* by C. R. Ashbee. London: Allen & Unwin.

172 The Problem of Armaments and a League of Nations. *Friends' Quarterly Examiner*, Fourth Month, pp. 193-7.

173 THE CHOICE BEFORE US. London: Allen & Unwin. Demy 8vo. pp. xi, 274. (New York: Dodd, Mead & Co.)

174 A New German State of Mind. Letter to *The Nation*, June 30, pp. 322-3.

175 LA GUERRA E IL MODO DI USCIRNE. Milan: Libreria Editrice Avanti! Translation of no. 134 by A. Calabi.

176 The Case against Persecution. Letter on the imprisonment of conscientious objectors to the *Manchester Guardian*, July 26, p. 8. Cf. another letter on "Death of C.O.'s in prison", Jan. 28, 1918, p. 3.

177 World Peace or World's End? The Solemn Choice before the Nations. *Sunday Pictorial*, Sept. 2, p. 5.

178 If Germany Does Not Repent. The After-War Problem of the Allied Nations. *Ibid.* Nov. 25, p. 5.

179 The Destruction of Liberty. Letter on the disfranchisement of conscientious objectors to the *Manchester Guardian*, Nov. 28, p. 3.

1918

180 Is It Possible to Abolish War? Permanent Peace Not a Utopian Dream. *Sunday Pictorial*, Jan. 13, p. 5.

181 Education and Patriotism. Letter to the *Morning Post*, Jan. 15, p. 6, in reply to criticism in a leading article of a lecture on "The

Educational Basis of Internationalism" reported in the issue of Jan. 9.

182 A League of Nations Now? [Contribution to a symposium.] *War and Peace*, Sept., pp. 327–8.

183 Amnesty for Political Prisoners. Letter in favour of the immediate release of conscientious objectors to the *Manchester Guardian*, Nov. 18, p. 3. An abbreviated version was published in the *Daily News*, Nov. 18, p. 4, under the title "Victory and Amnesty".

184 Introduction, pp. v–xix, to *Problems of the International Settlement*. London: Published for the National Peace Council by Allen & Unwin.

1919

185 Disarmament. *League of Nations Journal*, Jan., pp. 16–17. Cf. a letter on "The One Thing Needful" to *The Nation*, Nov. 30, 1918.

186 "Saul, Saul, why persecutest thou me?" [Unsigned article on the continued imprisonment of conscientious objectors.] *The Nation*, Feb. 8, pp. 539–40.

187 Introduction, pp. xi–xxvii, to *Documents and Statements relating to Peace Proposals and War Aims*. London: Allen & Unwin. (New York: The Macmillan Co.)

188 The Peace Terms. Letter to the *Manchester Guardian*, May 19, p. 12.

189 Review of J. L. Garvin: *The Economic Foundation of Peace*. *League of Nations Journal*, June, pp. 230–31.

190 Bolshevism [Review of L. Trotsky: *History of the Russian Revolution to Brest-Litovsk*; J. Reed: *Ten Days that Shook the World*; E. Buisson: *Les Bolcheviki, 1917–1919*; and A. Ransome: *Six Weeks in Russia in 1919*.] *The International Review*, July, pp. 544–8.

191 From Big Three to Big Four. Letter to *The Nation*, Sept. 6, p. 672.

192 The [Railway] Strike and some Morals. Letter to *The Nation*, Oct. 11, p. 37.

193 Either the League or the Doom of Mankind. *The Star*, Nov. 11, p. 2.

1920

194 The Choice before Us. *The Covenant*, Jan., pp. 182–95.

195 The U.D.C. Meeting. Letter to the *Cambridge Review*, March 12, p. 270, protesting against the breaking-up of a meeting.

196 Letter from Hungary. The Red Regime and the White. [Anonymous article purporting to be from a Hungarian correspondent.] *Manchester Guardian*, March 23, p. 6.

197 Review of L. Woolf: *Empire and Commerce in Africa*. *The Covenant*, April, pp. 439–41.

198 Review of Lord Eustace Percy: *The Responsibilities of the League*. *Ibid.* April, pp. 441–2.

199 The Future of British Liberalism. *Atlantic Monthly*, April, pp. 550–55.

200 Rousseau up to Date. [Review of G. D. H. Cole: *Social Theory*.] *The Athenaeum*, April 9, pp. 476–7.

201 An Episode in a Free Empire. [Unsigned article on native labour in British East Africa.] *The Nation*, April 17, pp. 62–3.

202 The Pilgrimage of Peace. [Review of C. L. Lange: *Histoire de l'Internationalisme*, tome 1.] *The Athenaeum*, April 30, pp. 586–7.

203 THE FUTURE OF THE COVENANT. [In a series of Study Circle Pamphlets.] London: The League of Nations Union. Demy 8vo. pp. 20. Some copies were published by British Periodicals, Ltd.

204 The Religion of Progress. [Review of J. B. Bury: *The Idea of Progress*; and W. R. Inge's Romanes Lecture with the same title.] *The Athenaeum*, June 18, pp. 791–2.

205 "Justum et Tenacem". [Review of G. P. Gooch's *Life of Lord Courtney*.] *Ibid.* July 23, pp. 105–7.

206 CAUSES OF INTERNATIONAL WAR. [No. 1 of the Swarthmore International Handbooks—a series of 8 volumes edited by Dickinson.] London: The Swarthmore Press Ltd. Cr. 8vo. pp. 110. (New York: Harcourt, Brace & Howe.)

207 Germany under the Treaty. Four articles in the *Manchester Guardian*. Nov. 29, p. 6, The Tragedy of the Children. Dec. 1, p. 11, The Destitution of the Worker. Dec. 3, p. 9, The Plight of the Middle Class. Dec. 4, p. 9, The Moral and a Remedy. A controversy arising out of these articles led to two letters on "The 'Round Table' and Germany", Dec. 4, p. 8, and Dec. 8, p. 16. Cf. also an earlier letter written from Berlin, on "The Allies and Germany's Milk Shortage", Oct. 23, p. 6.

208 The Plight of Germany. *The Nation*, Dec. 11, pp. 380–81.

209 THE MAGIC FLUTE. A Fantasia. London: Allen & Unwin. Sm. Cr. 8vo. pp. 128. (New York: The Macmillan Co.)

1921

210 Opinion in Germany. *Common Sense*, Jan. 8, p. 136.

211 Goethe. [Review of P. Hume Brown: *The Life of Goethe*.] *The Athenaeum*, Jan. 14, pp. 37–8, and 21, p. 68.

212 S.O.S.—Europe to America. *Atlantic Monthly*, Feb., pp. 244–9.

213 The Allies and Germany. Letter to the *Manchester Guardian*, March 31, p. 3.

214 Review of J. A. Hobson: *Problems of a New World. Sociological Review*, April, pp. 111–12.

215 The Internationalism of the Seas. [Review of J. A. Salter: *Allied Shipping Control*.] *The Nation and the Athenaeum*, July 30, pp. 651–2.

216 The Disease of War. [Review of R. Rolland: *Clerambault, Histoire d'une conscience libre pendant la guerre*.] *Foreign Affairs*, Aug., pp. i–ii.

217 The Russian Famine. Letters to the *Manchester Guardian*, Oct. 7, p. 14, and October 17, p. 3.

218 A German Looks at the League. [Review of W. Schücking and H. Wehberg: *Die Satzung des Völkerbundes*.] *Headway*, Nov., p. 38.

1922

219 Anglo-French Relations. Letter to the *Manchester Guardian*, May 26, p. 13.

220 Hofmannsthal's Mystery Play. ["Das grosse Welttheater" in the Kollegien-Kirche at Salzburg.] *Ibid*. Aug. 28, p. 12.

221 Dickinson went to Geneva as *Manchester Guardian* correspondent at the Third Assembly of the League of Nations. He wrote a preliminary survey of "Work before the Assembly", Sept. 4, p. 7; a daily dispatch, Sept. 7–Oct. 2; and articles entitled "A Week of the League of Nations", Sept. 14, p. 14, and "Final Impressions", Oct. 5, p. 8. "A Week of the League of Nations" was reprinted in *The Living Age*, Oct. 28, pp. 199–202, under the title "At the League Assembly".

222 Science and Goodwill. Letter to *The New Leader*, Oct. 27, p. 2.

223 On Sovereignty. *Youth*, Dec., pp. 178–9.

224 "British Mandates in the Pacific". Letter to the *Manchester Guardian*, Dec. 5, p. 4.

225 The Problem of the Straits [with reference to the Lausanne Conference]. Letters to the *Manchester Guardian*, Dec. 9, p. 9, and Dec. 30, p. 10.

1923

226 Peace. *Manchester Guardian Commercial. Reconstruction in Europe*, section 12. Jan. 4, pp. 739–40.

227 "Smashing Up Germany". Letter to the *Manchester Guardian*, Jan. 6, p. 6.

228 The French in the Ruhr. Letters to the *Manchester Guardian*, Jan. 30, p. 14, Feb. 5, p. 11, and Feb. 12, p. 5.

229 France on Organising Peace. [Review of *Les français à la recherche d'une Société des Nations depuis le Roi Henri IV jusqu'aux combattants de 1914*.] *Headway*, Feb., p. 276.

230 Mr Bonar Law and the League of Nations. Letter to the *Manchester Guardian*, Feb. 22, p. 4.

231 A Personal Impression of Tagore. *The New Leader*, Feb. 23, pp. 11–12.

232 Der Krieg, der Frieden und die Ruhrbesetzung. *Friedens-Warte*, March, pp. 68–70.

233 Causes of the Great War. *Foreign Affairs*, March, pp. 195–6. Reprinted as pp. 58–65 of no. 235.

234 "The European Outlook". Letter to the *Manchester Guardian*, March 2, p. 7.

235 WAR: ITS NATURE, CAUSE AND CURE. London: Allen & Unwin. Cr. 8vo. pp. 155. (New York: The Macmillan Co.) Cf. no. 233. For Danish and Swedish translations see nos. 243 and 260.

236 Mr Forster's New Book. [Review of E. M. Forster: *Pharos and Pharillon*.] *The Nation and the Athenaeum*, May 26, p. 273.

237 Goethe Once More. [In connection with E. Ludwig: *Goethe*,

Geschichte eines Menschen.] *Ibid.* June 23, pp. 390–92. Reprinted in *The Living Age*, Aug. 4, pp. 230–32.

238 "It is not to be thought of". [Review of Clive Bell: *On British Freedom.*] *The Nation and the Athenaeum*, July 7, pp. 457–8.

239 The Native, the Boer, and the Englishman. [Review of Olive Schreiner: *Thoughts on South Africa.*] *Ibid.* July 21, pp. 522–3.

240 Entente Diplomacy before the War. [Review of G. A. Schreiner: *Entente Diplomacy and the World.*] *Ibid.* Aug. 11, p. 613.

241 What the Issues Are at Geneva. [Article about the Corfu incident written from Geneva.] *Daily Herald*, Sept. 8, p. 3.

242 Three articles in *The Nation and the Athenaeum* written from Geneva. Sept. 15, pp. 738–9, Italy and the League; Sept. 22, pp. 769–70, The Competence of the League; Sept. 29, pp. 800–802, Can These Bones Live? The third article was reprinted in the *New Republic*, Oct. 24, pp. 228–30.

243 Krigen, Freden og Fremtiden. Copenhagen: P. Haase & Sons. Translation of no. 235 by D. Grünbaum.

244 Vale. [Review of Sir Walter Raleigh: *Some Authors.*] *The Nation and the Athenaeum*, Nov. 3, p. 189.

245 Goethe. [Review of B. Croce: *Goethe.*] *Ibid.* Dec. 1, p. 347.

246 The Perfect Friend. [Review of *Some New Letters of Edward Fitzgerald*, edited by F. R. Barton.] *Ibid.* Dec. 8, p. 378.

1924

247 The [Proposed] Treaty of Mutual Assistance. Two letters to *The Nation and the Athenaeum*, Jan. 5, pp. 511–12, and Jan. 19, pp. 567–8.

248 Shelley and Science. [Review of O. W. Campbell: *Shelley and the Unromantics.*] *Ibid.* Feb. 16, p. 703.

249 The League and German Universities. Letters to the *Manchester Guardian*, Feb. 22, p. 16, and March 1, p. 7.

250 The Making of the Treaty of Versailles. [Review of R. S. Baker: *Woodrow Wilson and World Settlement.*] *Foreign Affairs*, March, pp. i–iv.

251 Distress in Germany. The Facts. Letter to the *Manchester Guardian*, March 7, p. 16.

252 A Vision of England. [Review of E. L. Grant Watson: *English Country.*] *The Nation and the Athenaeum*, March 8, p. 802.

253 M. Poincaré. [In connection with Sisley Huddleston: *Poincaré: a Biographical Portrait.*] *Ibid.* March 29, pp. 913–14.

254 A Woman of Genius. [Review of S. C. Cronwright-Schreiner: *The Life of Olive Schreiner.*] *The Nation and the Athenaeum*, April 26, p. 116. Reprinted in *The Living Age*, June 21, pp. 1203–5.

255 The Modern Caligula. [Review of Count R. Zedlitz-Trützschler: *Twelve Years at the Imperial German Court.*] *The Nation and the Athenaeum*, June 28, p. 414.

256 Review of F. C. S. Schiller: *Problems of Belief. Proceedings of the Society for Psychical Research*, July, pp. 196–9. Cf. a letter to the *Journal of the S.P.R.*, Oct., p. 324.

257 An Appeal to British Fair Play. [In connection with a pamphlet issued by a number of German intellectuals on the question of the origin of the War.] *The Nation and the Athenaeum*, Aug. 30, pp. 660–61.

258 Europe: 1890–1898. [According to the *Grosse Politik*, vols. 8–12.] *Contemporary Review*, Sept., pp. 316–22.

259 Disarmament and Security. Letter to the *Manchester Guardian*, Sept. 8, p. 14.

260 KRIGET, FREDEN OCH FRAMTIDEN. Upsala: J. A. Lindblad. Translation of no. 235 by E. Lundquist.

261 "Victory". [Review of A. Fabre-Luce: *La Victoire*.] *The Nation and the Athenaeum*, Oct. 4, pp. 19–20.

262 A Field Marshal's Memoirs. [Review of F. Whyte: *A Field-Marshal's Memoirs*, from the Diary, Correspondence and Reminiscences of Alfred, Count von Waldersee.] *Ibid.* Nov. 1, p. 188.

263 Life after Death. Do We Desire Immortality? [In connection with Sir James Marchant's symposium on *Immortality*.] *The New Leader*, Nov. 14, p. 8.

264 Exporting Munitions. Letter to the *Manchester Guardian*, Nov. 21, p. 16.

265 A short contribution to a symposium on "E. D. Morel: the Man and his Work". *Foreign Affairs*, Dec., p. 124.

1925

266 Mr Wells Prophesies. [Review of H. G. Wells: *A Year of Prophesying*.] *The Nation and the Athenaeum*, Jan. 17, p. 554.

267 Egypt and the League. [A Criticism of British action after the assassination of the Sirdar.] *Headway*, Feb., p. 25. Cf. a letter to the *Manchester Guardian*, Nov. 27, 1924, p. 7.

268 BRIEFE EINES CHINESISCHEN GELEHRTEN. Celle: N. Kampmann. Translation of no. 48 by A. Malata.

269 INDIEN, CHINA UND JAPAN. Celle: N. Kampmann. Translation of no. 132 by A. Malata.

270 The League under Fire. [Review of F. Kellor: *Security against War*.] *Foreign Affairs*, May, pp. 262–3.

271 The Perfect Militarist. [Review of *Politische Dokumente von A. von Tirpitz*, vol. 1.] *The Nation and the Athenaeum*, May 16, pp. 208–9.

272 The Export of Arms. Letter to the *Manchester Guardian*, May 20, p. 18.

272 SHINA NO ICHI KANRI YORI Ô-BEIJIN NI ATÔRU SHO. Tokyo:
·1 Hokuseidô Shoten. Translation of no. 48 by Jirô Nagura.

273 The Situation in China. Letter to the *Manchester Guardian*, July 14, p. 20.

274 Mr Santayana's Dialogue. [Review of G. Santayana: *Dialogues in Limbo.*] *The Nation and the Athenaeum,* Aug. 29, pp. 650–51.

275 The Bombardment of Damascus. Letter to the *Manchester Guardian,* Oct. 31, p. 12.

276 The Serajevo Murder. [Review of M. E. Durham: *The Serajevo Crime.*] *The Nation and the Athenaeum,* Dec. 26, pp. 471–2.

1926

277 THE INTERNATIONAL ANARCHY, 1904–1914. London: Allen & Unwin. Demy 8vo. pp. xiv, 516. (New York: The Century Co.) Cf. no. 280. Reissued as no. 337.

278 The Failure at Geneva. Letter to the *Manchester Guardian,* March 29, p. 8.

279 "Who is on our side, who?" [In connection with D. A. Peat's "Arbitrate First" Bureau.] *The Nation and Athenaeum,* Aug. 28, p. 605. Cf. a letter on "Personal Service for Peace" to the *Manchester Guardian,* Aug. 24, p. 18.

280 Die wirkliche Moral der Ereignisse. *Europäische Gespräche,* Sept., pp. 463–72. Translation of pp. 472–81 of no. 277 by A. H. R. Wach.

1927

281 Review of vol. 11 of *British Documents on the Origins of the War.* *Journal of the Royal Institute of International Affairs,* Jan., pp. 52–3.

281 CHINNO AVAJ. Ahmedabad: D. B. Kalelkar. [Reissued by Navajiban
·1 Press, 1938.] Translation of no. 48 by Chandrashankar Shukla.

282 "British Hypocrisy". [Review of H. Luz: *Lord Grey und der Weltkrieg.*] *The Nation and Athenaeum,* April 16, p. 52.

283 French and British Disarmament Plans. *Foreign Affairs,* May, pp. 299–300.

284 Oscar Browning. [In connection with H. E. Wortham's biography.] *Cambridge Review,* May 20, pp. 425–6.

285 Macchiavelli. [On the occasion of the quatercentenary of his death.] *The Nation and Athenaeum,* June 18, pp. 366–7.

286 Review of A. Ebray: *A Frenchman Looks at the Peace*; O. Hammann: *The World Policy of Germany, 1890–1912*; and E. Brandenburg: *From Bismarck to the World War. Journal of the Royal Institute of International Affairs,* July, pp. 253–5.

287 Contribution, pp. 40–42, to *Russell Hillard Loines, 1874–1922. A Selection from his Letters and Poems with Biographical Sketch and Recollections by his Friends.* New York: privately printed.

288 Two articles in *The Nation and Athenaeum* written from Geneva. Sept. 3, pp. 712–13, The Eighth Assembly; Sept. 24, pp. 796–7, The Debate in the Assembly.

289 REVOLUTION AND REACTION IN MODERN FRANCE. London: Allen & Unwin. Cr. 8vo. pp. 256. (New York: Brentano.) Revised edition of no. 33, with a new preface and conclusion.

289 CHÊNG I YÜ TZǓ YU. Shanghai: The Commercial Press. Translation
·1   of no. 88 by Ch'eng Chên-chi.
290 East and West. [Review of Hwuy-ung: *A Chinaman's Opinion of Us
      and of His Own Country*.] *The Nation and Athenaeum*, Nov. 26, p. 322.
291 Introduction, pp. v–xxii, to *A Project of Perpetual Peace. Rousseau's
      Essay*. Translated by Edith M. Nuttall. London: Richard
      Cobden-Sanderson.
292 Armed Anarchy. [In connection with vols. 1 and 2 of *British Docu-
      ments on the Origin of the War*.] *Foreign Affairs*, Dec., pp. 173–4.

                              1928
293 Bismarck. [In connection with E. Ludwig: *Bismarck, the Story of a
      Fighter*.] *Foreign Affairs*, Jan., p. 217.
294 Goethe's View of Nature. [In collaboration with Miss F. M.
      Stawell.] *Hibbert Journal*, April, pp. 399–409. Reprinted as ch. 2
      of no 297.
295 The Real Moral. [Review of P. Renouvin: *The Immediate Origins of
      the War*.] *The Nation and Athenaeum*, April 28, pp. 111–12.
296 On the Discovery of Good—a Dialogue. *Journal of Philosophical
      Studies*, July, pp. 279–84. Partly incorporated in nos. 309 and
      315.
297 GOETHE AND FAUST. An Interpretation. With Passages newly
      translated into English Verse. [In collaboration with Miss F. M.
      Stawell.] London: G. Bell and Sons, Ltd. Demy 8vo. pp. 291.
      (New York: The Dial Press.) Cf. no. 294.
298 Goethe Again. [Review of E. Ludwig: *Goethe, the History of a Man*.]
      The Nation and Athenaeum, Oct. 27, pp. 146–8.
299 Anglo-American Relations. A Very Real Danger [of hostility
      through naval competition]. Letter to the *Manchester Guardian*,
      Nov. 29, p. 20.
300 Obscene Books and the Law. [The dangers of police censorship.]
      Letter to the *Manchester Guardian*, Dec. 29, p. 7.

                              1929
301 Reviews of F. Stieve: *Germany and Europe*; and of *The Memoirs of
      Prince Max of Baden*. *Journal of the Royal Institute of International
      Affairs*, Jan., pp. 52–4.
301 CHIN TAI LUN T'AN. Shanghai: The Spring Tide Bookshop. Trans-
·1   lation of no. 65 by Liang Yü-ch'un.
302 "All Quiet on the Western Front". [Review of E. M. Remarque's
      book.] *Cambridge Review*, May 3, p. 412.
303 Our Knowledge of Other People. *Ibid.* June 5, pp. 515–17.
304 Goethe's View of Nature. *The Realist*, Aug., pp. 97–106.
305 Introduction, pp. xi–xiv, to *The Ascent of Humanity* by Gerald Heard.
      London: Jonathan Cape.
306 Points of View. [A series of broadcast talks of which Dickinson gave

the first and last.] *The Listener*, Oct. 9, pp. 465–6 and 490, and Nov. 20, pp. 679–81. Reprinted in no. 313.

307 Arthur Berry. [Obituary.] *Cambridge Review*, Oct. 11, p. 10.

308 On Translation. [In connection with Tu Fu: *The Autobiography of a Chinese Poet, A.D. 712–770*, arranged and translated by F. Ayscough.] *The Nation and Athenaeum*, Nov. 23, pp. 282–3.

1930

309 A Political Dialogue. *The Political Quarterly*, Jan., pp. 70–85, and April, pp. 248–64. Reprinted as pp. 11–54 of no. 315. Cf. also no. 296.

310 C. P. Sanger. [Obituary.] *The Nation and Athenaeum*, Feb. 22, p. 701.

311 Euripides and the *Bacchae*. *Cambridge Review*, Feb. 28, pp. 298–9.

312 The Ascent of Humanity. [In connection with Gerald Heard's book.] *Antiquity*, March, pp. 5–11.

313 Introduction, pp. 9–18, and two talks, pp. 21–32 and 129–43, in *Points of View. A Series of Broadcast Addresses*. London: Allen & Unwin. A reprint of no. 306, with the addition of the Introduction. (Freeport, N.Y.: Books for Libraries, 1969.)

314 Goethe. [Broadcast talk.] *The Listener*, April 23, pp. 713–14.

315 After Two Thousand Years. A Dialogue between Plato and a Modern Young Man. London: Allen & Unwin. Cr. 8vo. pp. 213. (New York: W. W. Norton & Co.) Cf. nos. 296 and 309.

316 The Abyss. [Review of K. A. Bratt: *That Next War*.] *The Nation and Athenaeum*, Nov. 8, pp. 211–12.

1931

317 Then and Now. [A broadcast discussion with John Maud on the ideas of young men in the early 'eighties and today.] *The Listener*, Jan. 7, pp. 23–4.

318 We Hear a Great Deal about Plato. *The Radio Times*, Feb. 13, pp. 349 and 398.

319 The Dialogues of Plato. [A series of six broadcast talks.] *The Listener*, Feb. 18, pp. 264–5 and 286; Feb. 25, pp. 320–21; March 4, pp. 369–70; March 11, pp. 422–3; March 18, pp. 464–5; March 25, pp. 511–12; April 1, pp. 559–60. Reprinted in an expanded form as no. 329.

320 Russian Foreign Policy. [Review of L. Fischer: *The Soviet in World Affairs*.] *The Political Quarterly*, April, pp. 278–83.

321 Edward Carpenter as a Friend. An essay, pp. 34–46, in *Edward Carpenter. In Appreciation*, edited by G. Beith. London: Allen & Unwin.

322 Would *You* Fight for the League? *The Clarion*, June, pp. 167–8.

323 Reflections of Spiritualism. [Review of G. O. Leonard: *My Life in Two Worlds*.] *The New Statesman and Nation*, Sept. 26, p. 376.

324 The Essential Issue. [Contribution to a symposium of "Reflections on the Crisis".] *The Political Quarterly*, Oct., pp. 470–72.

325 The Issue. [Socialism and Capitalism.] *The Highway*, Nov., pp. 5–7.

326 J. McT. E. McTaggart. [With chapters by Basil Williams and S. V. Keeling.] Cambridge University Press. Cr. 8vo. pp. viii, 160. (New York: The Macmillan Co.)

327 Mr Nevinson on Goethe. [Review of H. W. Nevinson: *Goethe, Man and Poet.*] *The New Statesman and Nation*, Nov. 14, p. vii.

328 If I Were Dictator. [One of a series of articles under this title.] *The (New York) Nation*, Nov. 25, pp. 567–8.

329 Plato and his Dialogues. London: Allen & Unwin. Cr. 8vo. pp. 228. [Paperback edition published by Penguin Books, 1947.] (New York: W. W. Norton & Co.) An expanded version of no. 319.

330 What I Would Do with the World. [The last of a series of broadcast talks under this title.] *The Listener*, Dec. 16, pp. 1048–9.

331 B.B.C. Talks. [Dissent from the proposed policy of attempting to avoid all possible offence.] Letter to *The Times*, Dec. 23, p. 4.

1932

332 Dialogue as a Literary Form. A paper read on Feb. 17 and published posthumously in *Essays by Divers Hands, being the Transactions of the Royal Society of Literature of the United Kingdom*, New Series, vol. 11, pp. 1–19. [Issued in separate form by Melford, 1932.]

333 Goethe—the Man. Goethe Revealed in *Faust*. [Two broadcast talks.] *The Listener*, April 6, pp. 481–4 and 513, and April 13, pp. 519–20 and 552.

334 The Political Background. *Scrutiny*, May, pp. 40–46. Reprinted under the title "Two Issues" in *The Living Age*, Aug., pp. 539–43.

335 Mencius. [Review of A. Lyall's translation of Mencius; I. A. Richards: *Mencius on the Mind*; and L. S. Hsü: *The Political Philosophy of Confucianism.*] *The New Statesman and Nation*, June 18, pp. 801–2.

336 The Contribution of Ancient Greece to Modern Life. Being the Inaugural Lecture delivered at the Local Lectures Summer Meeting of the University of Cambridge, 1932. London: Allen & Unwin. Fcap. 8vo. pp. 32. Reprinted in no. 340.

1937

337 The International Anarchy, 1904–1914. New edition of no. 277, with a foreword by Sir Arthur Salter. London: Allen & Unwin. pp. xviii, 516.

338 Article on Oscar Browning, pp. 126–7, in *The Dictionary of National Biography, 1922–1930*. London: Oxford University Press.

1938

339 Brieven van een Chinees. 's-Gravenhage: L. J. C. Boucher. Translation of no. 48 by J. W. Schotman.

251

1946

340 LETTERS FROM JOHN CHINAMAN AND OTHER ESSAYS. London: Allen & Unwin. (Toronto: Thomas Nelson.) pp. 216. A reprint of nos. 48, 117, 336, 60 and 102, with an introduction by E. M. Forster.

1947

341 UN "BANQUETE" MODERNO. Buenos Aires: Espasa-Calpe. Translation of no. 65 by R. Vázquez-Zamora.

1957

342 THE GREEK VIEW OF LIFE. London: Methuen & Co. pp. xv, 261. (Ann Arbor: University of Michigan Press.) New edition of no. 90, with a preface by E. M. Forster. [Re-issued in University Paperbacks series, 1962. pp. xii, 177.]

1959

343 MODAN SHINPÔJIAMU; ICHI CHÛGOKUJIN NO TEGAMI. Tokyo: Nan'-undô. Translation of nos. 65 and 48 by Isamu Muraoka.

1962

344 A MODERN SYMPOSIUM. New York: Frederick Ungar Publishing Co. pp. xv, 160. New edition of no. 65, with an introductory essay, The Uses of G. Lowes Dickinson, by Louis Filler.

345 A MODERN SYMPOSIUM. London: Allen & Unwin. pp. 95. (New York: Barnes & Noble.) New edition of no. 65, with an introduction [or rather, extracts from *Goldsworthy Lowes Dickinson*] by E. M. Forster.

1967

346 A MODERN SYMPOSIUM: BASIC POLITICAL VIEWPOINTS DEBATED. New York: Hart Publishing Co. pp. 160. New edition of no. 65, with a foreword by Harold Taylor.

OBITUARY NOTICES

This list contains only such obituary notices as were written by friends who knew Dickinson personally and who are therefore able to give original impressions of his character.

The Times, Aug. 4. Followed by short appreciations from E. M. Forster, Aug. 6, and Syed Ross Masood, Aug. 9.

Manchester Guardian, Aug. 4. With an appreciation by Professor Ernest Barker.

The New Statesman and Nation, Aug. 6, editorial paragraph. Also a paragraph by "Critic", Aug. 13.

The Week-End Review, Aug. 13. Letter from Gerald Heard.

The Spectator, Aug. 13. A tribute by E. M. Forster. Reprinted in *The Living Age*, Oct.

The (New York) Nation, Aug. 17. Editorial paragraph.

The New Clarion, Aug. 27. Article by H. M. Tomlinson.

Sunday Times, Aug. 28. Review of no. 336 by Desmond MacCarthy, under the title "Liberal Culture".

Headway, Sept. Paragraph by Professor Gilbert Murray.

Cambridge Review, Oct. 14. Obituary by J. T. Sheppard.

The Listener, Oct. 19. Broadcast talk by E. M. Forster.

The Political Quarterly, Oct.–Dec. Article on "Lowes Dickinson and Graham Wallas" by Professor H. J. Laski.

The Journal of Education, Nov. Letter from a former pupil at the London School of Economics.

Journal of the S.P.R., Nov. Obituary by Miss F. M. Stawell.

The Criterion, Jan. 1933. Article on "Goldie Dickinson: the Latest Cambridge Platonist" by N. Wedd.

Goldsworthy Lowes Dickinson. A Memoir by Roger Fry. Privately printed (together with J. T. Sheppard's obituary) for distribution to members of King's College, Cambridge. pp. 28.

Annotated Index

Although *Goldsworthy Lowes Dickinson* was published with an index which I guess to be Forster's own handiwork, there is no proof of this. In any case it was a strictly functional affair with no individual touches, and I have felt free to alter, re-group or even ignore its chosen headings and sub-headings, as well as to expand it considerably. Nevertheless, it has provided a starting-point, and has suggested that certain topics—Dickinson's feeling for flowers, for example—are more significant than I had realized. Occasionally, also, it has supplied initials or a forename for what would otherwise have had to remain as an unadorned surname.

The present index is intended to serve the three purposes expounded at the head of the index to *Two Cheers for Democracy* (Abinger Edition, vol. 11). Briefly, these are "(1) the tracing of any given passage or *obiter dictum*, however imperfectly remembered . . . (2) the pinpointing of what Forster has said on any given topic . . . (3) the provision, in an unobtrusive yet accessible form, of brief expository notes . . .". In addition, an attempt has been made to chart the various aspects of the subject of this biography. These are all grouped under Dickinson's own name, in six slightly arbitrary sections: summary accounts, main events, characteristics, interests, attitudes, and writings. Most of these are themselves arranged alphabetically. It should be noted that attitudes, opinions and sayings indexed directly under their subjects are Forster's rather than Dickinson's—although, obviously, many of these would have been endorsed by Dickinson, just as many of *his* attitudes etc. are recorded by Forster with evident approval.

Less annotation has been attempted than in *Two Cheers for Democracy*, largely because Forster is less allusive as a biographer than as an essayist, and has himself provided, on this occasion, most of the annotation that seems called for. I have, however, ventured to ignore his remarks at the bottom of p. xxii and the top of p. xxiii to the extent of providing bad literal translations of quotations from Goethe and others. I have indexed the preliminary pages sparingly, the appendices only in so far as they do not repeat or paraphrase information given elsewhere in the volume, and the Bibliography not at all.

Dickinson is abbreviated throughout to D., and Forster to F.

OLIVER STALLYBRASS

Ackerley, J. R. (1896–1967), 181; *Hindoo Holiday*, 115
Acton, Lord (1834–1902), 77
Albany Review, 68
Alexander, Alice, *see* Dickinson
All Souls Place, 2, 20, 28, 75–6, 89, 97, 103
Allen, Clifford, later Baron Allen of Hurtwood (1889–1939): letter to, 172–3
"alles vergängliche . . .", *see* Goethe
Alpine Journal, 63
America, 75, 100, 104–10, 134, 138–9; F. optimistic on, 114
Anglo-Chinese Society, Cambridge, 120
Ariel, the world of, 13, 18–19, 147
Aristophanes (*c.* 450–385 B.C.): *Birds*, 18, 20
Ashbee, Charles Robert (1863–1942; architect, designer, town planner and writer; founder of the Guild and School of Handicraft, London, later Chipping Camden; involved in designing modern Jerusalem), 29, 36, 130, 138–9; letters to, 41, 43–4, 47, 50, 96, 107, 150
Ashbee, Janet, 130; letters from, 34; letters to, 34, 131–2
Asplin, Mrs, 166
Athenaeum, The, 146
Athens, 90
Atlantic crossing, 105
Atlantic Monthly, 144, 145
Auden, W. H. (1907–): on *Goldsworthy Lowes Dickinson*, vii–x, xv
Austen, Jane (1775–1817), 146

Bach, Johann Sebastian (1685–1750), 69, 161, 188
Baker, Joseph Allen (1852–1918; Liberal M.P. from 1905), 138
Baker, P. H., 130

Bancroft, Sir Squire (1841–1926) and Marie Effie, *née* Wilton 1839–1921), 20
barber, an informative, 188–9
Barger, George (1878–1939; Professor of Medical Chemistry at Edinburgh), 85
Barnwell, 24
bathing-costumes: a middle-class fetish, 16; not used in Cambridge in the 1880s, 26
Beaufort Street, 152, 185
Beethoven, Ludwig van (1770–1827), 20, 69; Moonlight Sonata, 8, 13, 18–19; Seventh Symphony (*not* Sonata), 25; Ninth (Choral) Symphony, 69, 78, 149, 188
Behrens, Adolf, 69
Békássy, Ferenc (*c.* 1893–1915), 132
Belgion, Montgomery (1892–), xv
Bell, Julian (1908–37; killed in Spanish Civil War), 142; letters to, 173 and plate facing 168
Benares, 116
Bentham, Jeremy (1748–1832), 79
Beomonds school, 12–16, 19, 103
Berenson, Bernhard (1865–1939; authority on Italian art); letter to, 174
Bergson, Henri (1859–1941; his "élan vital" was popularized by, notably, G. B. Shaw as the "life force"), 112, 155
Berkeley, George (1685–1753; Bishop of Cloyne), 91
Berkeley, California, 106
Berlin, 154, 155
Bernhardi, Friedrich von (1849–1930; German general and military writer), 144
Berry, Arthur (1862–1929; Vice-Provost of King's from 1924), 54, 78

as a child, 11; nonsense, love of, 113; open-mindedness, 112; personal appearance, 80, 83–5, 207–8; Chinese cap, 118, 128, 207; physical disabilities, 69, 153; piety, as a boy, 10, 18; a rebel (own account of how he became), 14–15; rebuke, buoyant reaction to, 156; remorse, capacity for, 13, 16; resentment, lack of, when snubbed, 128; sensitiveness, 15, 151, 171; sexual nature and problems, xiv, 47, 56, 63, 103, 151; Socratic quality, *see* Socrates; strength, 151, 197; tactlessness, occasional, 166; teachability, 12; toughness: moral, 15, 131; and physical, 64; unselfishness, 25, 97, 151, 167, 171, 197; vitality in old age, 159

interests, activities and accomplishments: the four gifts he loved most: people, music, books, scenery (*q.v. below in each case*), 22; acting, 16, 19–20; art, 57–58; bell-ringing, 24; bicycling, 23, 72, 130; books: reading (*see also names of authors; and for writing see separate section below*), 22; bridge, 181, 184; broadcasting, 82, 94, 169, 170; chess, 113, 141, 146, 186; editorial work: *Cambridge Magazine*, 145; *Independent Review*, 85–7; farming, 42–5; flowers, 56, 78, 168; home life, 75–6; lecturing and teaching: University Extension, 46–8, 79; at Cambridge, 75, 77–83, 85, 160, 180; at London School of Economics, 80–1, 160; in America, 104, 106–9; for the League of Nations Society, later Union, 139–40, 143, 157–8; letter-writing, *see section on writings below*; mountaineering, 63–

64, 67; music (*see also names of composers*), 20, 22, 25, 69, 77, 185–6; people (*see also under individual names*), 22; piquet, 146; politics, *see section on attitudes below*; psychical research, 100–2; riding, 64, 83; rowing, 23, 54, 64, 67; scenery (*and for associated visionary experiences see* Frensham; Heidelberg; Mistra; Snowdon; T'ai Shan; Yosemite), 22; social work, 24; swearing, 61, 166; swimming, 64; typing, 171–2, 193

attitudes, opinions, sayings (for attitudes etc. to individuals see their names): America, 107, 109–110, 139–40; Anglo-Indians, 114, 117; authority, 97; Cambridge, 42, 78, 86–8, 175; China, 117–18, 120–3; Christ, Christianity and Christian churches (*see also* religion *below*), 28, 131, 133–4, 150, 168, 175, 176, 180; and Platonism, 177; culture, 41, 73; "daemonic" men, 170; death (*see also* immortality *below*), 197; diarist style, the ideal, 113; education, 82–3; egotism and egoism, 178, 189; England and the English countryside, 56, 172; euthanasia, 97; experience, 182; feminism, 88; France and Paris, 58, 154; freedom, 88; Germans and Germany, 40, 154, 155–6, 185–186; God, 98–9; Greece and the Greeks, 89–90, 170, 213–15; history, 66, 87–8; humility, 97; immortality, 100, 152, 182; India, 114, 116–17, 122–3; intellect and intelligence, 105; IT, xv, 190, 196; Italy, 64; knowledge, 99; the League as established, 152–4, 191; London, 58; love and personal

267